BAYSWATER TO LITTLE VENICE

THROUGH TIME

Brian Girling

AMBERLEY

Acknowledgements

Books consulted during this compilation include *The Buildings of England, London 3, North West* by Bridget Cherry and Nikolaus Pevsner; *Dial M for Maida Vale* by Kevin O'Sullivan; *Little Venice* by James Dowsing, and *Guide to Bayswater* by James Dowsing and John Wittich.

Grateful thanks are offered to Maurice Friedman who has kindly contributed images from his collection. Additional assistance by Amanda Borwick and Ian Vanlint has been very helpful and thanks are due to them too.

First published 2016

Amberley Publishing
The Hill, Stroud, Gloucestershire, GL5 4EP
www.amberley-books.com

ISBN 978 1 4456 4717 3 (print)
ISBN 978 1 4456 4718 0 (ebook)

British Library Cataloguing in Publication Data.
A catalogue record for this book is available from the British Library.

Typesetting by Amberley Publishing.
Printed in Great Britain.

Introduction

This book is a new and colourful celebration of a diverse slice of inner-west London that takes in areas of the former Metropolitan Borough of Paddington before they became included in the City of Westminster in 1965.

A quick glance at a London street map will show two arrow-straight main roads that converge at Marble Arch (the site of the former gallows at Tyburn). The straightness of the roads hints at their Roman origins. For centuries they ran through open countryside, but by the early 1800s the advancing tide of London's expansion was bringing new streets into the angle formed by the convergence of what we now know as Edgware Road and Bayswater Road.

These were new suburbs for London: westward extensions of housing that was being laid out in Marylebone, with Tyburnia to the west and Bayswater further on. With Royal Hyde Park close at hand, these were well-to-do areas; the houses embraced the fashionable late Georgian style in squares, terraces and crescents. The houses built later also followed fashion with a more decorative Italianate mode, then popular in west London's grander squares and terraces.

While Tyburnia was new (only a scattering of shanties called Tomlin's Town had briefly stood there), Bayswater along the old road to Uxbridge and Oxford was older, originating as 'Bayard's Watering' after a local spring where animals were watered. Modest buildings were the order here until the Victorians capitalised on its wonderful location that overlooks the royal parks with spectacular colonnaded terraces at Lancaster Gate. Away from the park, however, there were slummy patches, notably behind Queen's Road (Queensway) where poverty lingered on into the 1900s.

In the rural areas north of Bayswater, isolated for centuries, lay the villages of Westbourne Green and Paddington. In the early 1800s they were at the forefront of transport revolutions, which would set the pattern for what we see today.

The first was the arrival in 1801 of the Grand Junction Canal; canals were then seen as the most effective means of moving heavy freight in an age of poor roads. Wharves sprang up along the canal banks and a dock was created at Paddington Basin. The system was extended via the Regent's Canal in 1821, forming a link with the River Thames.

The railways arrived in 1838 and under the influence of Isambard Kindom Brunel went on to establish a great railway terminus for the capital. In 1863, Paddington (by now urbanised) witnessed another transport landmark with the opening of the world's first underground railway, the Metropolitan. The trains were originally steam-powered, but in 1900 a deep-level electric Tube line beneath Bayswater Road, the Central London Railway, was a taste of the future. Road congestion had increased during the 1900s, and in the '60s an elevated motorway above the rooftops was built, creating a new link to the west.

These transport improvements led to a decrease in the commercial traffic on the canals, which had increasingly become the domain of pleasure craft and houseboats along the tree-shaded waterways that were styled 'Little Venice'.

Badly battered by war and the austerity that followed it, parts of Paddington became drab and rundown, but gradually the potential for it as a desirable inner-city location was realised.

The worst of the slum housing was replaced by bright new housing estates and old properties were revitalised, Tyburnia's Hyde Park Estate was also smartened up with opulent new apartment complexes.

Through these pages we can see parts of Paddington as our ancestors once saw them and with comparison photographs from the present day, see how much (or little) the area has developed. Along the way are lost streets, pubs, shops and cinemas, together with the transport of yesteryear and a unique school in Bayswater. The other worldly delights of Little Venice are observed as are the grand Victorian townscapes of Bayswater's Victorian heyday. It is hoped that the resident and visitor alike will find much to interest and intrigue along the way!

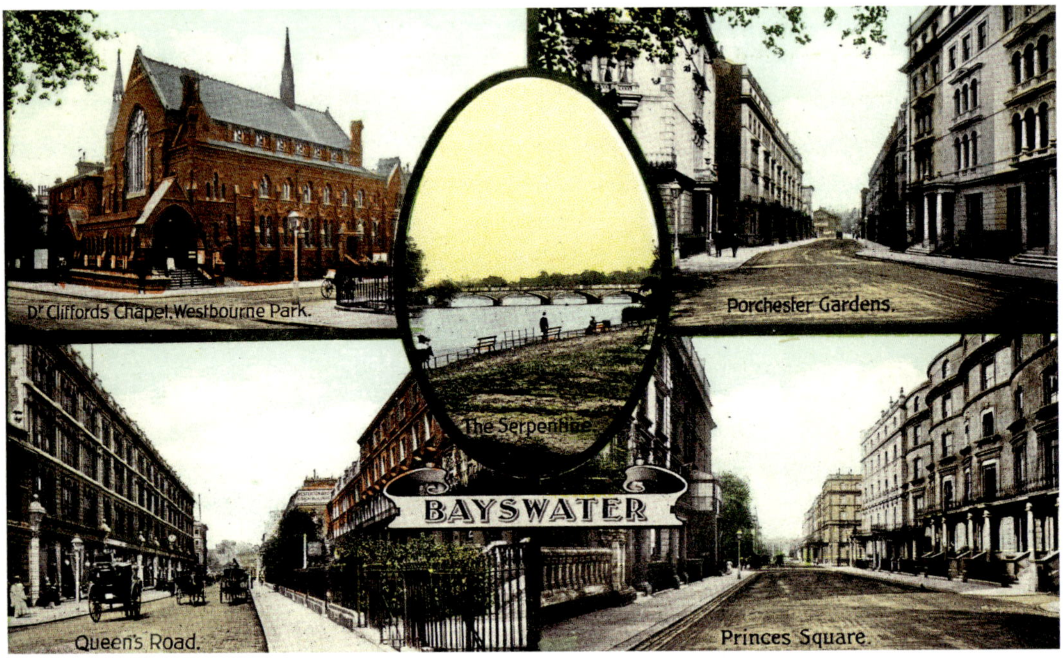

A vintage postcard showing some of Bayswater's most well-known locations.

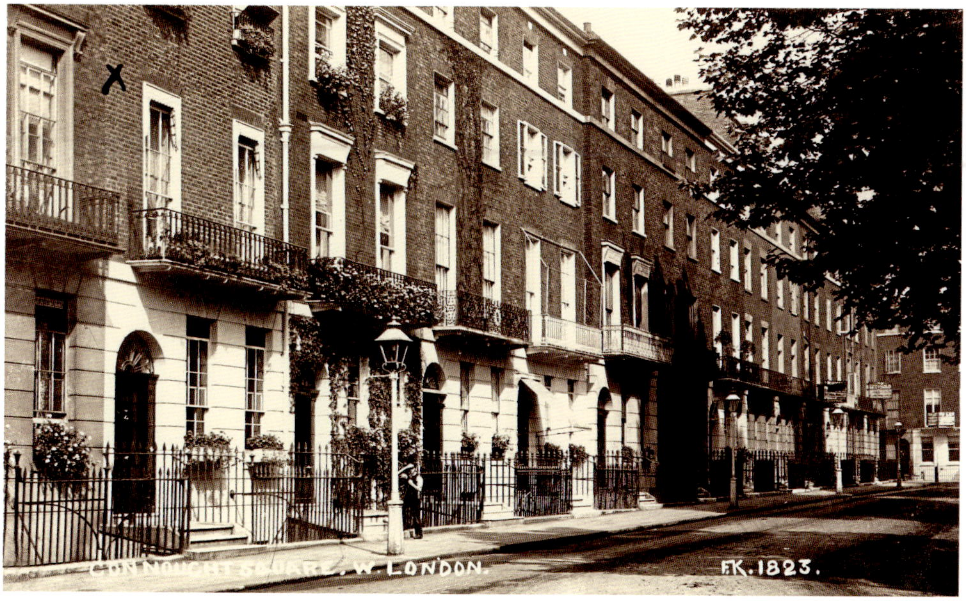

Connaught Square, West Side, *c.* 1906

In the 1820s London was expanding into its surrounding countryside, and among the new suburbs that arose was Tyburnia. It was located by the two Roman roads that met at the Tyburn crossroads (now Marble Arch), and there were elegant new streets to oust the temporary bungalow housing of Tomlin's Town that had briefly occupied the fields. The earliest houses were in the latest version of the Georgian style, plain brick with painted stucco embellishments. The wonderfully preserved houses of Connaught Square show the best of the style.

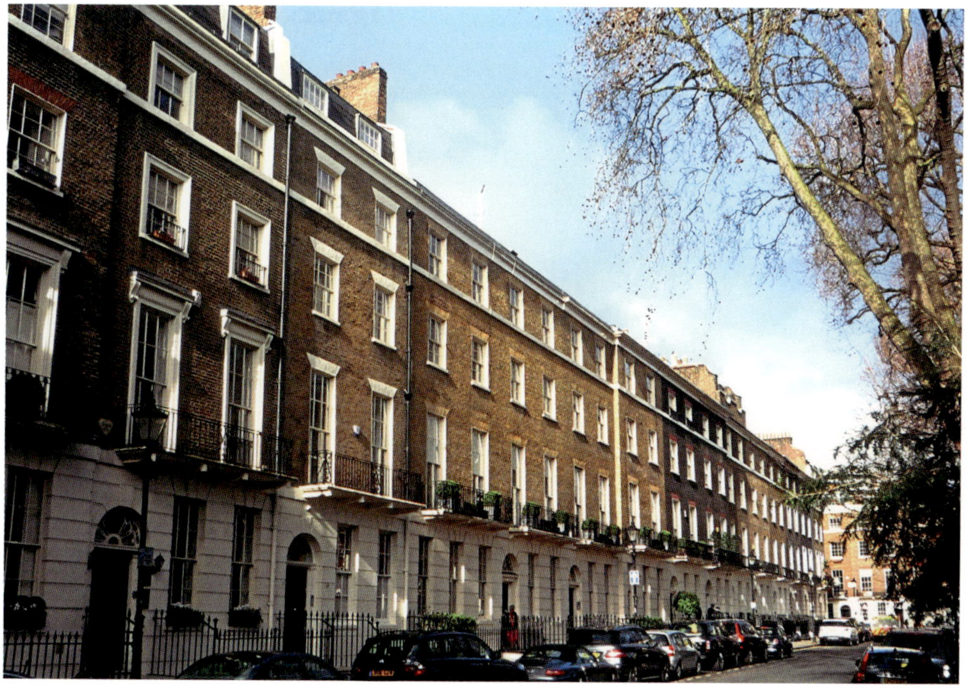

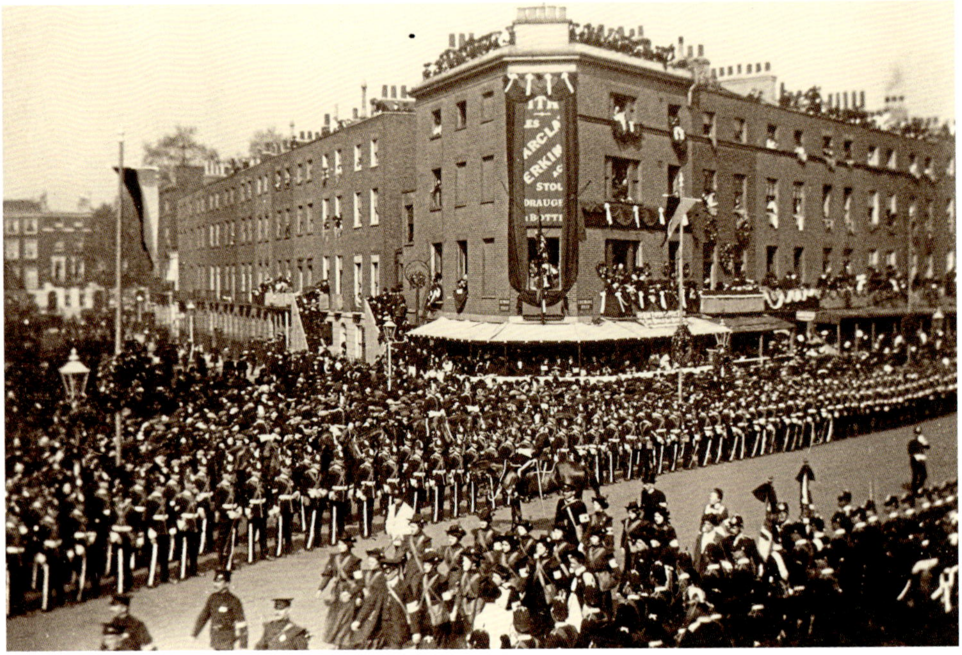

Edgware Road and Seymour Street, 20 May 1911

The plain style of Tyburnia's buildings continued into Edgware Road with its tall houses and ground floor shops. Despite its humble aspect, Edgware Road sometimes witnessed scenes of grand royal pageantry as it lay on the ceremonial route from Buckingham Palace to Paddington station and that of the royal train. In the above image the crowds can be seen assembled on the occasion of Edward VII's funeral when the body of the much-loved king was taken in procession to the royal train for the journey to Windsor for interment. The view looks along Seymour Street to the distant Connaught Square.

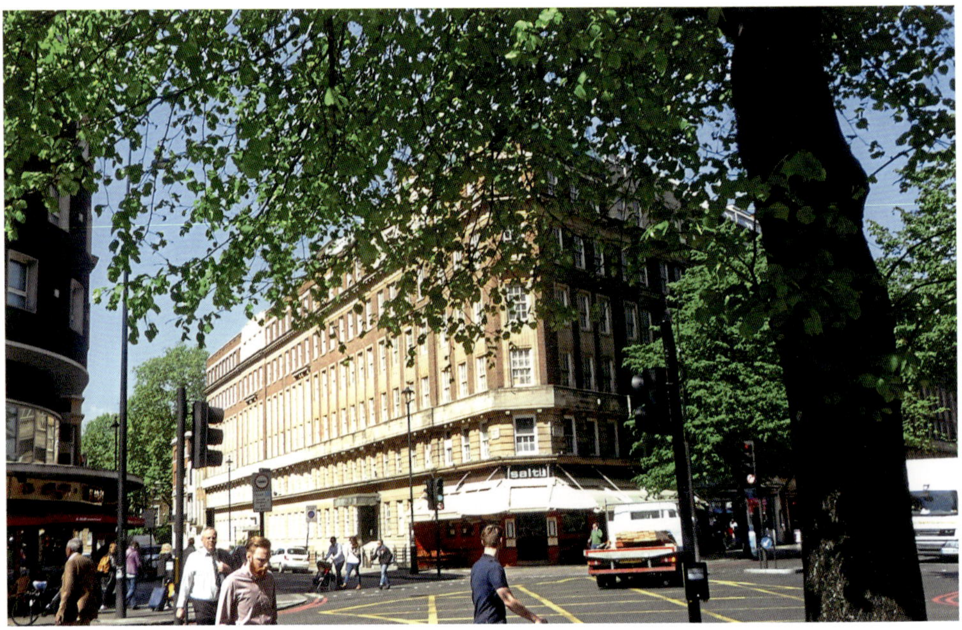

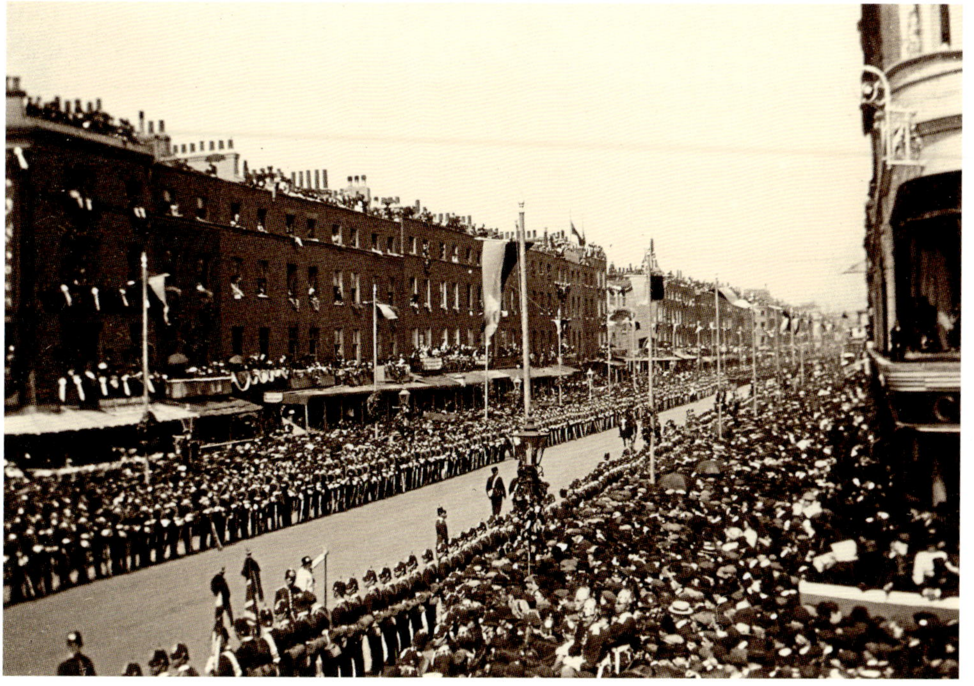

Edgware Road seen from Seymour Street, 20 May 1911

The above image shows more of the vast throng that lined Edgware Road for Edward VII's funeral. Much of this street was rebuilt from the 1930s with smart apartment blocks and in later years a vibrant Middle Eastern community has created a range of exotic shops and restaurants, giving a unique flavour to the street. One of the last properties to be rebuilt was the Mitre pub, which can be seen to the far left.

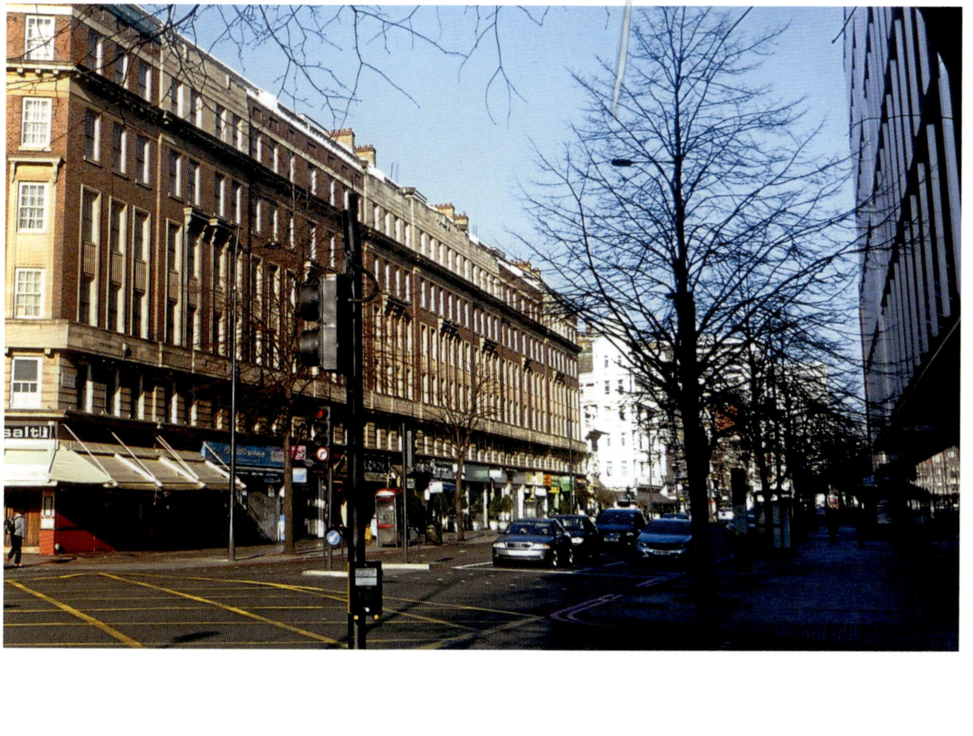

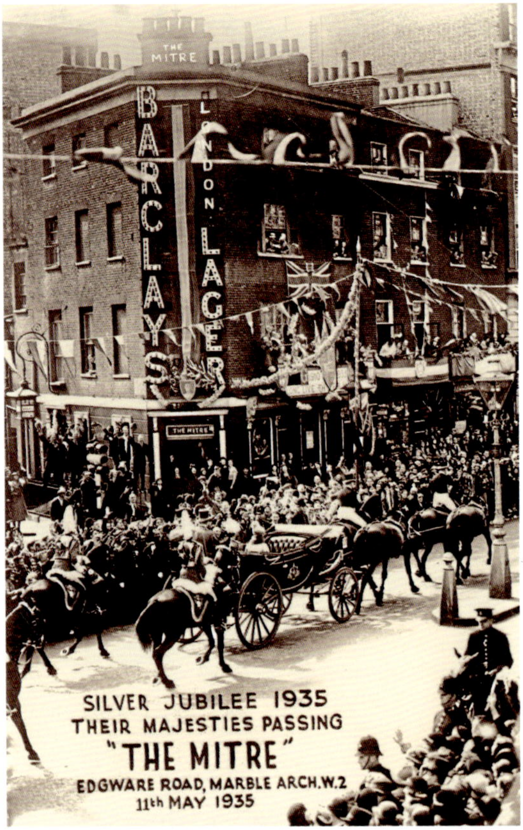

The Mitre, Edgware Road by Seymour Street, 11 May 1935

The Silver Jubilee of George V and Queen Mary brought another spectacular royal parade, with the Mitre pub suitably adorned with patriotic decor. The pub is seen above in the final years of its old building before a fine new Mitre arose to match the grander buildings already surrounding it.

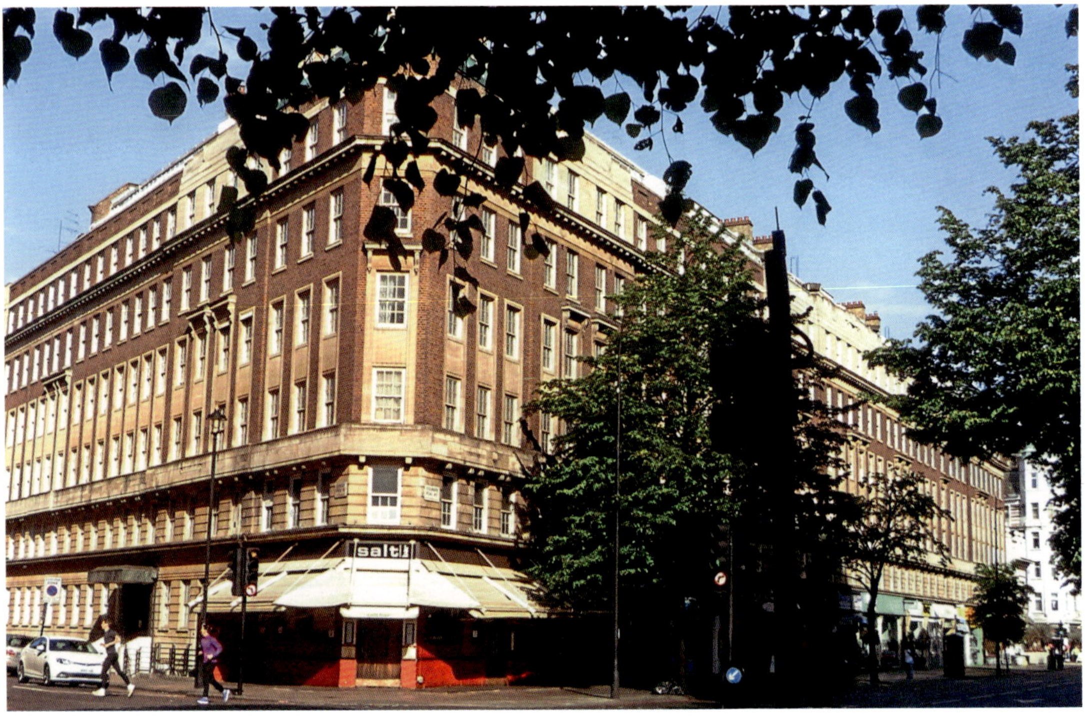

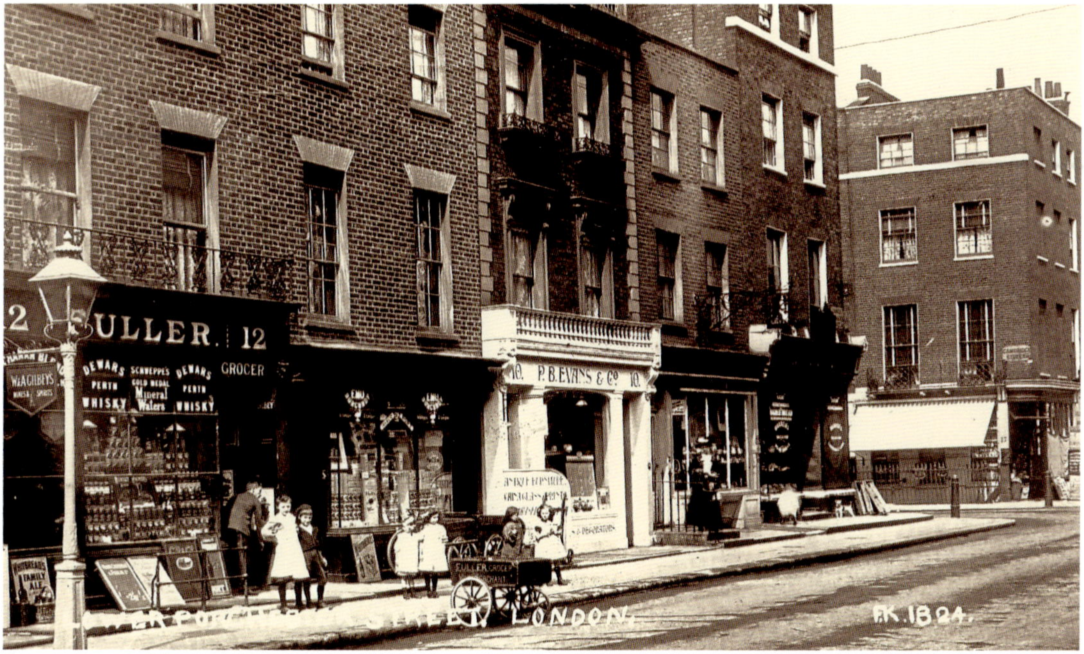

Lower Porchester Street (Porchester Place) by Cambridge (Kendal) Street, *c.* 1905
Tyburnia was generously endowed with local shops, ranging from the continuous rows along the Edgware Road boundary to the hinterland where corner shops and groups like this were scattered among the terraces. Here, Percival Evans, baker, and William Fuller, grocer, supplied local households in Edwardian days. Fuller's handcart is standing in readiness for its delivery service. (The above image is courtesy of Maurice Friedman.)

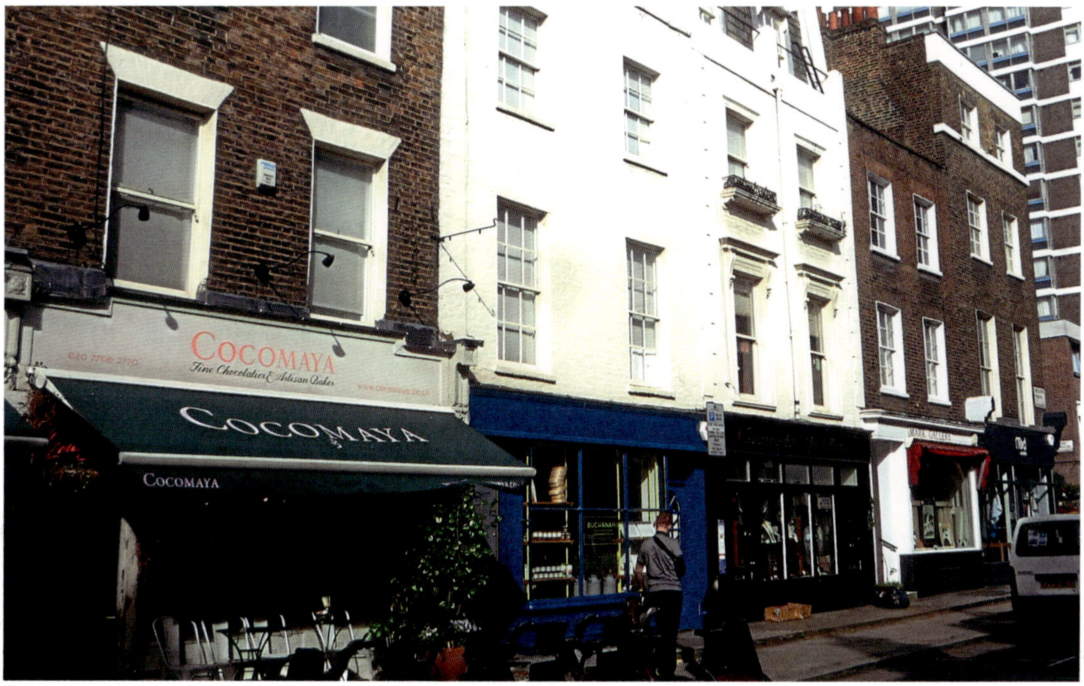

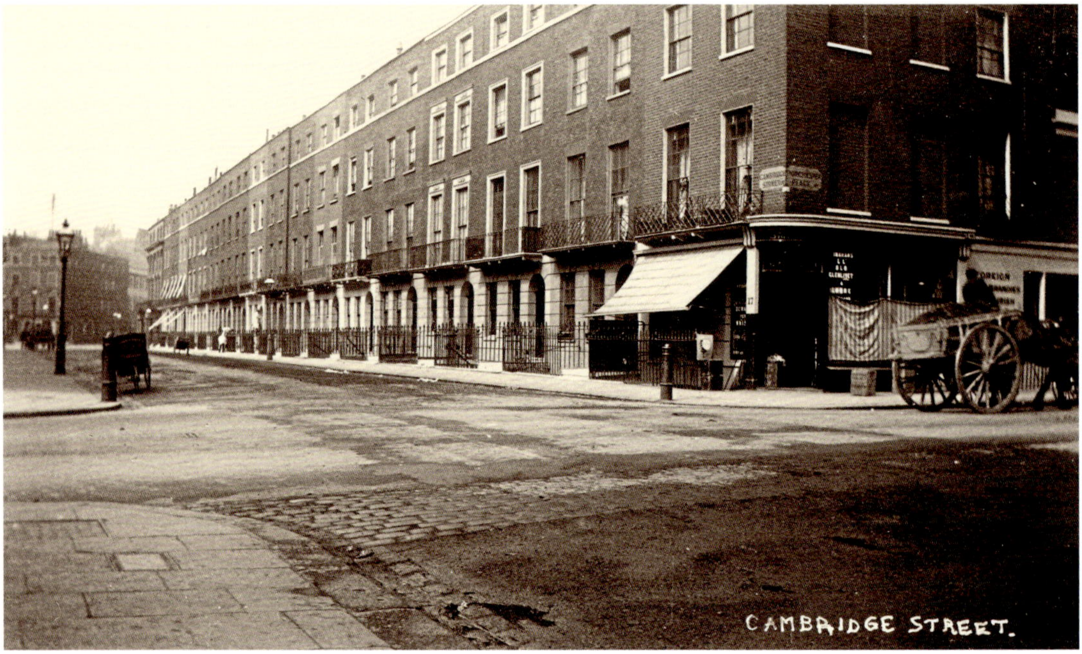

Cambridge Street (Kendal Street), *c.* 1906

An impressive terrace of typical Tyburnia houses can be seen above, complete with the grocer Thomas Smith's corner shop. It all changed in the post-war years with the building by the Hyde Park Estate of Coniston Court. Cambridge Street was renamed Kendal Street in the late 1930s when the London County Council sought to abolish many duplicated street names across the capital.

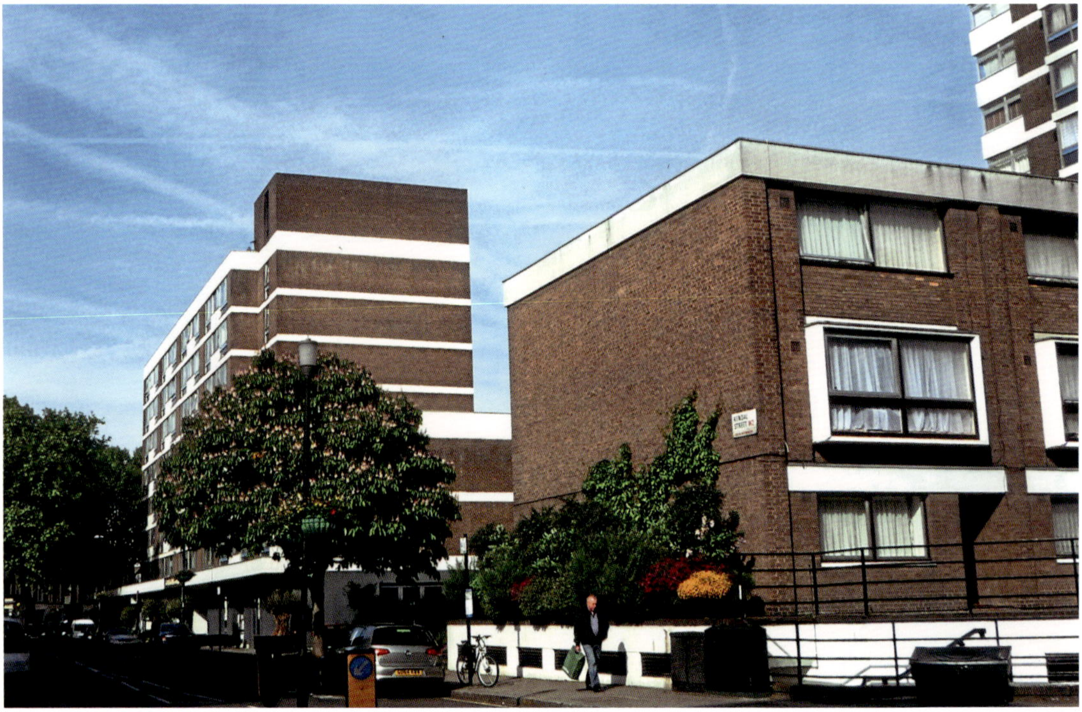

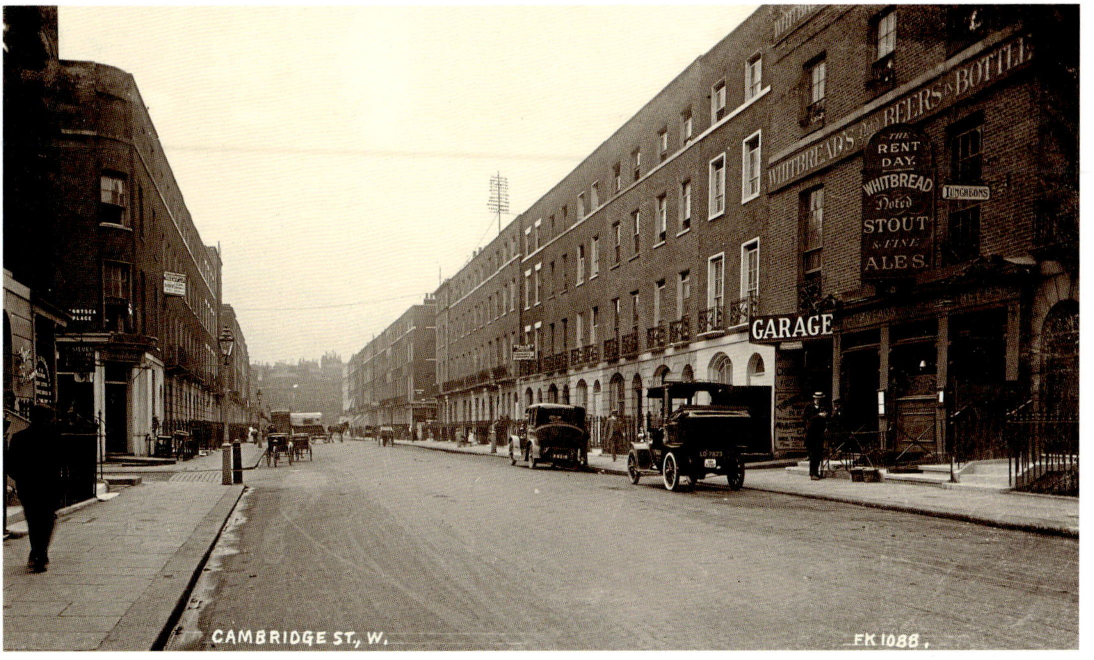

Cambridge Street (Kendal Street) seen from Edgware Road, *c.* 1912

Portsea Place is on the left, while to the right the curiously named 'Rent Day' pub stands above an entrance to Sovereign Mews. These former stables accommodated Joseph Brown, chimney sweeper, an essential service in that era of domestic coal fires. The Marble Arch Garage can also be seen: a typical mews enterprise as the new private motoring craze gradually replaced the old equine trades in backwaters like this. The transformation of the street began in the 1930s with the construction of smart neo-Georgian flats.

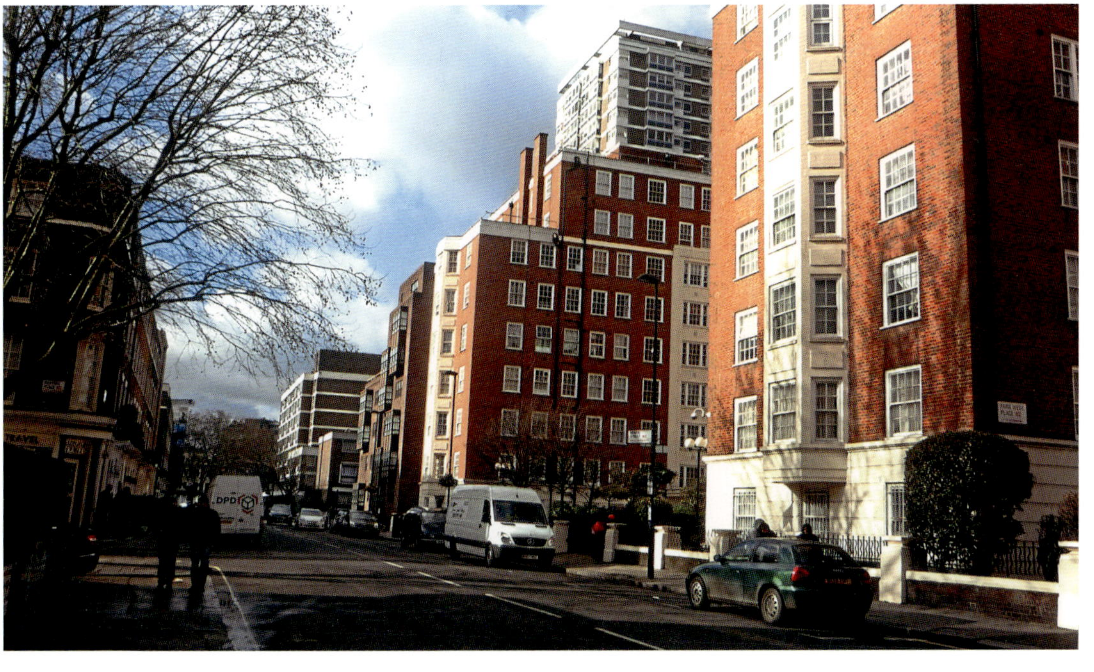

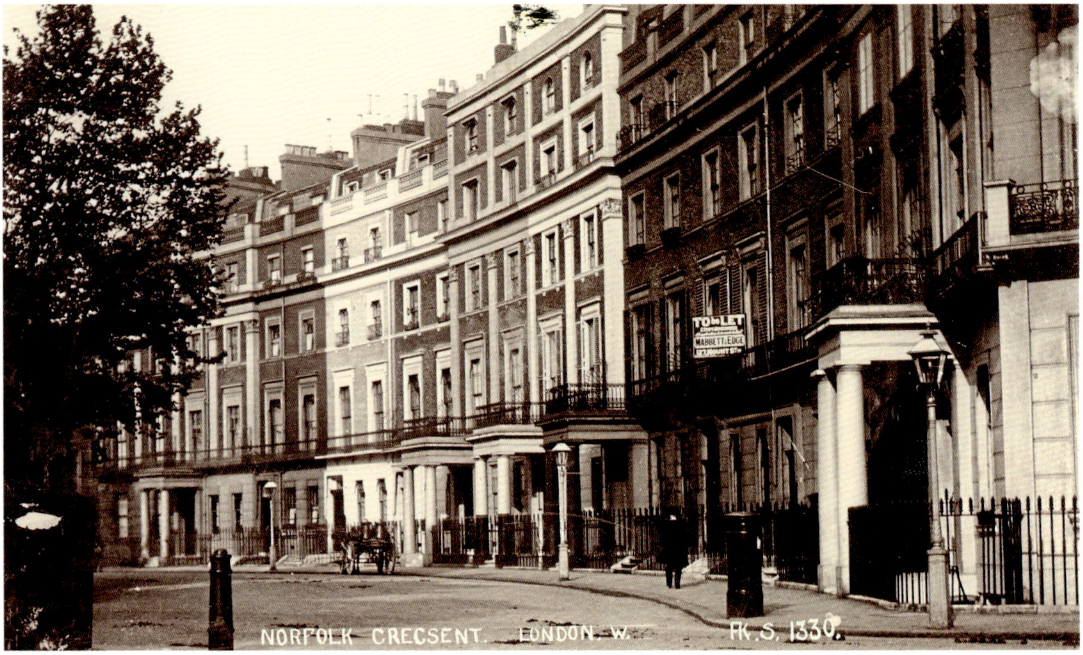

Norfolk Crescent, *c.* 1903

By the time Norfolk Crescent was built in the 1840s architectural tastes had moved on and a more flamboyant Italianate style was becoming popular. The new houses were marked by prominent columned porches and a greater use of painted stucco, although the effect was sometimes diminished by ill-matched painting schemes for individual houses. The 1960s brought a continuance of the rebuilding of parts of Tyburnia's Hyde Park Estate, which had begun before the war. Norfolk Crescent is one such example as modern low-rise town houses replaced their Victorian forebears.

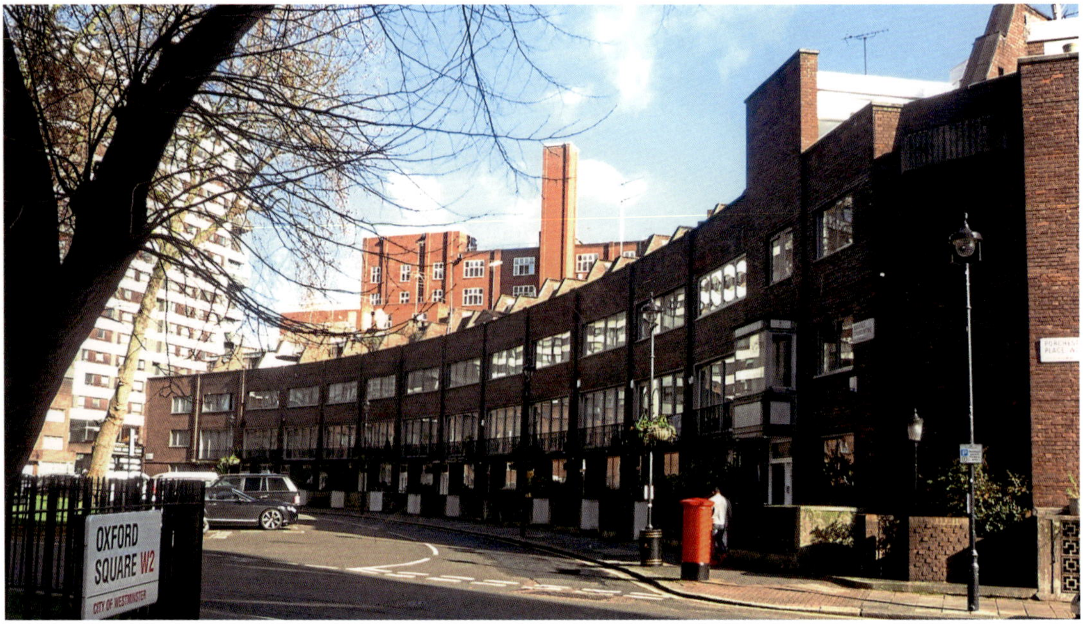

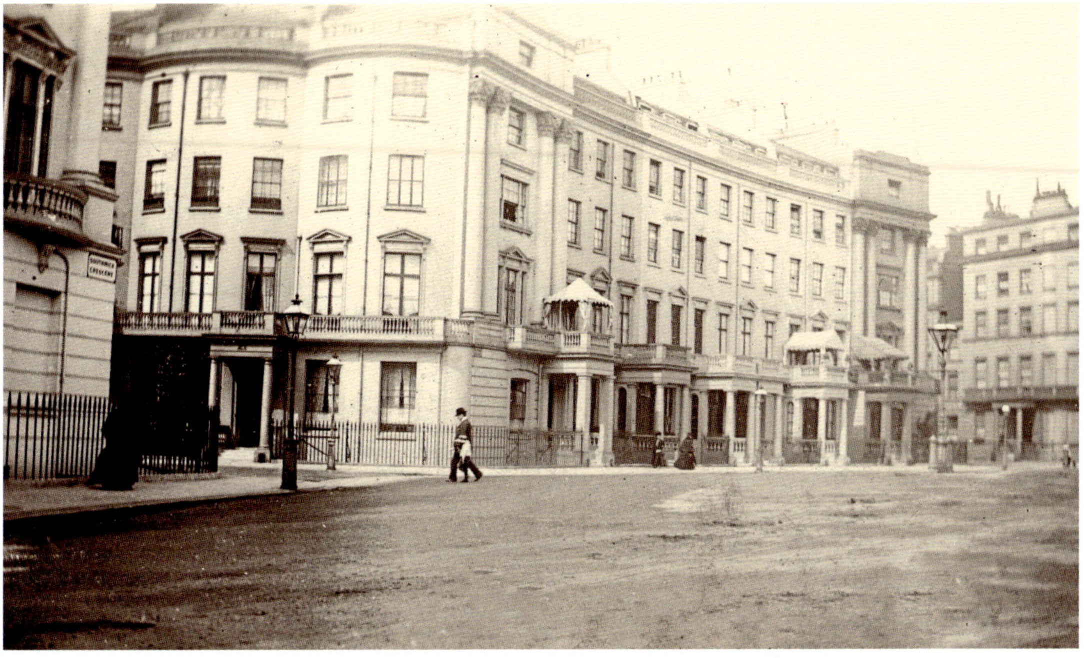

Southwick Crescent (Hyde Park Crescent), *c.* 1906

In the above image the crescent can be seen with its original houses, before these were replaced by the neo-Georgian ones more familiar today. The spacious crescent is also the location of the church of St John the Evangelist, formerly the Connaught Chapel (1832).

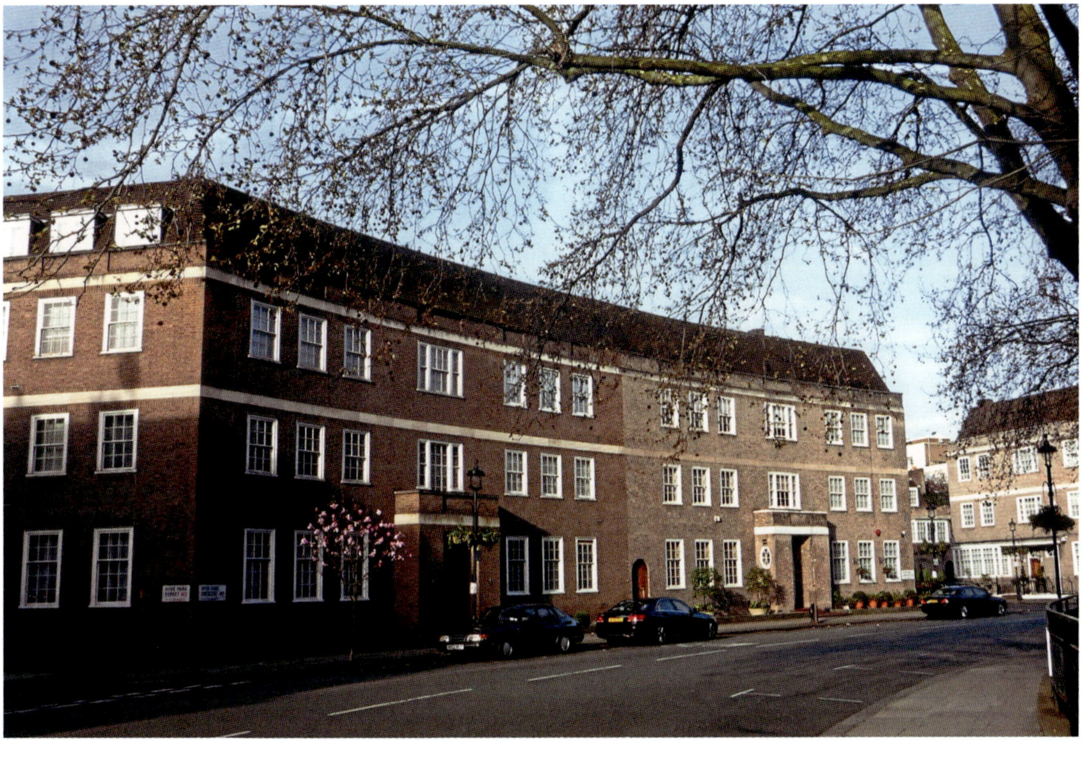

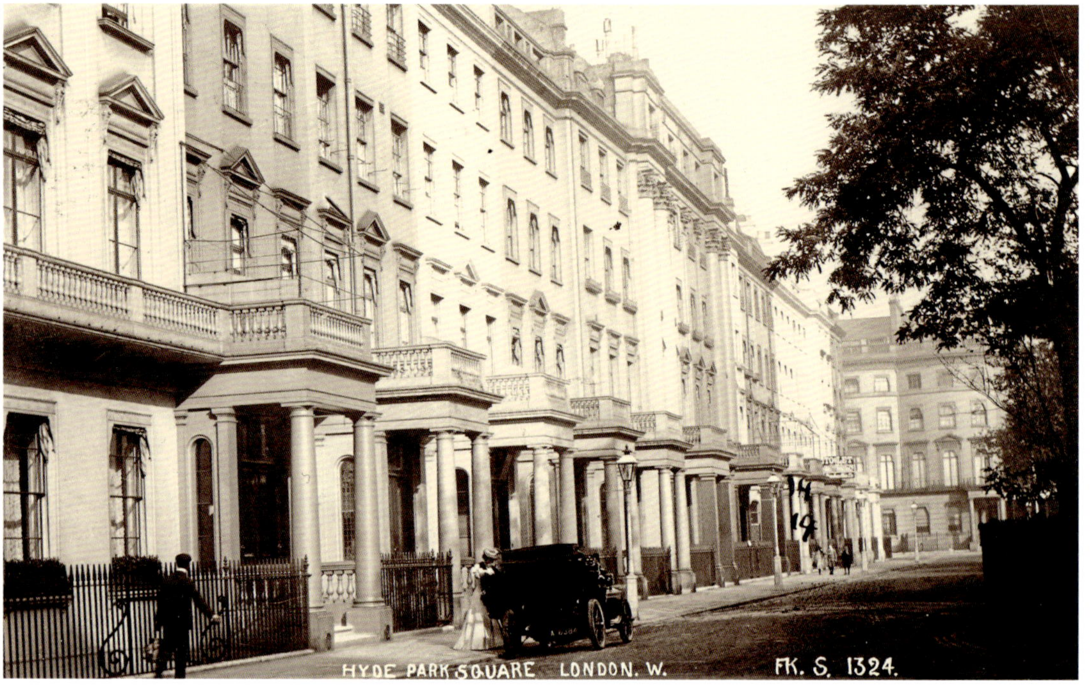

Hyde Park Square, *c.* 1903

The grand Italianate houses seen above are from the 1840s and are representative of a style that was becoming popular in west London's grander squares and terraces.

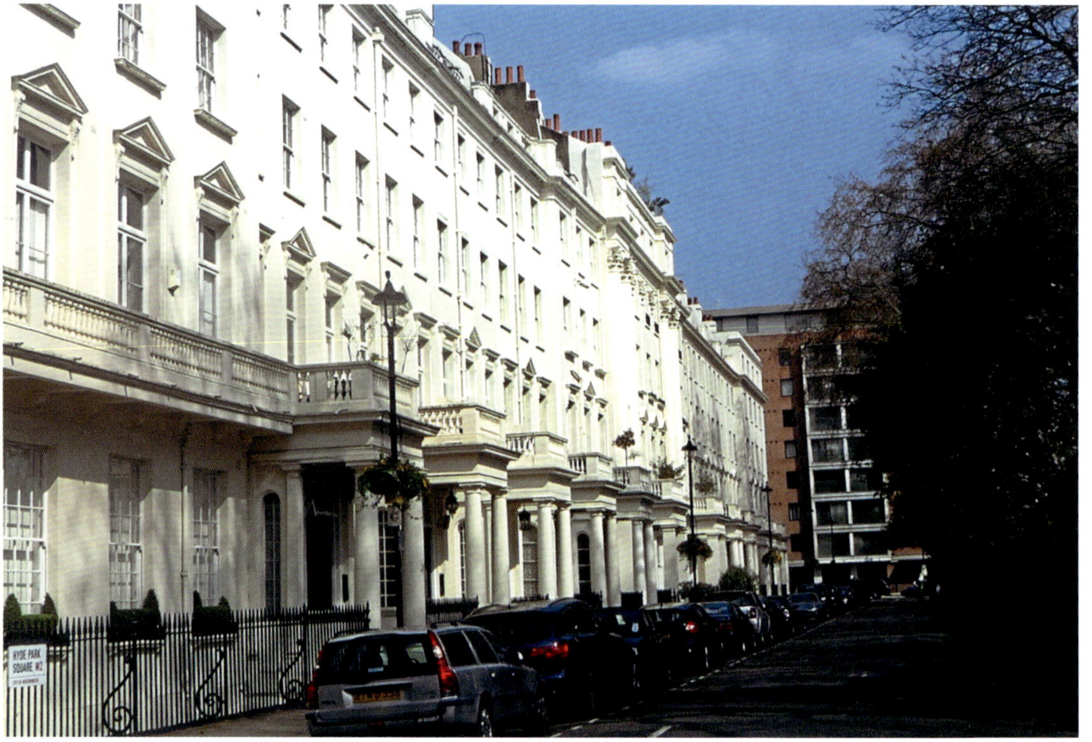

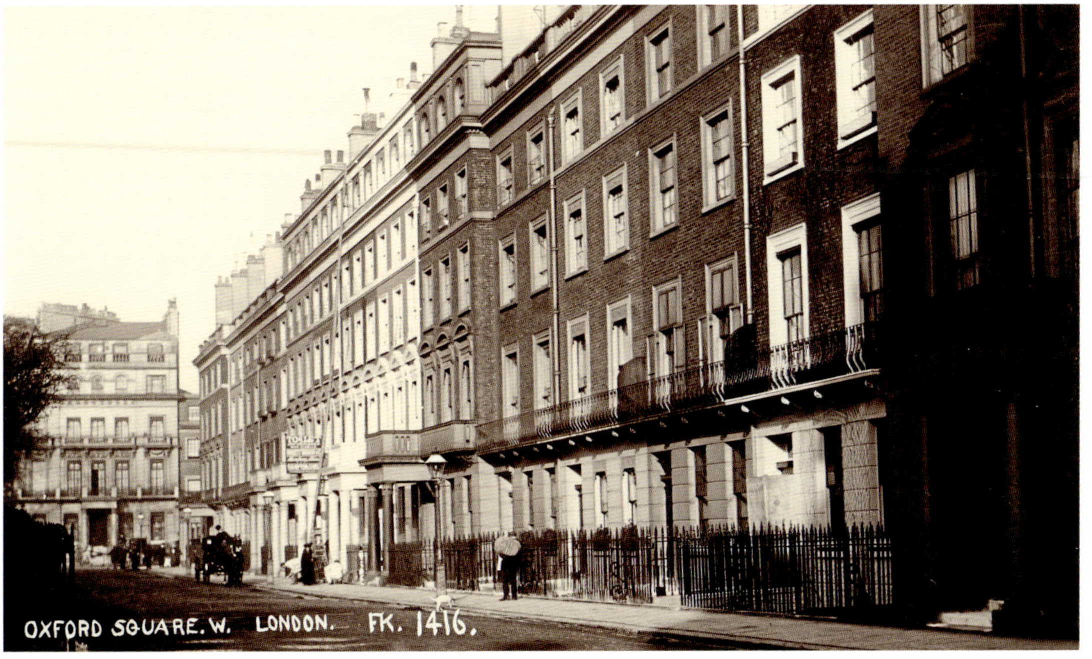

Oxford Square, *c.* 1904

The Edwardian scene in the above image shows a variety of housing designs for Tyburnia, with the earlier sparsely adorned properties leading on to a group in the later Italianate mode. This was another part of the Hyde Park Estate that lost all of its original houses in the 1960s.

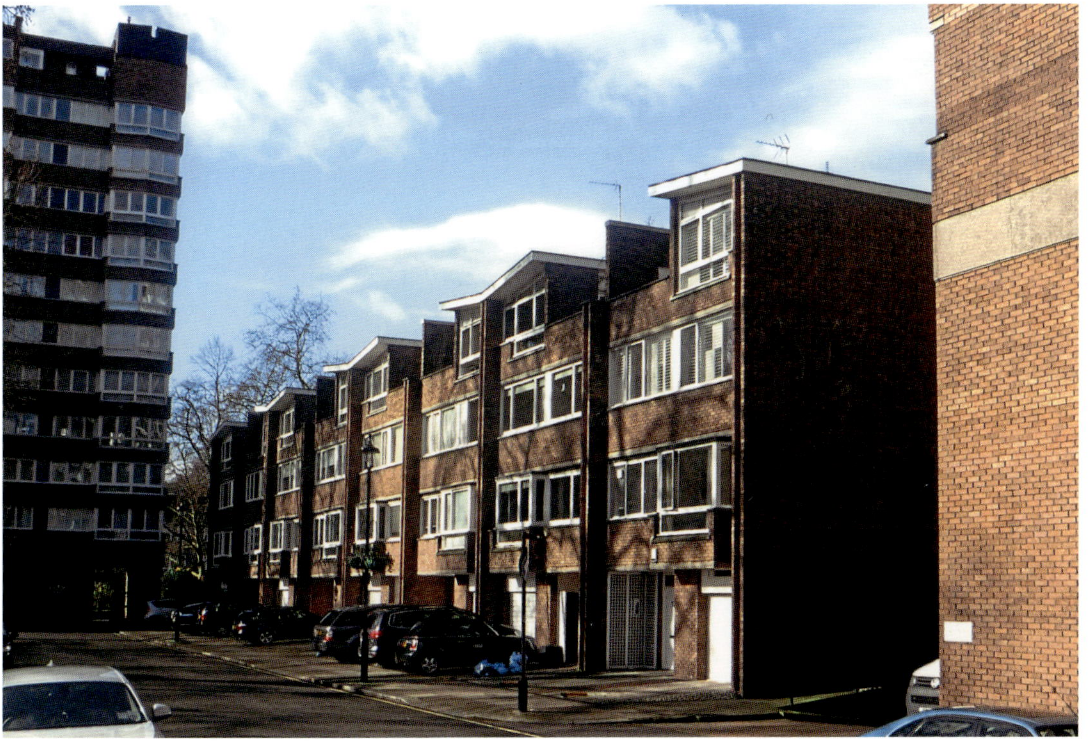

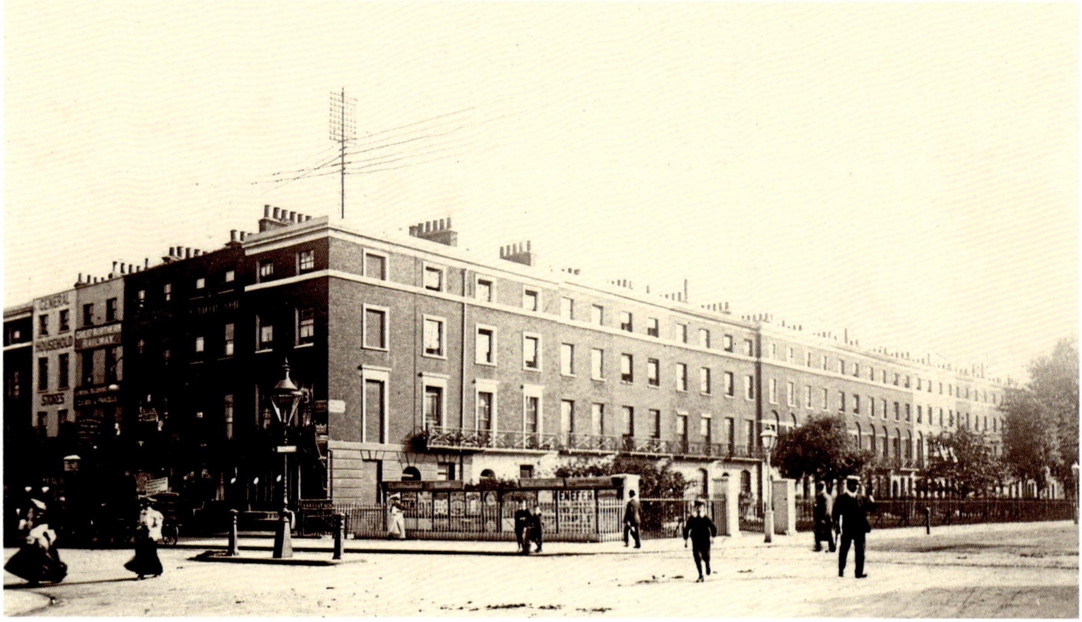

Edgware Road and Oxford Terrace (Sussex Gardens), ***c.*** **1903**

Here, Edgware Road's long and plain terraces clung on until the 1960s, when they were replaced by the ultra-modern apartments of the Water Gardens alongside a lengthy road widening. The lively Middle Eastern community now thrives here, but in Edwardian days Albert Ginger's butcher's shop graced the corner. To the right, the Oxford and Cambridge Terraces border the boulevard-like Grand Junction Road, now known as Sussex Gardens.

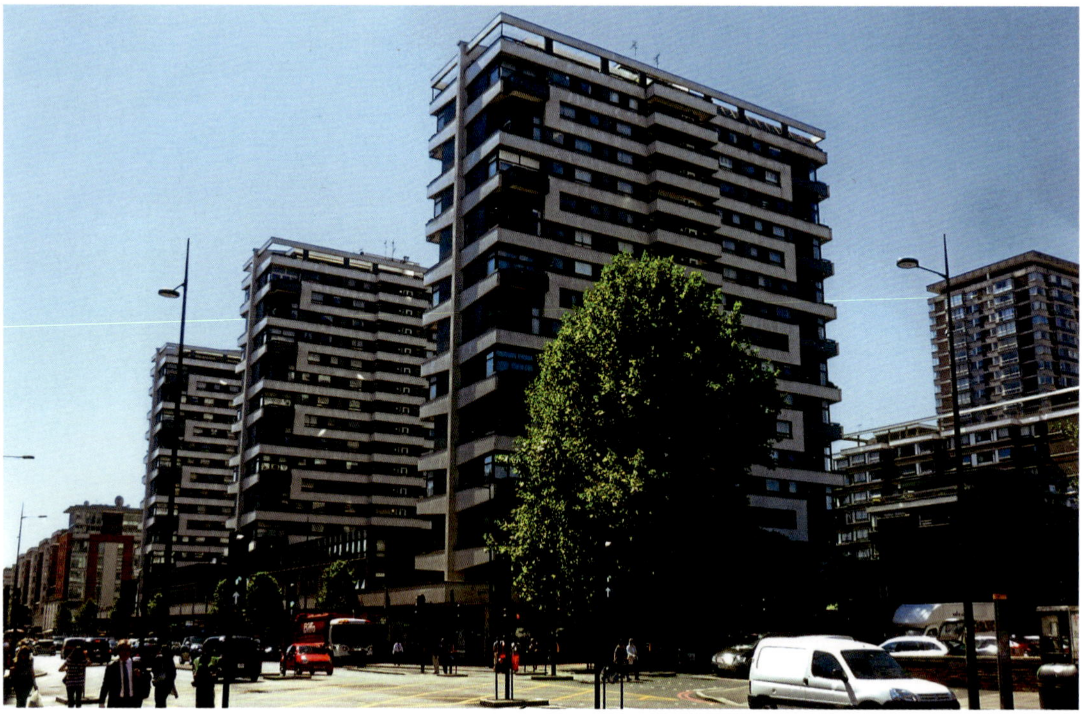

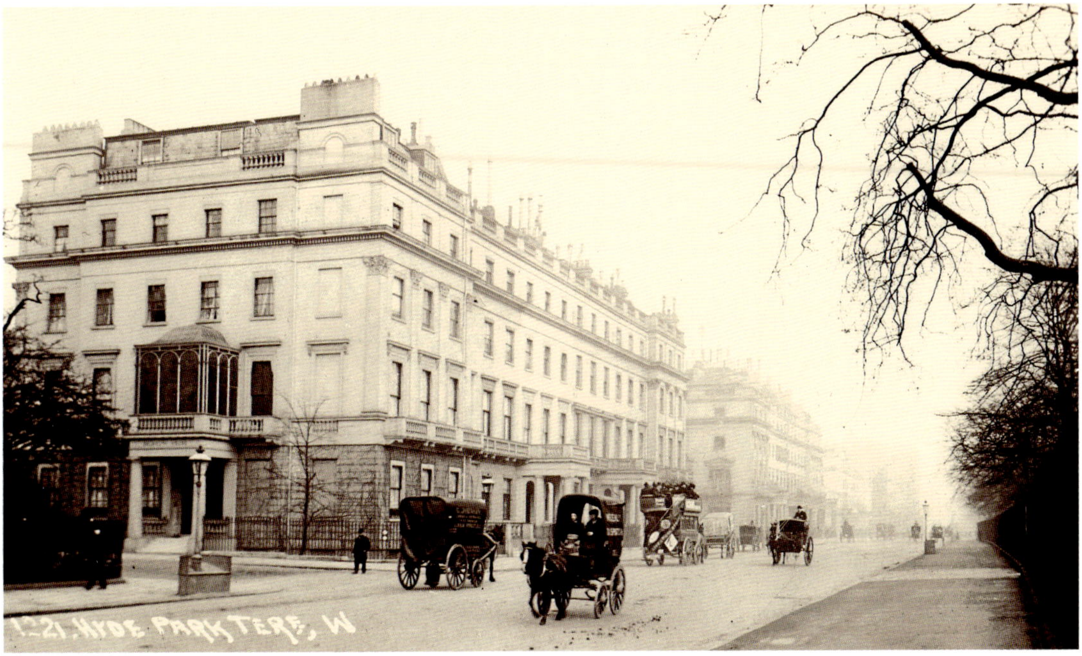

Hyde Park Terrace, Bayswater Road, by Clarendon Place, *c.* 1903

Tyburnia and Bayswater's southern boundary was once a more grandiose affair, with showpiece terraces in stucco overlooking the former royal hunting ground of Hyde Park and Kensington Gardens also. Bayswater Road, the old road to Uxbridge, was made up of a series of individually named terraces of which this was an early arrival. The first to be built was Connaught Place in 1807.

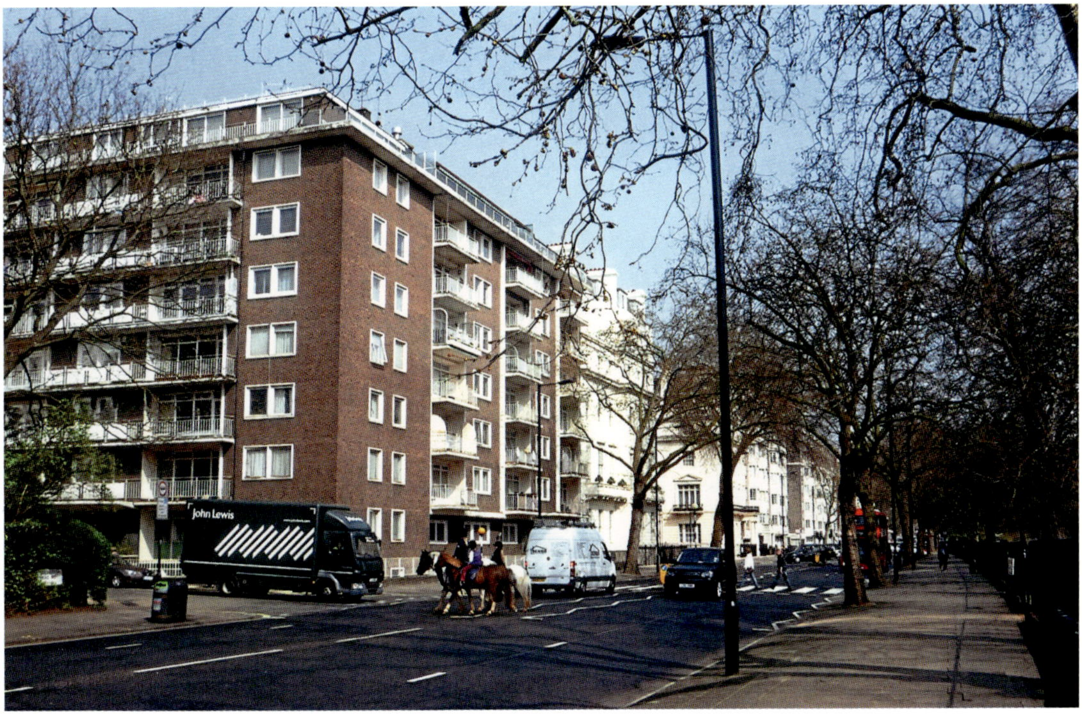

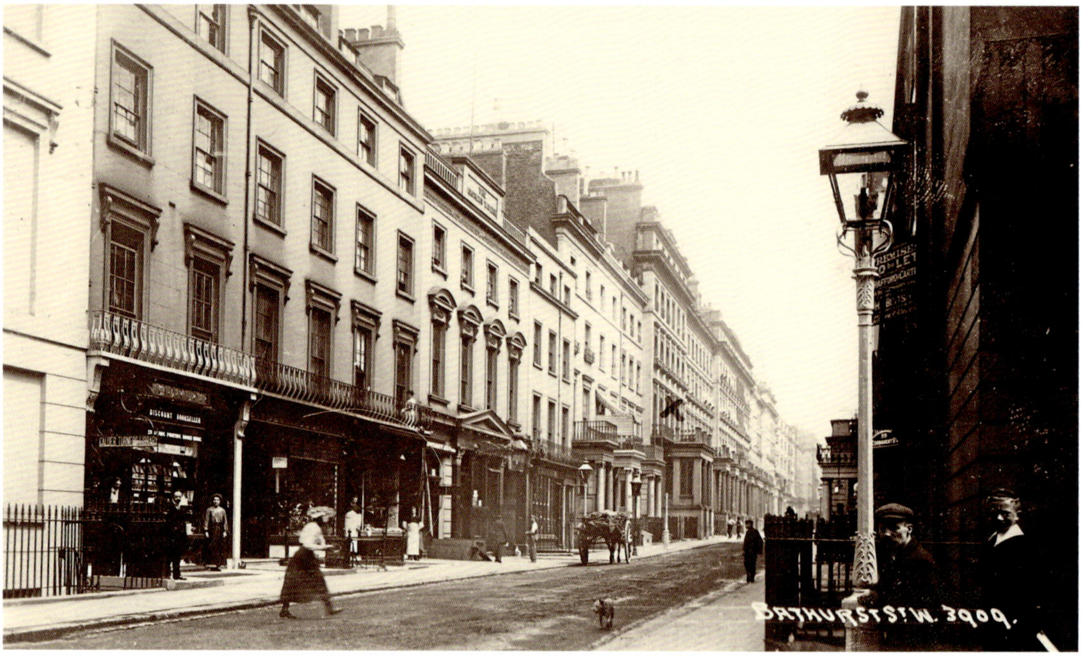

Bathurst Street and Sussex Square, *c.* 1905

In the above image an atmospheric Bayswater side street is visible, showing the Archery Tavern whose name recalls a popular local sport in Regency times. The pub stood above an entrance to Bathurst Mews where a working stables survives into the present day. The shops included those of Calder Turner's Library, a discount bookseller, and that of John Brumbridge the dairyman.

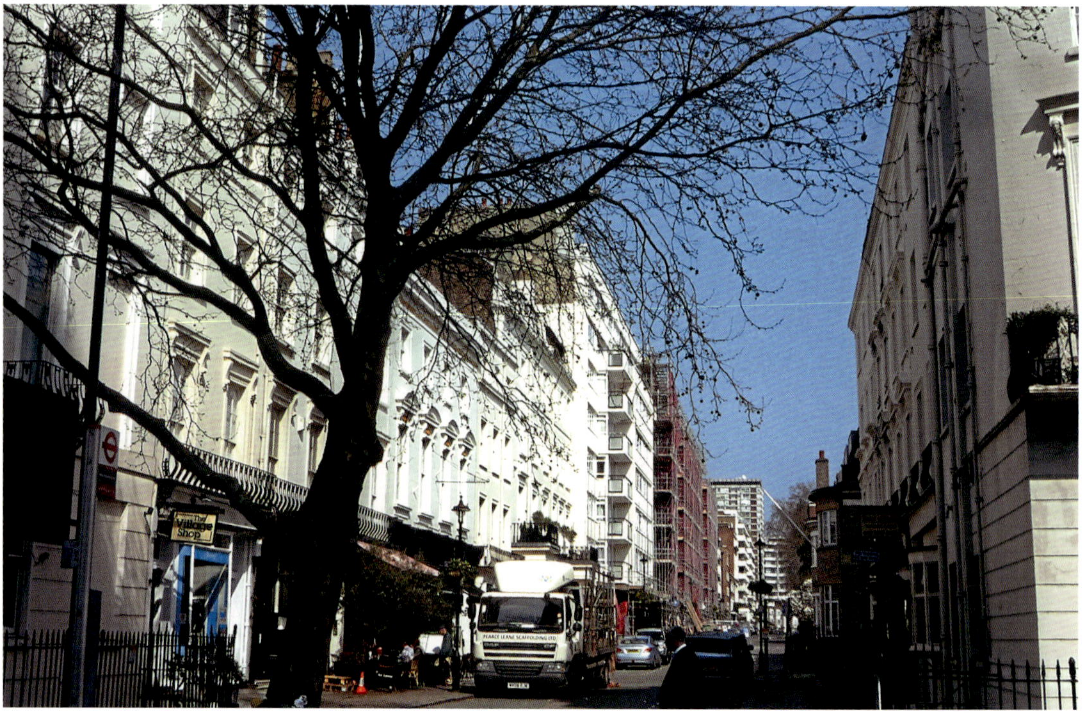

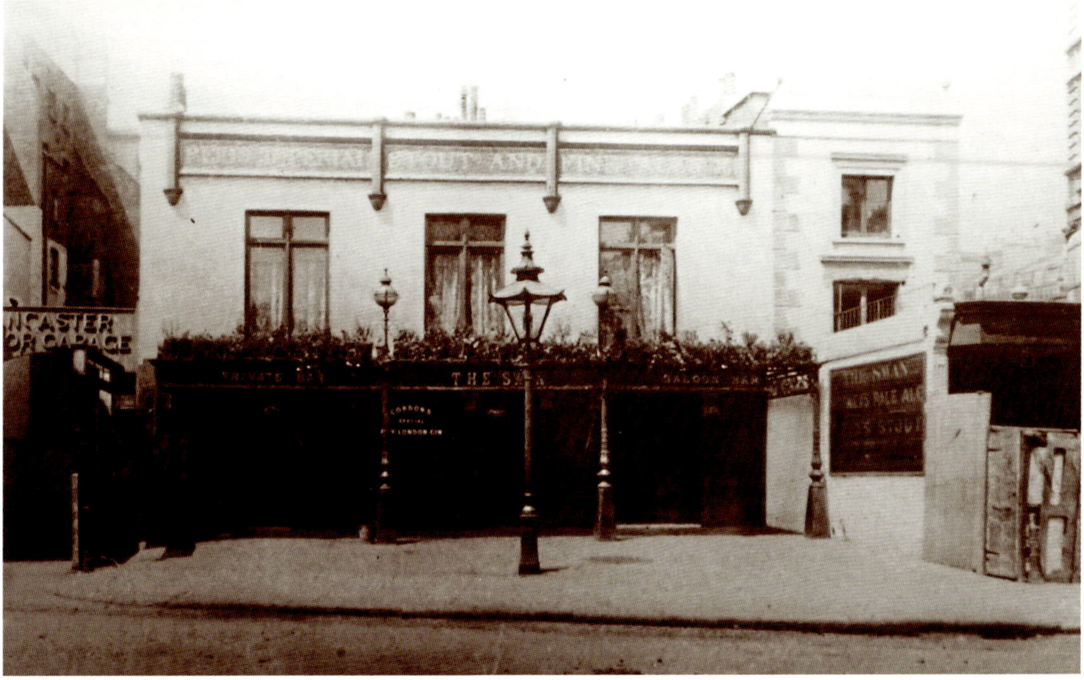

The Swan, Bayswater Road by Elms Mews, *c.* 1910

A sole survivor of the modest buildings that were scattered along Bayswater Road before the Victorians built their grand terraces. This venerable tavern had its origins around 1775 and reputedly gave a final refreshment to some of the miscreants en route to meet their fate on the Tyburn gallows. Travellers on the old rural road to Uxbridge found a welcome at The Swan, as did the cab and omnibus drivers who watered their horses at the drinking fountain opposite.

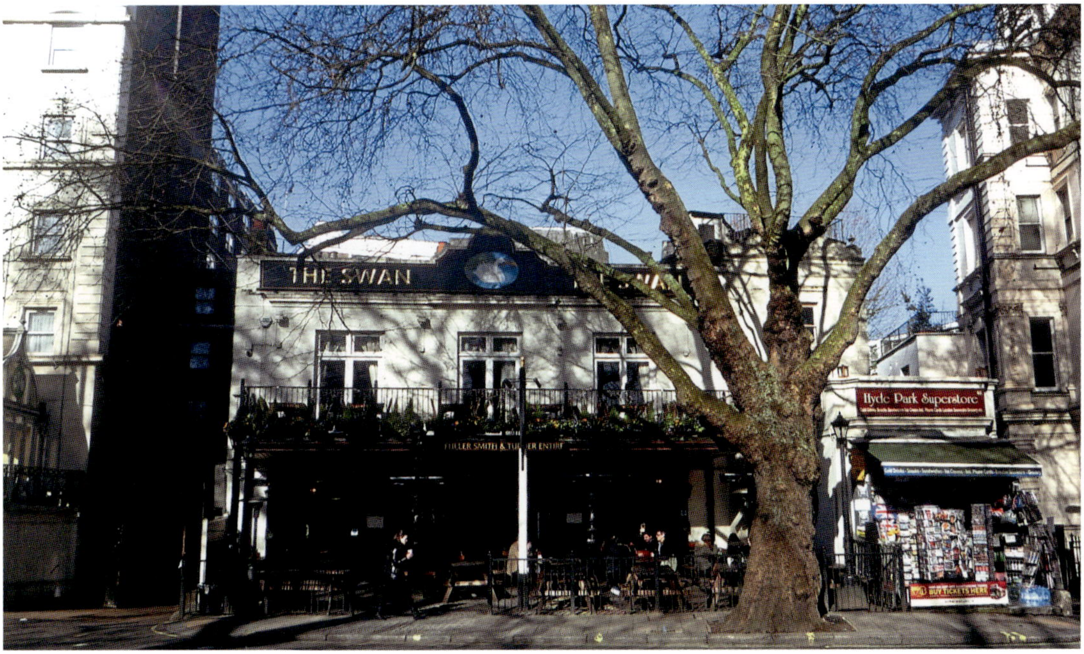

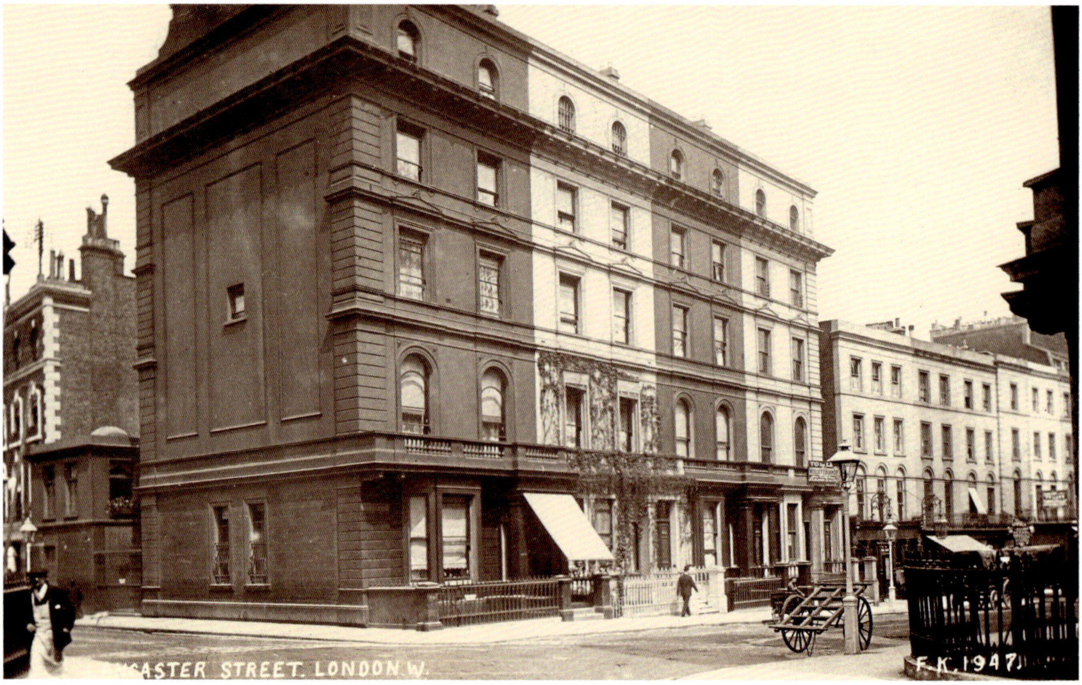

Lancaster Street, *c.* 1906

This mixed residential and shopping street, which ran from Lancaster Gate to Gloucester Terrace, no longer features on the London street map, having been abolished following war damage in 1940. In 1939 the street was briefly known as Barrie Street after local author J. M. Barrie, creator of Peter Pan. The multi-storey Carroll House now covers the street's old site.

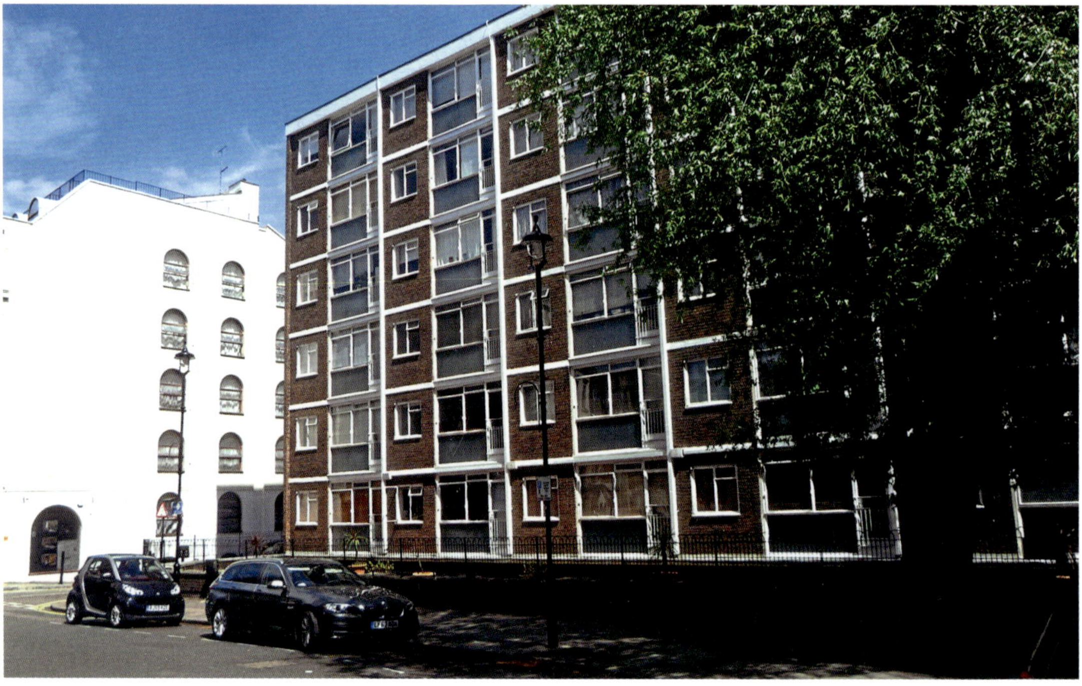

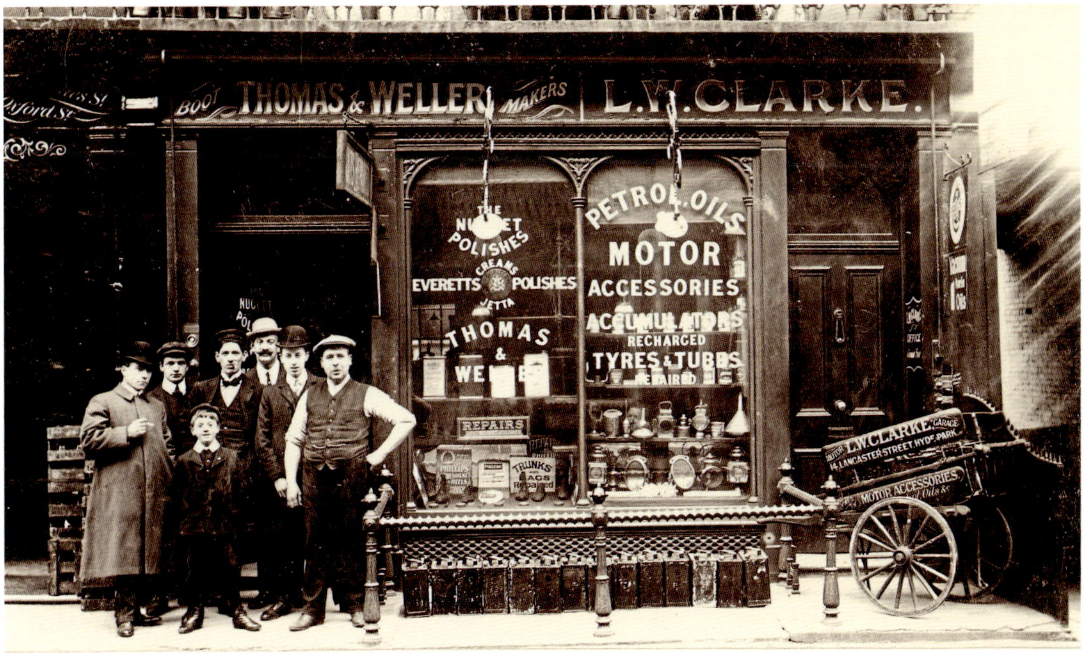

No. 14 Lancaster Street, by Brookes Mews, *c.* 1910

A lost shop in a lost street, the premises were shared by boot makers Thomas & Weller and Levi Clarke's motor garage. Here the window is filled by a variety of motor lamps and in those days when filling stations were rare, 'motor spirit' (petrol) was sold over the counter in shops like this. Following Lancaster Street's demise, Carroll House took the site, as seen here from Elms Mews.

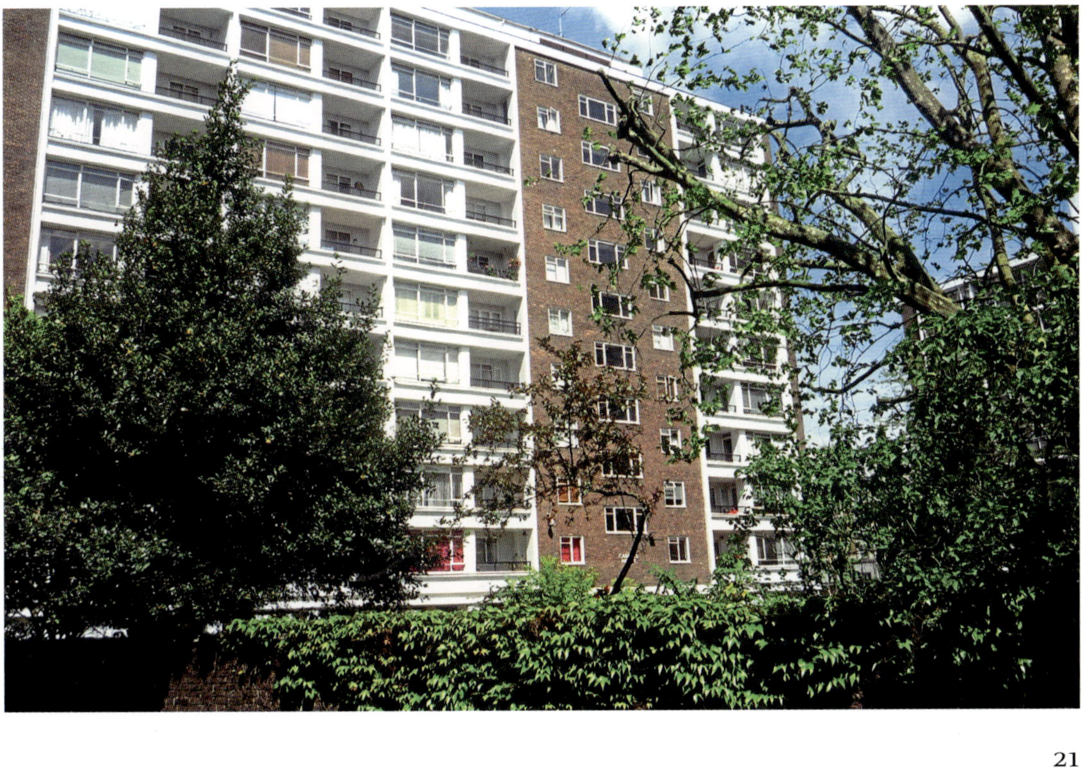

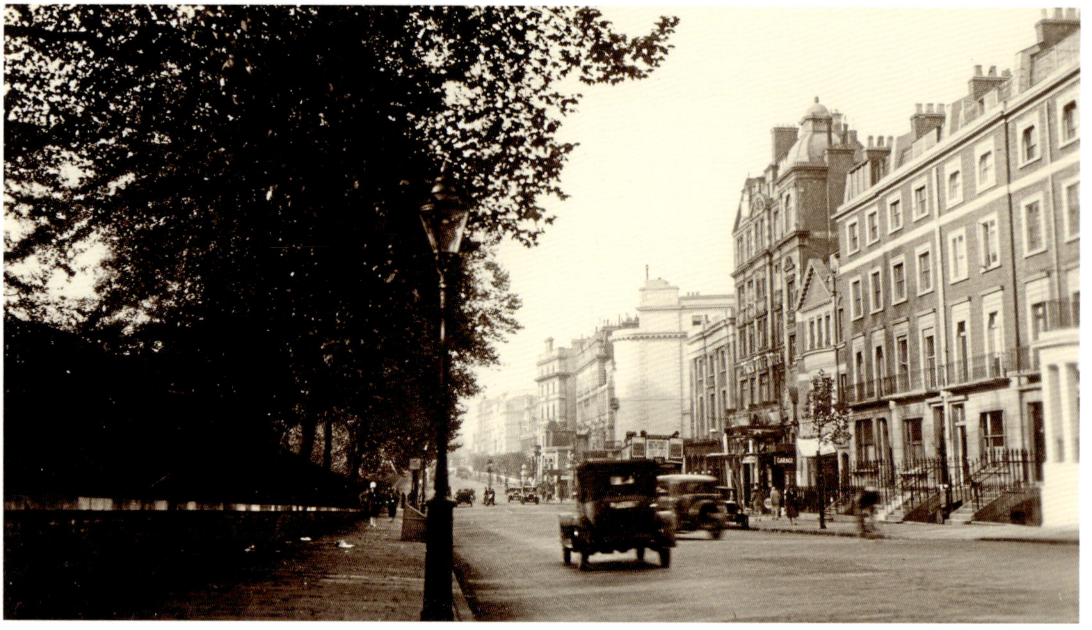

Stanhope Terrace, Bayswater Road, 1928

The erection of the Royal Lancaster Hotel in 1967 replaced this Bayswater terrace, together with the prominent Park Gates Hotel that stood above Lancaster Gate Tube station. The station was rebuilt and the road widened at the same time. A slight dip in the road is perceptible here: this is the former valley of the Westbourne stream, whose waters emerge in Kensington Gardens as the lake known as the Serpentine.

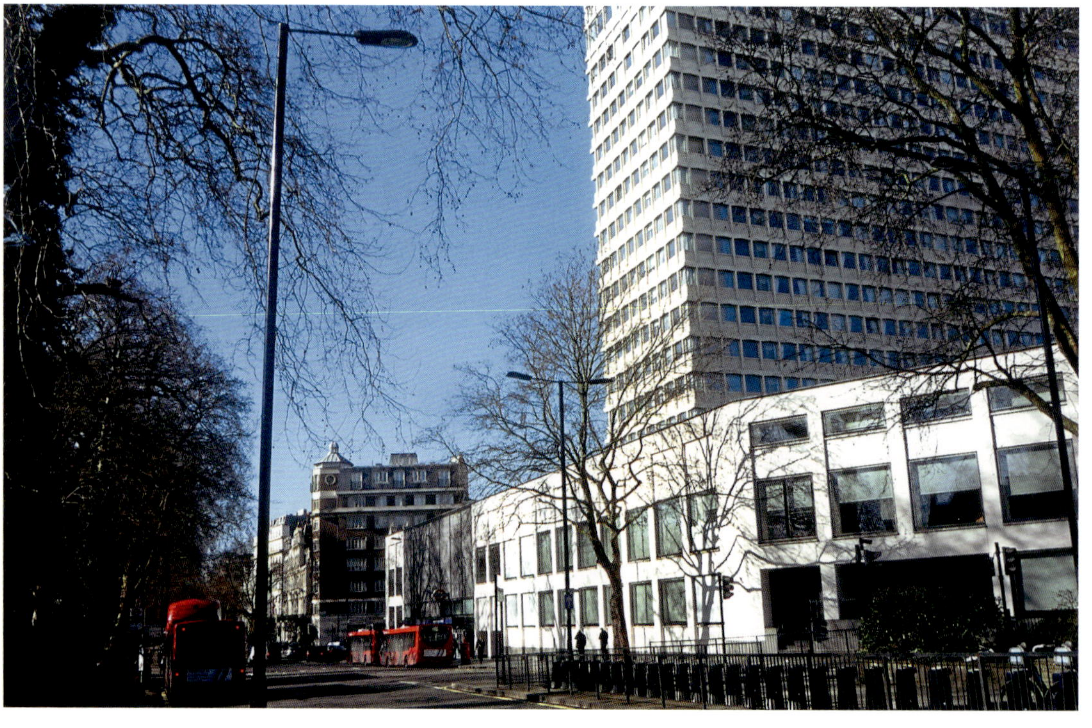

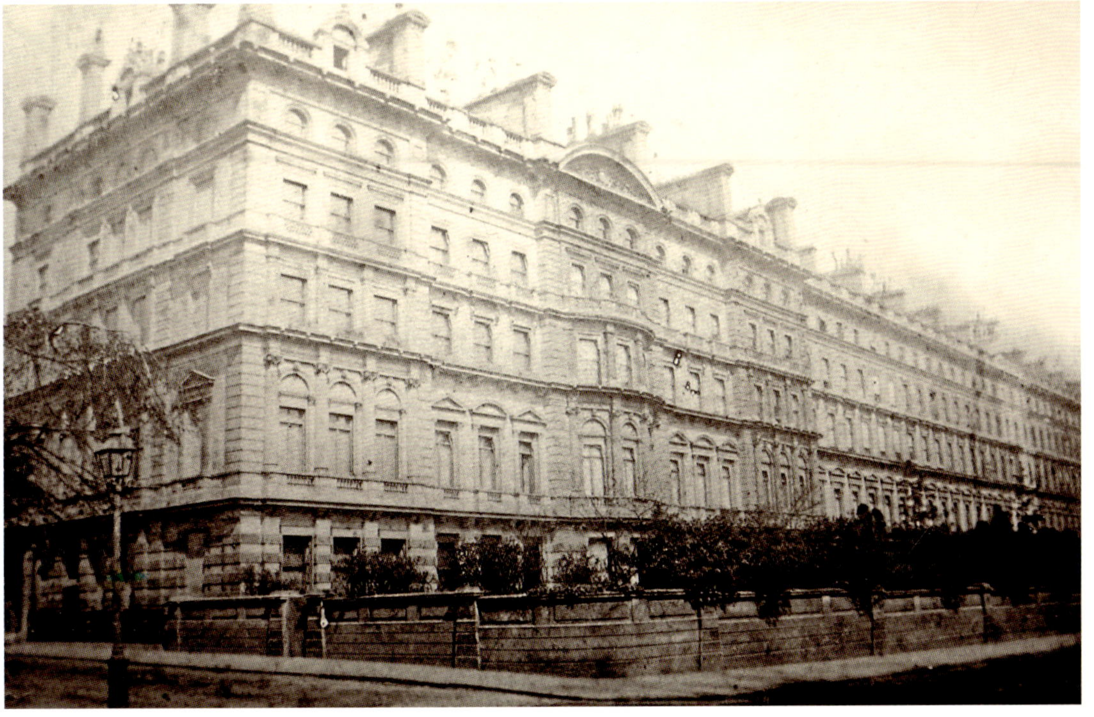

Lancaster Gate by Leinster Terrace, Bayswater Road, *c.* 1875

In the above image a grand terrace from the 1850s can be seen. Builders had begun to capitalise on Bayswater Road's fine outlook over the royal park. The view catches the houses in the early years of their lives; a modern restoration has given the houses a sparkling new look.

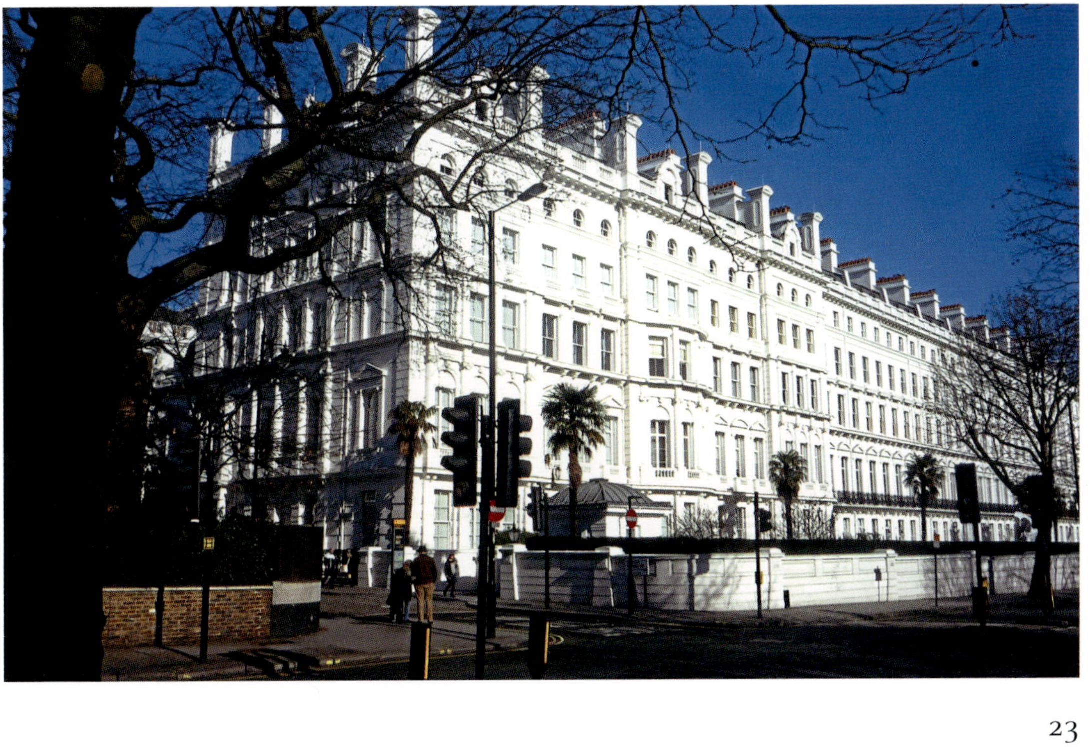

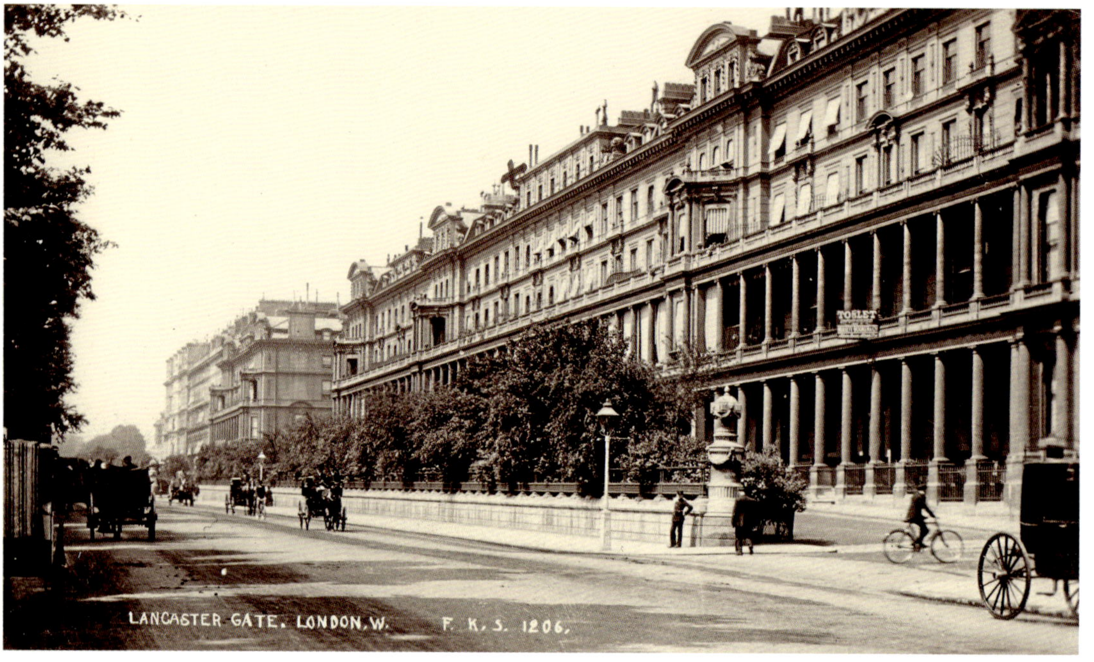

Lancaster Gate, Bayswater Road, *c.* 1903

The Victorians created these spectacular colonnaded terraces in around 1856 to the designs of Sancton Wood. Sadly, such grand Victoriana has not always been held in the highest esteem, and in the 1930s a modern design was allowed to intrude.

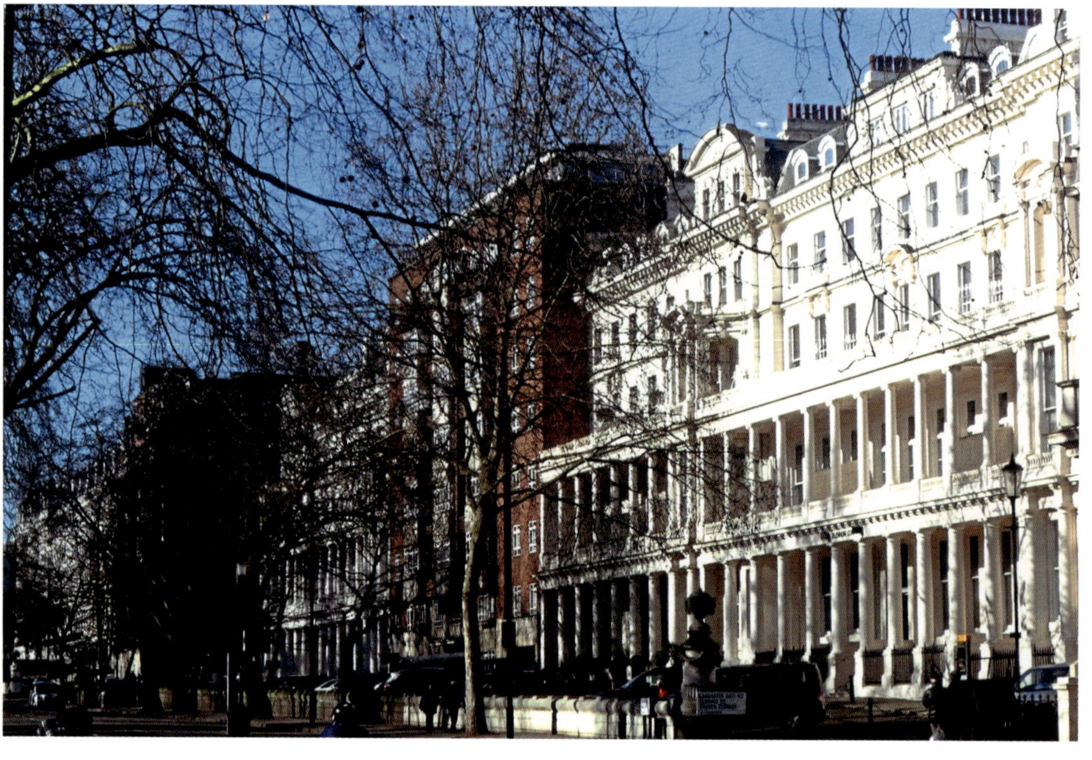

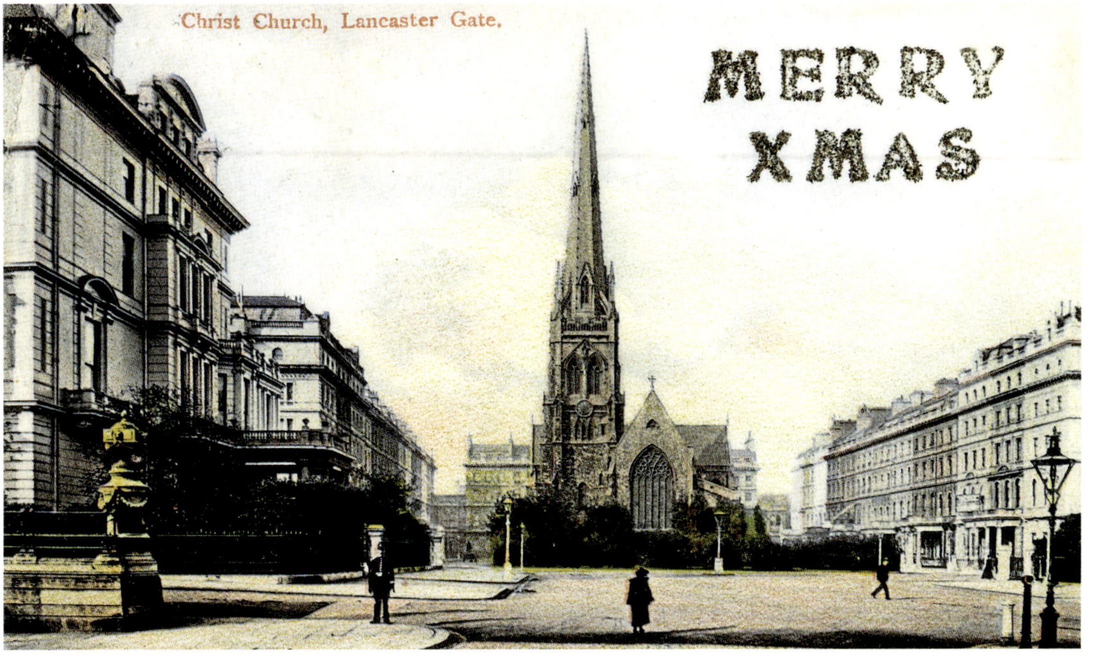

Christ Church, Lancaster Gate, *c.* 1906

The church was built in the Gothic Revival style from 1854–55 to designs by F. & H. Francis. The congregation was drawn from the occupants of the new town houses being built at the time in Bayswater. The spire is a notable landmark, especially when seen from Kensington Gardens, and it survived when much of the church was replaced in 1983 by Spire House (a residential conversion).

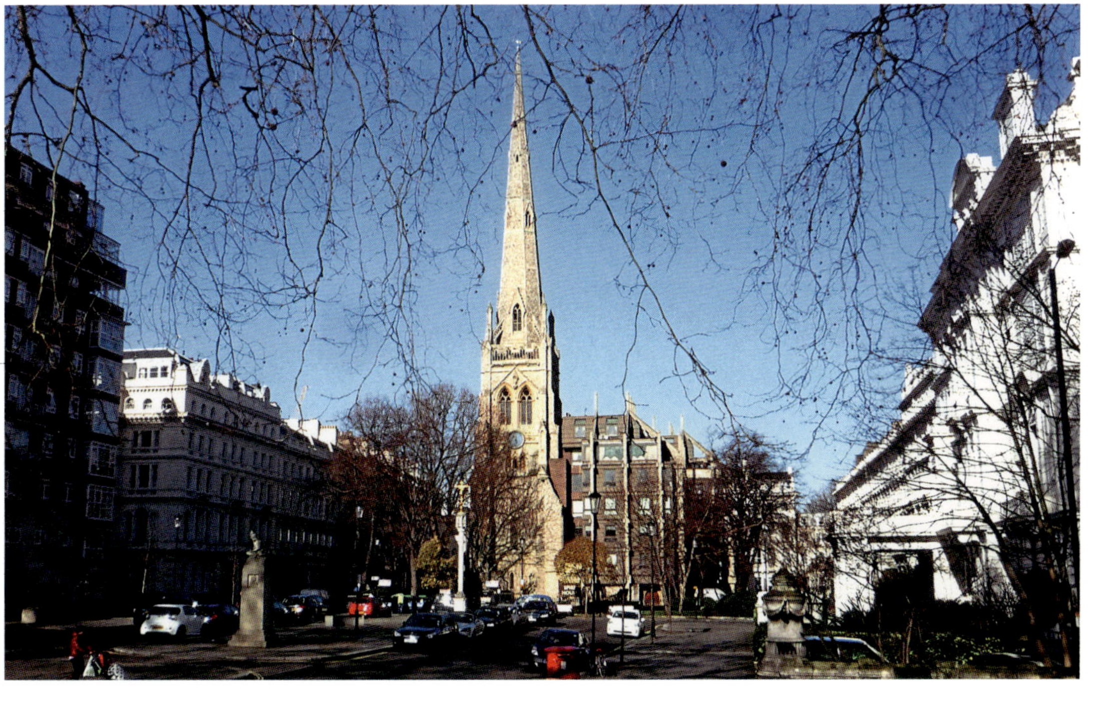

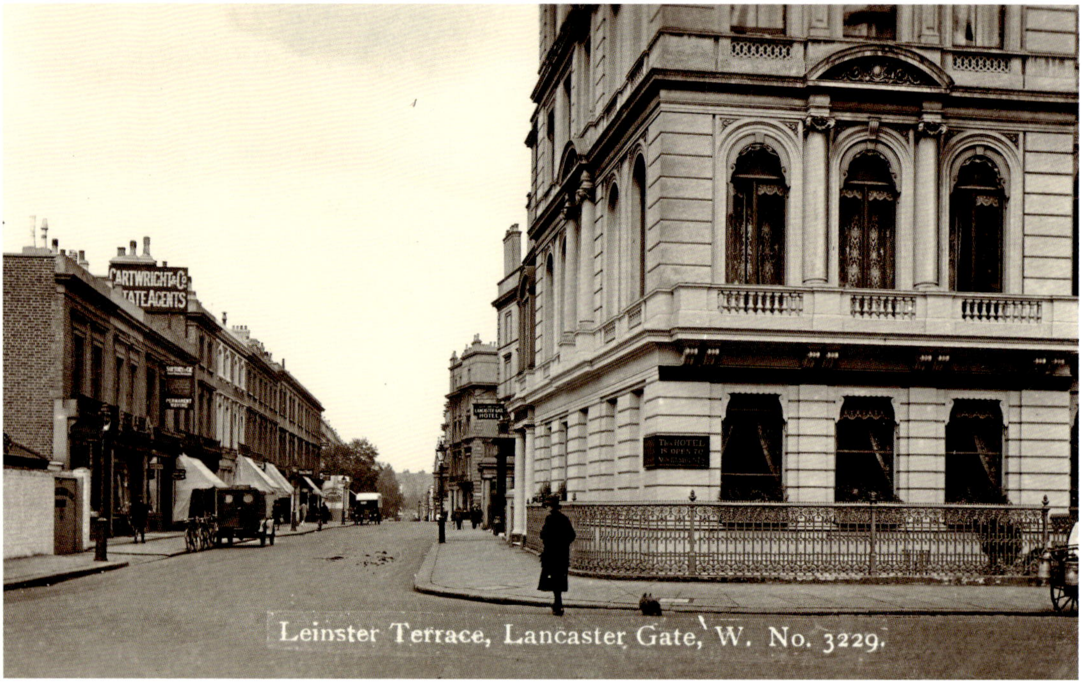

Leinster Terrace, *c.* 1920

The above image shows a street of shops that were built to serve the well-to-do residents of Bayswater's new houses, including local author J. M. Barrie whose house was just off-camera to the left. The street is now part of a well preserved conservation area.

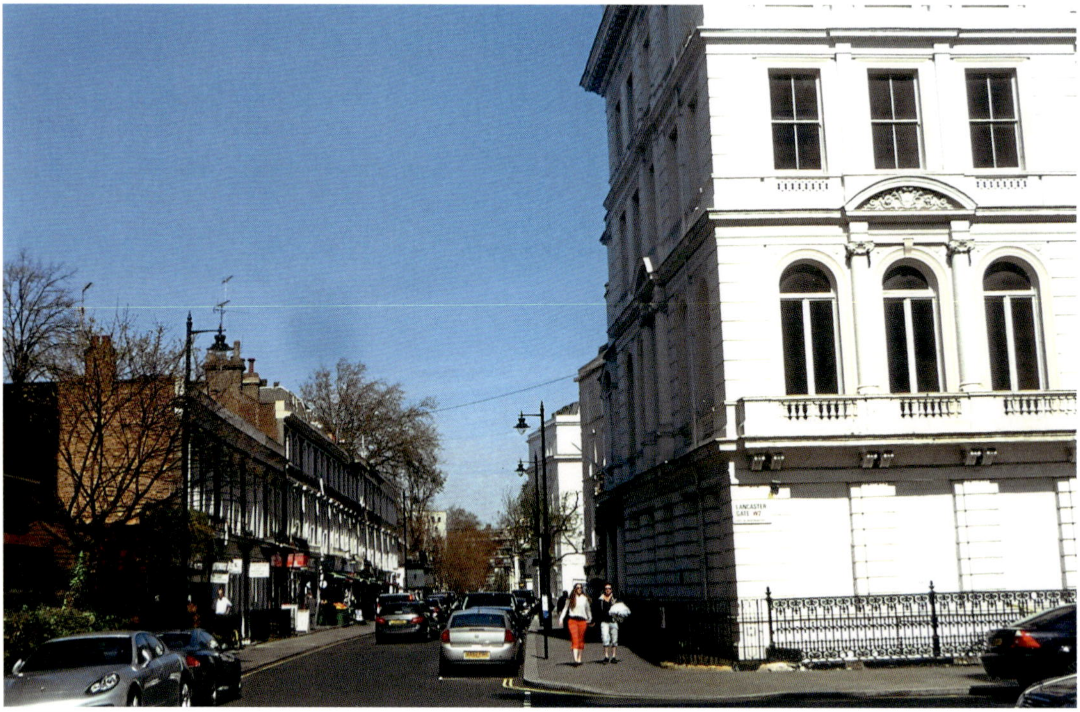

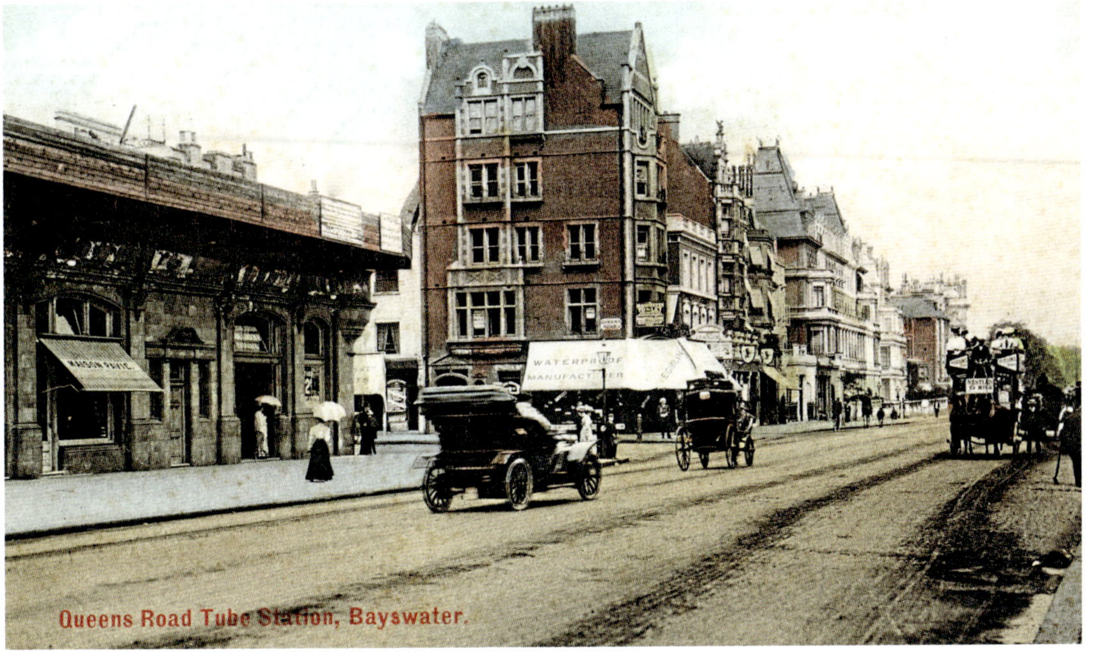

Queen's Road (Queensway) Tube station, *c.* 1903

Above is an early view of a station on what was then London's latest wonder – the Central London Railway (the Central Line), which opened on 30 July 1900. The line ran between Bank and Shepherd's Bush and offered fast cross-city transportation for a flat fare of 2*d*. The line was a vision of the future for late Victorian Londoners, with its deep-level electric trains in a city more used to steam locomotives and horse powered omnibuses. The image above was captured as work began on the Coburg Court Hotel above the station. The Tube stop retained its Queen's Road name until 1946.

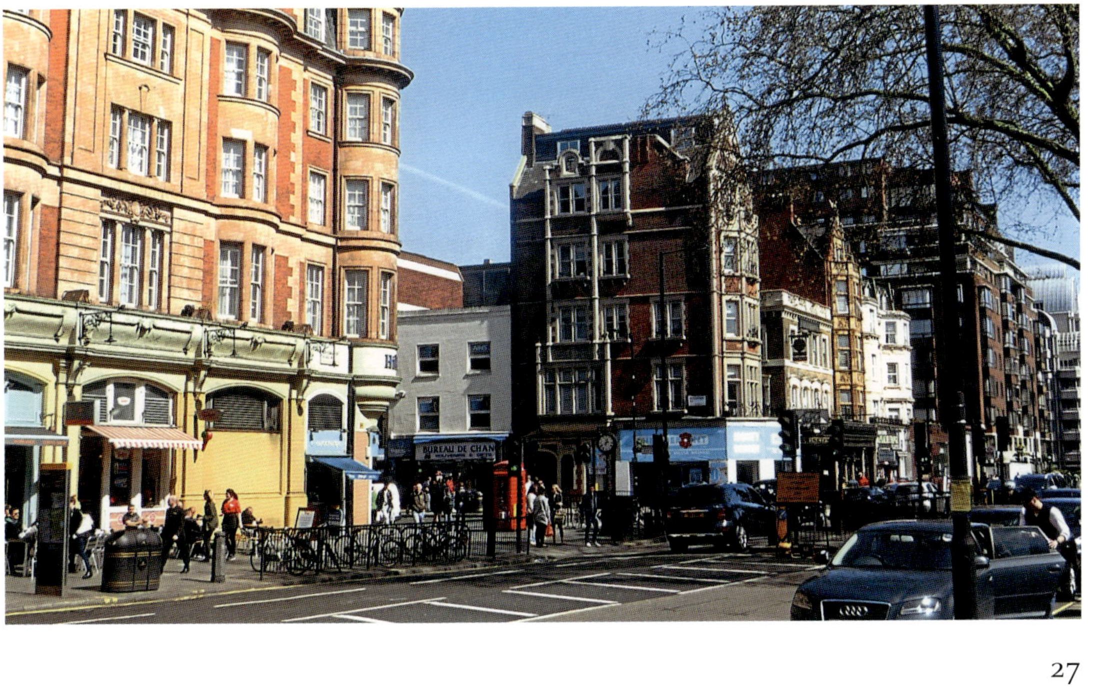

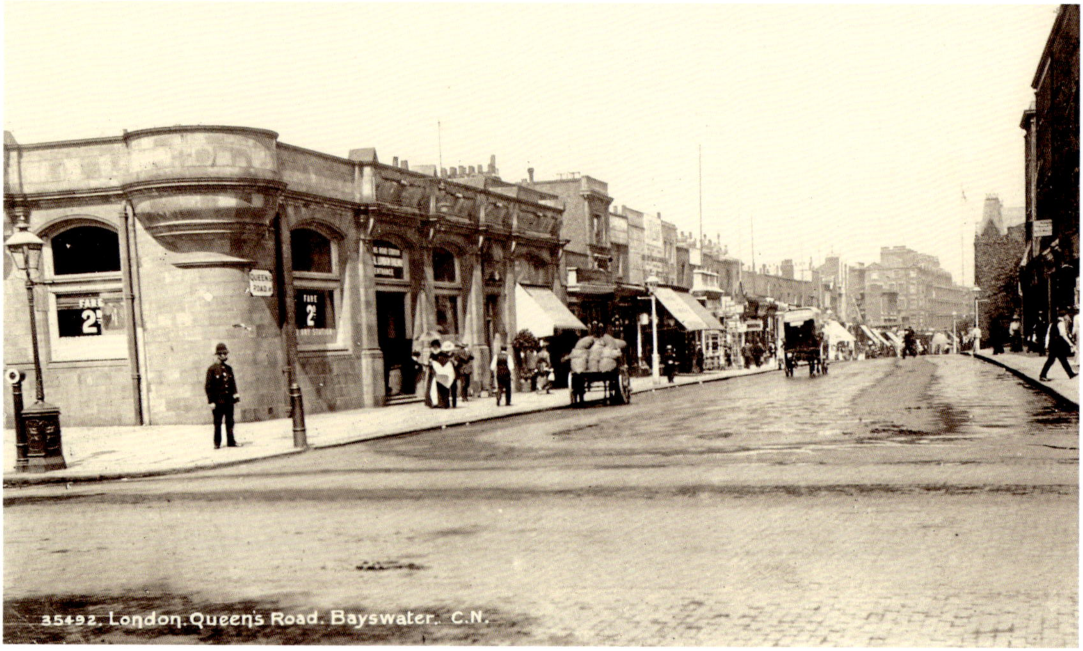

Queen's Road (Queensway) from Bayswater Road, *c.* 1902

The terracotta faced stations on the 'Twopenny Tube' were designed to take tall buildings above street level. Here, above, work had yet to begin on the Coburg Court Hotel. This was a part of Bayswater that had yet to be influenced by the close by Victorian grandeur, with Queen's Road and its hinterland home to a ragged assembly of lowly properties in which poverty existed. The great change came in 1928 with the construction of new flats called Queen's Court and an ice skating rink. Queen's Road was renamed Queensway in the 1930s.

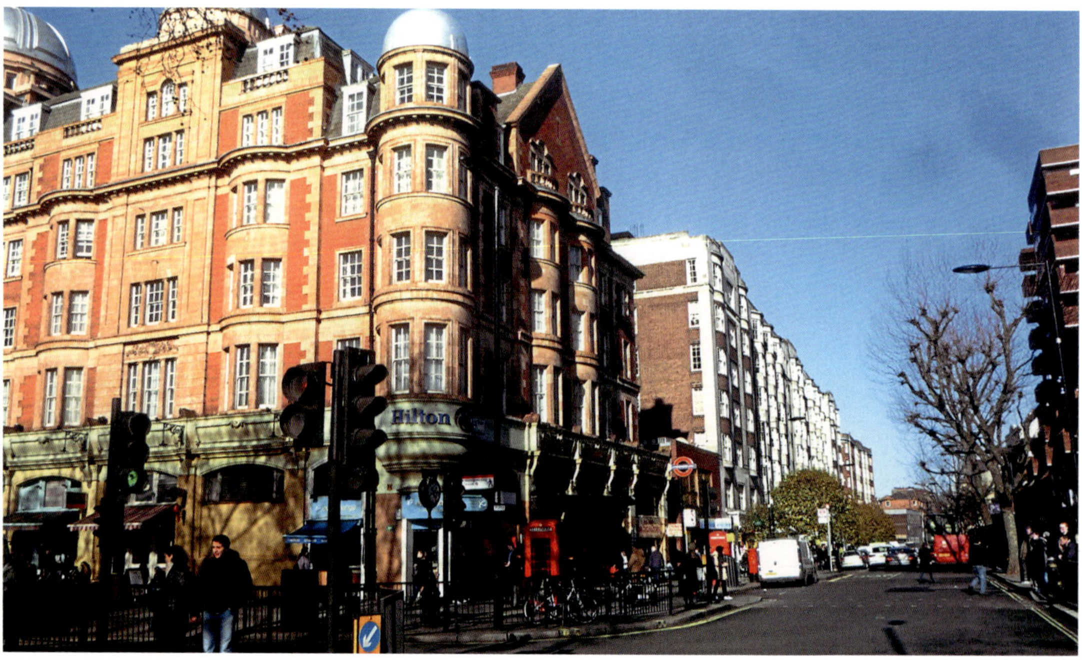

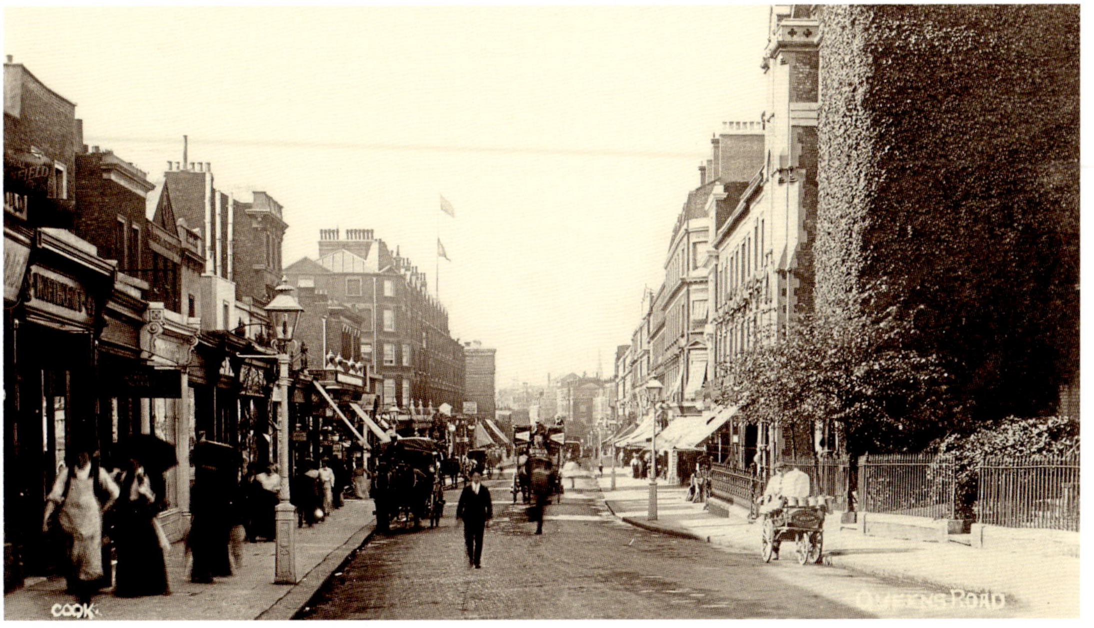

Queen's Road (Queensway) *c.* 1905

This street began as a rural track called Black Lion Lane, it was later renamed in honour of Queen Victoria. However, the royal influence did not extend to the architecture, seen here with shops built on the former front gardens of its early houses. The later Victorians brought new shopping rows as the street evolved into Bayswater's high street, but it was the Edwardians who firmly established this as a prime shopping destination with the rebuilding of the mighty Whiteley's department store.

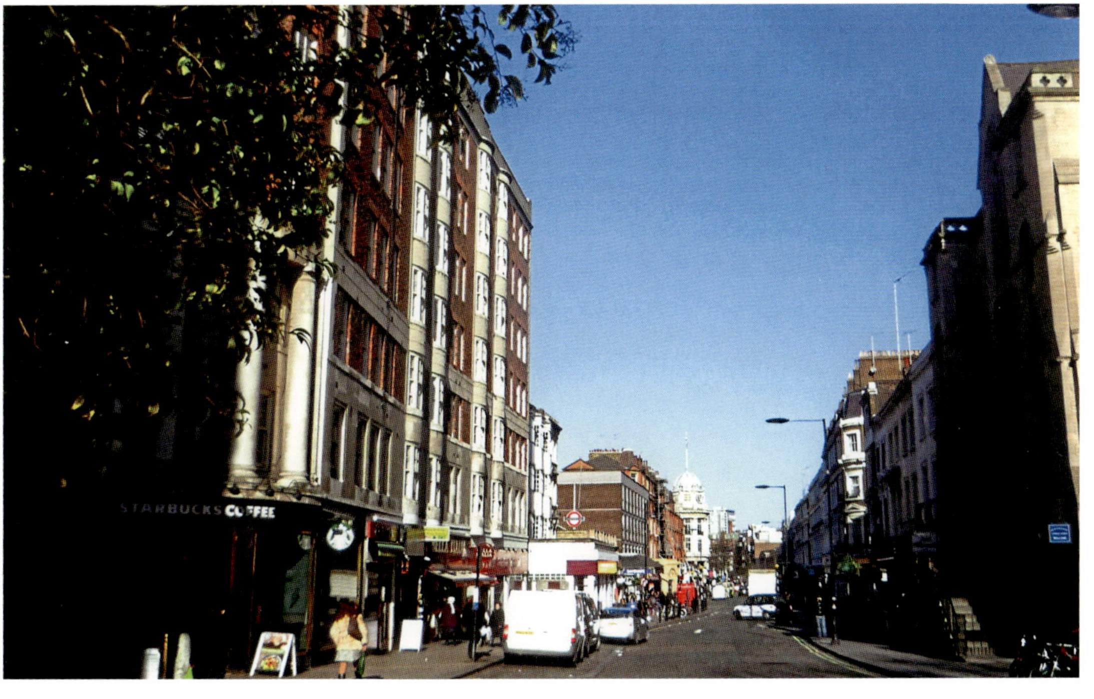

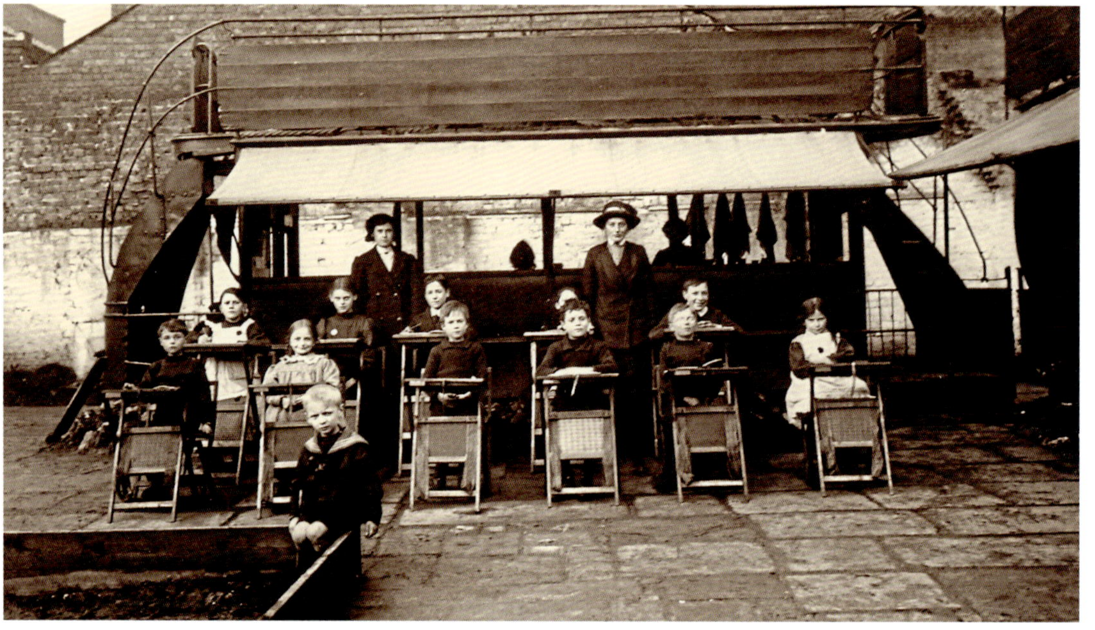

Poplar Square School, Poplar Place, 1912

Poplar Square was a transient address consisting of four lowly cottages built in the 1820s. The poverty afflicted area also contained a Ragged School. In 1912 this became the location for a temporary infant school, its classrooms were housed in a pair of redundant horse trams. Old horse trams were put to a variety of uses following their withdrawal from passenger service – their application at Poplar Square was possibly unique. No doubt the children appreciated the novelty of such an unusual school, but they would have needed to wrap up well in the winter months. The modern view of the approximate site is seen from Caroline Place Mews in the bottom image.

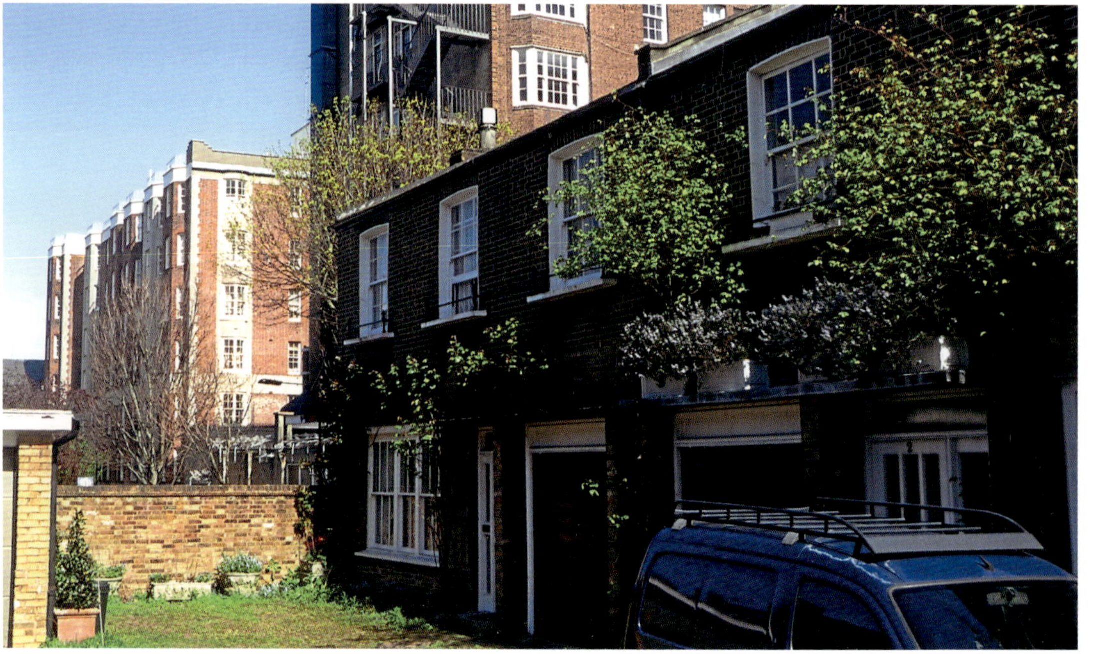

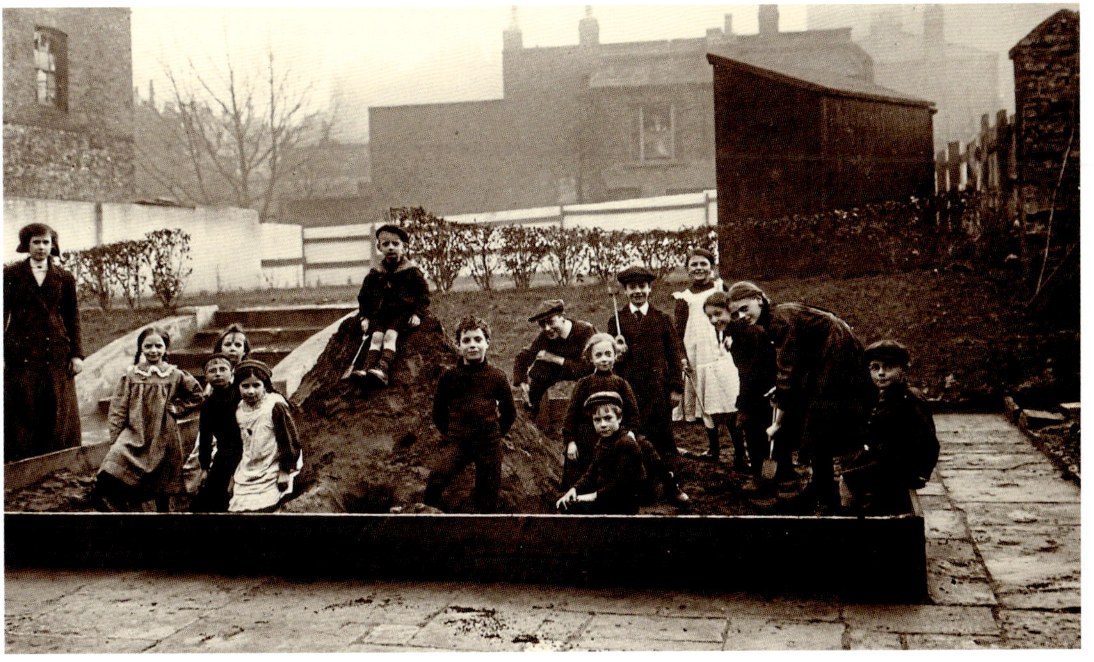

Poplar Square School, Poplar Place, 1912

The photograph above was taken a fortnight after the school opened in November 1912, its popular sandpit can be seen, as can steps leading to a grassy playground. The image captured something of the modest nature of the neighbourhood as it was then, with its run-down cottages, but with the grander world of Bayswater Road visible in the far distance. Luxury modern housing has long since transformed the area.

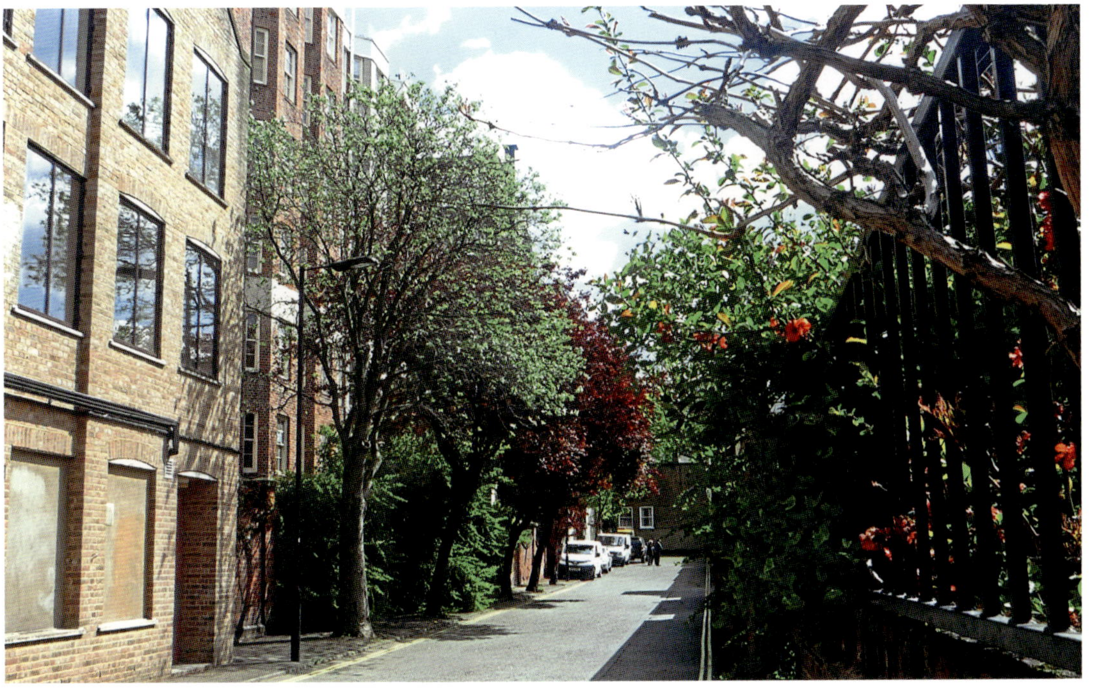

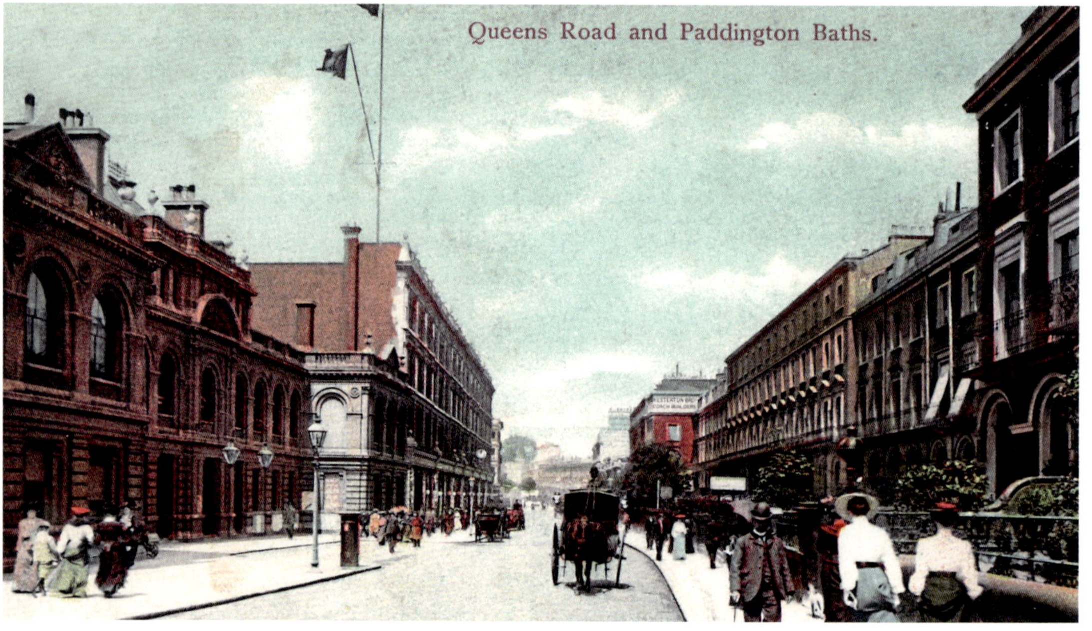

Paddington Baths and Whiteley's, *c.* 1906

The mid-Victorian draper William Whiteley opened his first shop in Westbourne Grove before making a move to Queen's Road where he established a large department store. 'The Universal Provider' rebuilt this on an epic scale in 1911, completing the project in 1925. By the 1980s the vast store was deemed too large for a location which had declined somewhat as a major shopping area. The store closed, but reopened in 1981 as a multiple outlet called Whiteley's Shopping Centre. Paddington Baths (visible in the above image to the left) had opened in 1874 but gave its site for the 'New Whiteley's' in 1911.

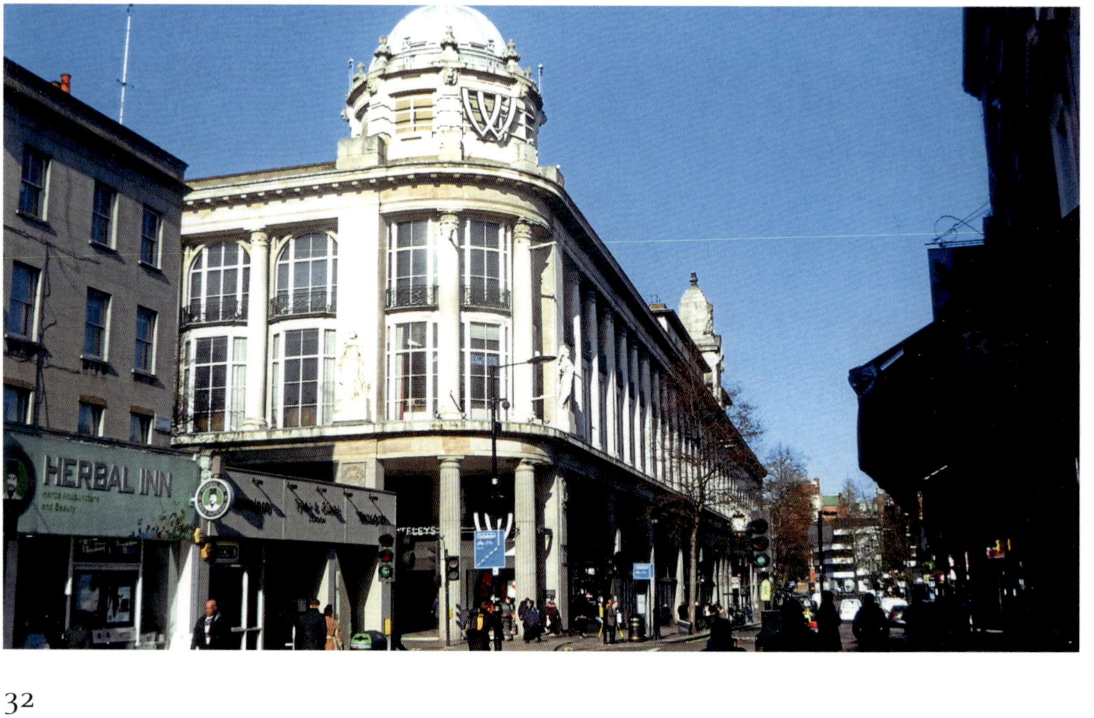

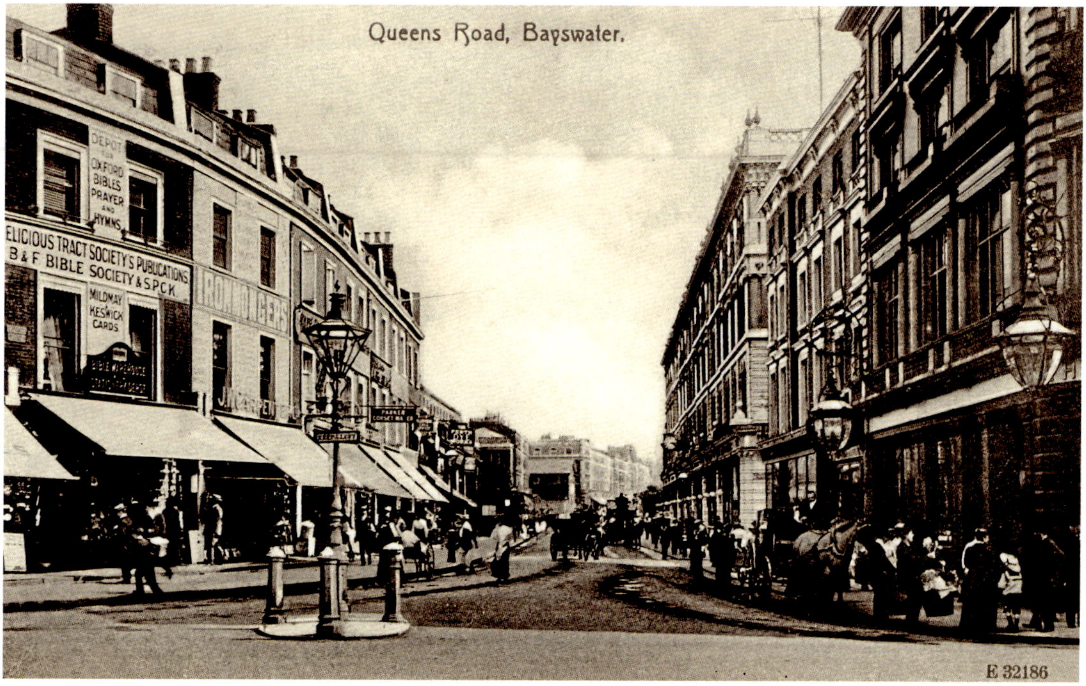

Queen's Road (Queensway) from Bishop's Bridge Road, *c*. 1906

Road widening and the replacement of the buildings on the left by flats has given a new look to this old shopping street. 'Old' Whiteley's is seen centre right, and the Redan pub has been caught in both views.

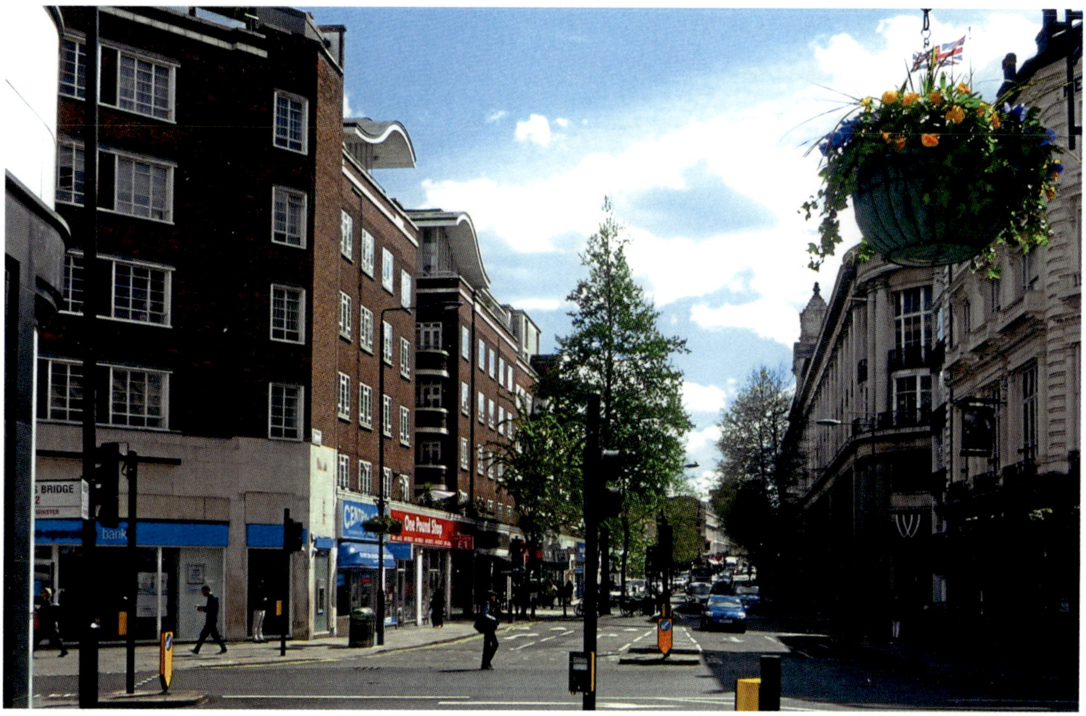

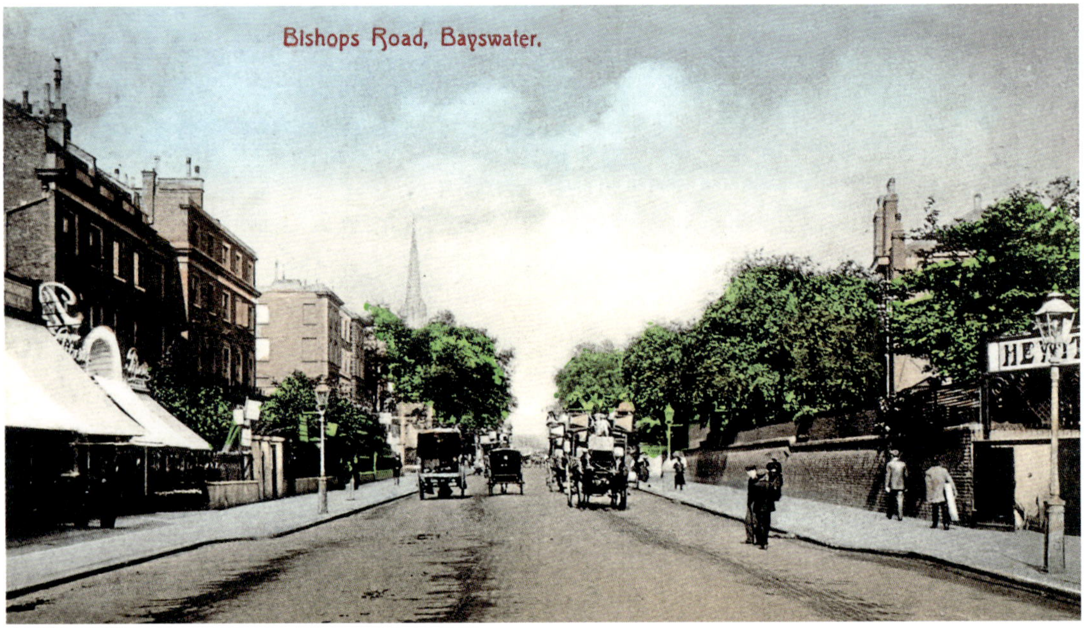

Bishop's Road (Bishop's Bridge Road), *c.* 1906

The residential section of Bishop's Road was made up of large houses and terraces (visible to the above left) and by the extensive gardens surrounding the vast houses of Porchester Terrace (seen to the right). It all changed in dramatic fashion from the end of the 1940s with the construction for the Borough of Paddington and one of the great post-war housing schemes, the Hallfield Estate. This abolished the old street pattern as new blocks by the renowned Tecton, Drake and Lasdun arose. The partnership's work espoused continental modernism, then rare in London. The first phase was completed in 1955.

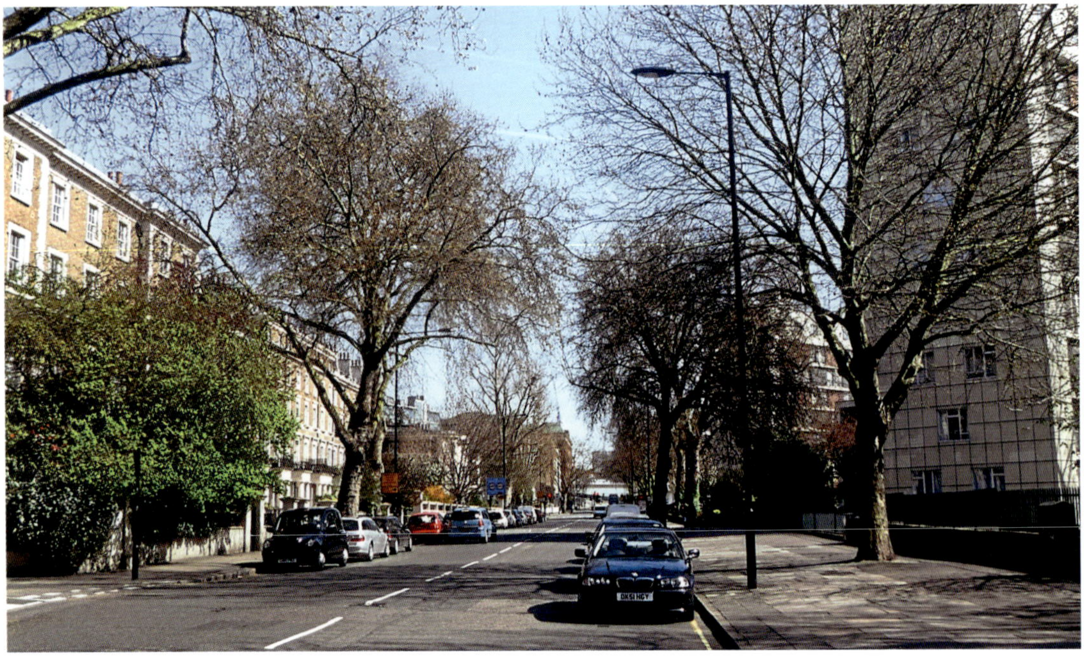

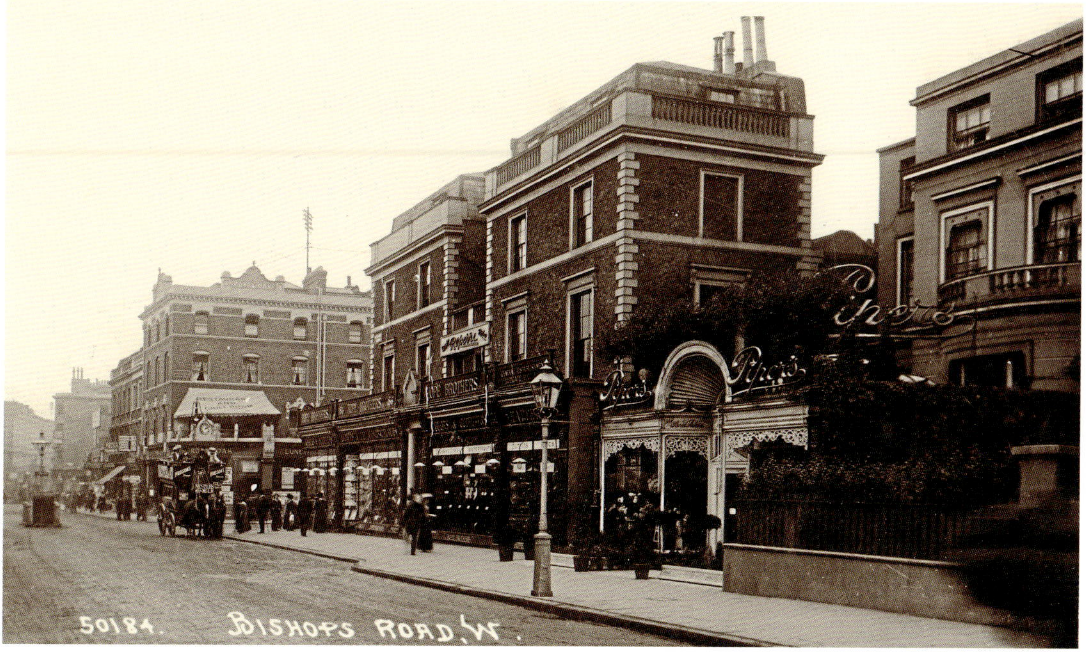

Bishop's Road (Bishop's Bridge Road), ***c.*** **1906**

This street evolved from a rural track called Bishop's Walk, but we see it in the above image when a range of shops lined its western end. The shop of John Piper & Sons (a florist), stands out here with its shell-like entrance. There is a distant sight of Porchester Road with the Royal Oak pub on the corner.

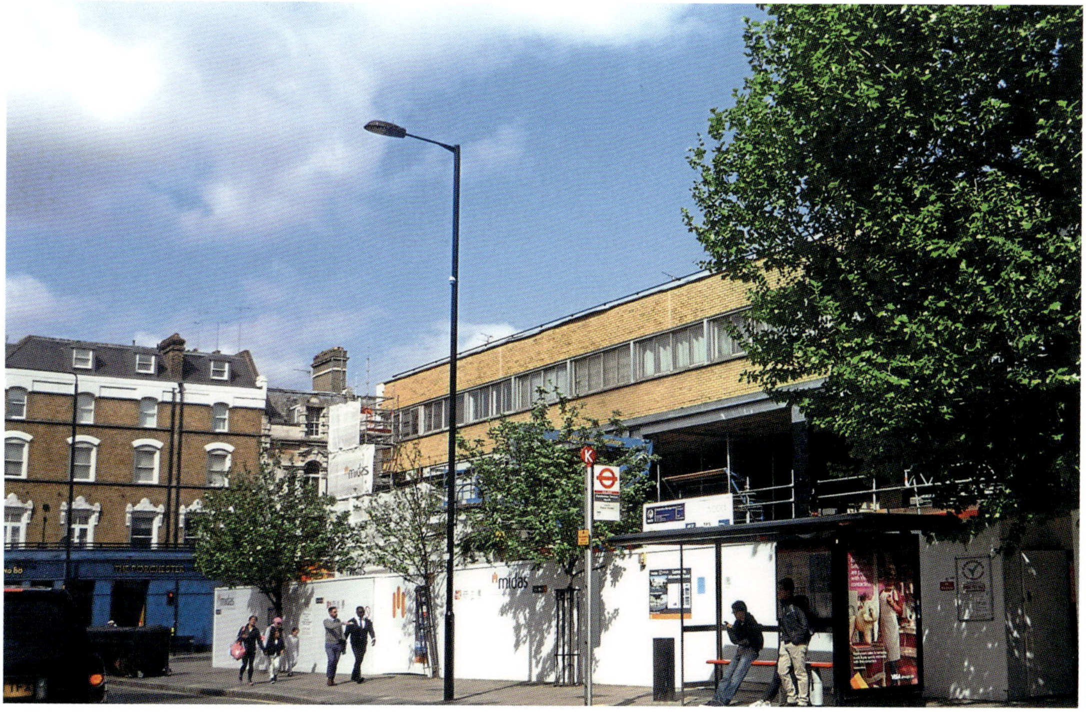

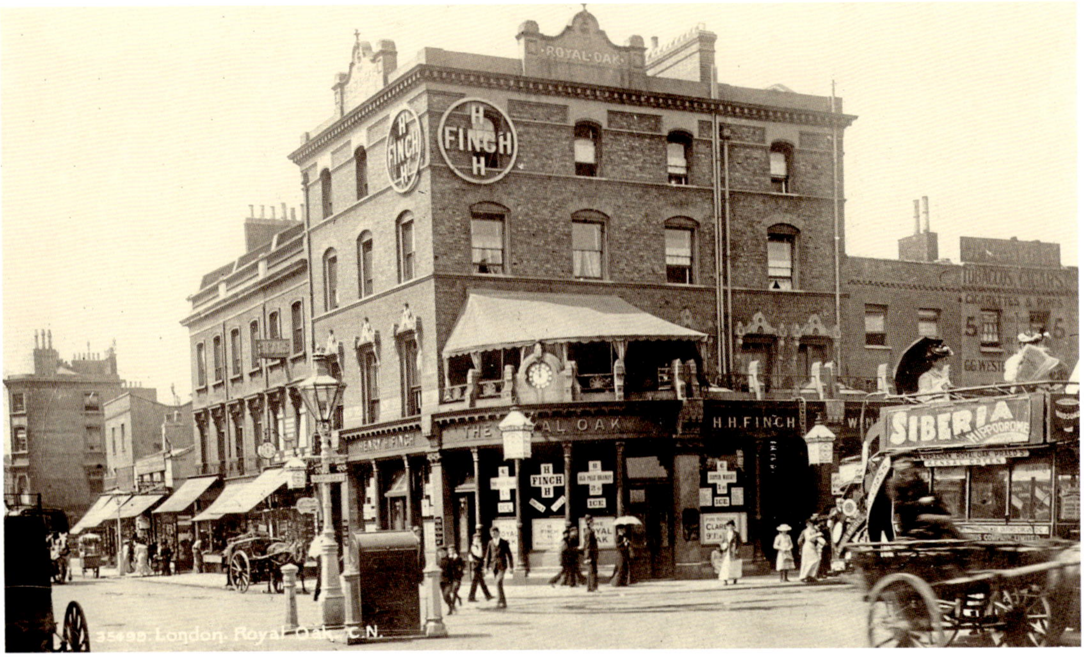

The Royal Oak, Bishop's Road by Porchester Road, *c.* 1903

This historic pub, dating from the 1870s, is a rebuilding of the original Royal Oak, a tavern and tea gardens that enjoyed a rural setting near the village of Westbourne Green. To the right of the above image, a row of aged shops would shortly be rebuilt.

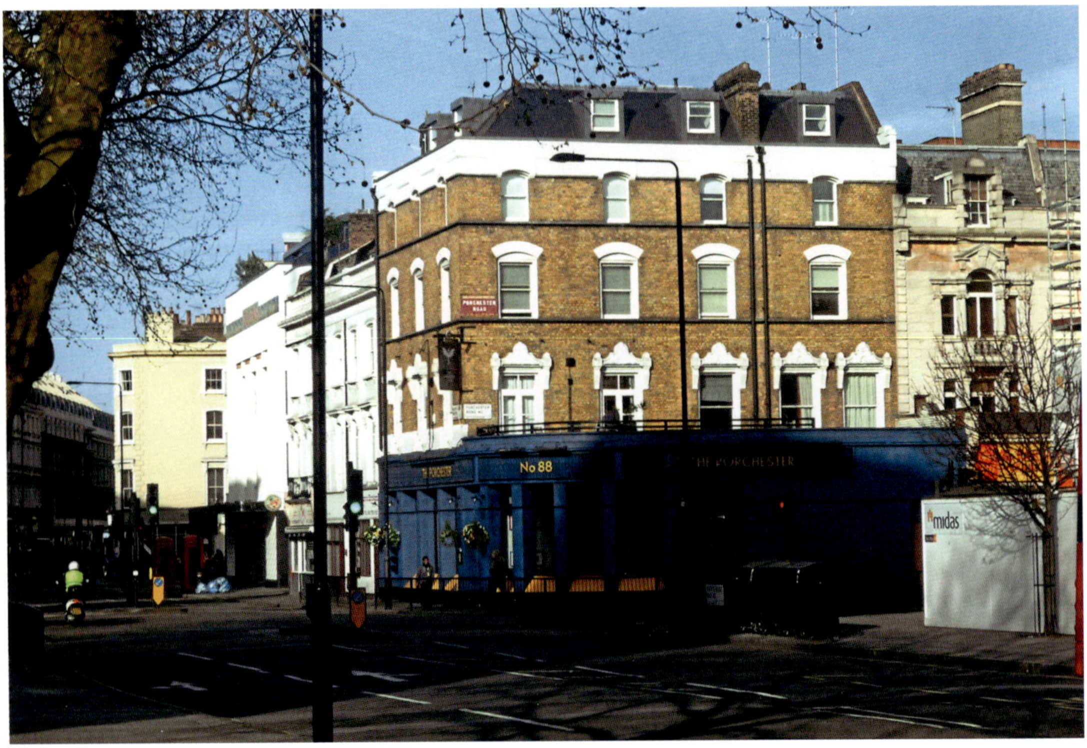

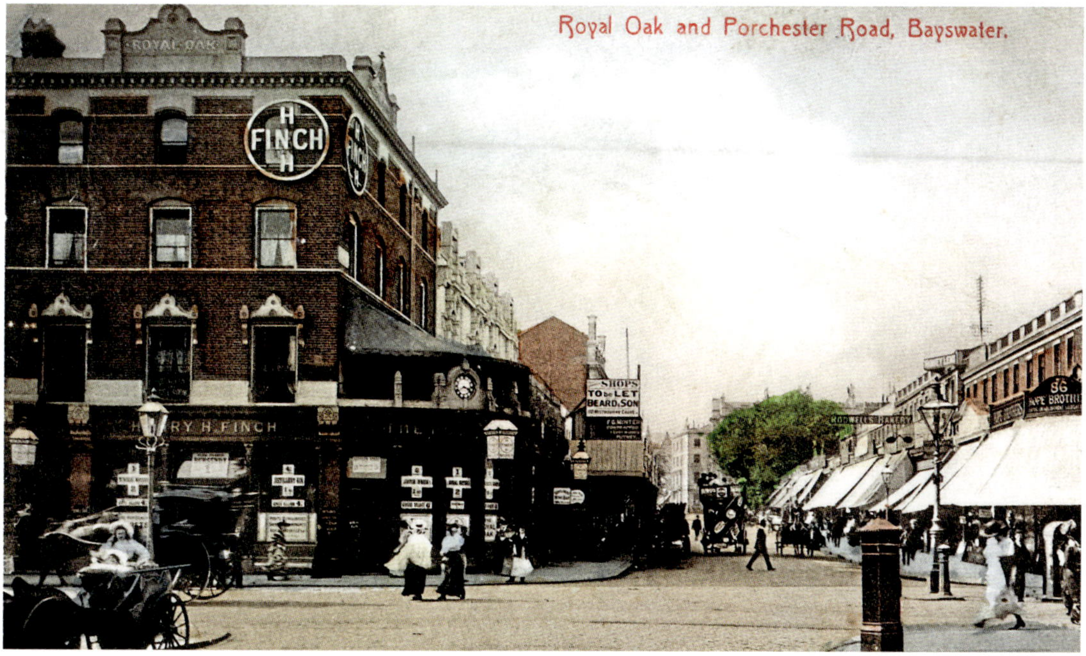

The Royal Oak and Porchester Road, *c.* 1906

This shows the Royal Oak's new neighbouring shops emerging from the builder's hoardings. Their construction extended the shopping facilities in the district. The pub currently has a new modern look and a new name, but the early octagonal pillar box in the foreground has been removed.

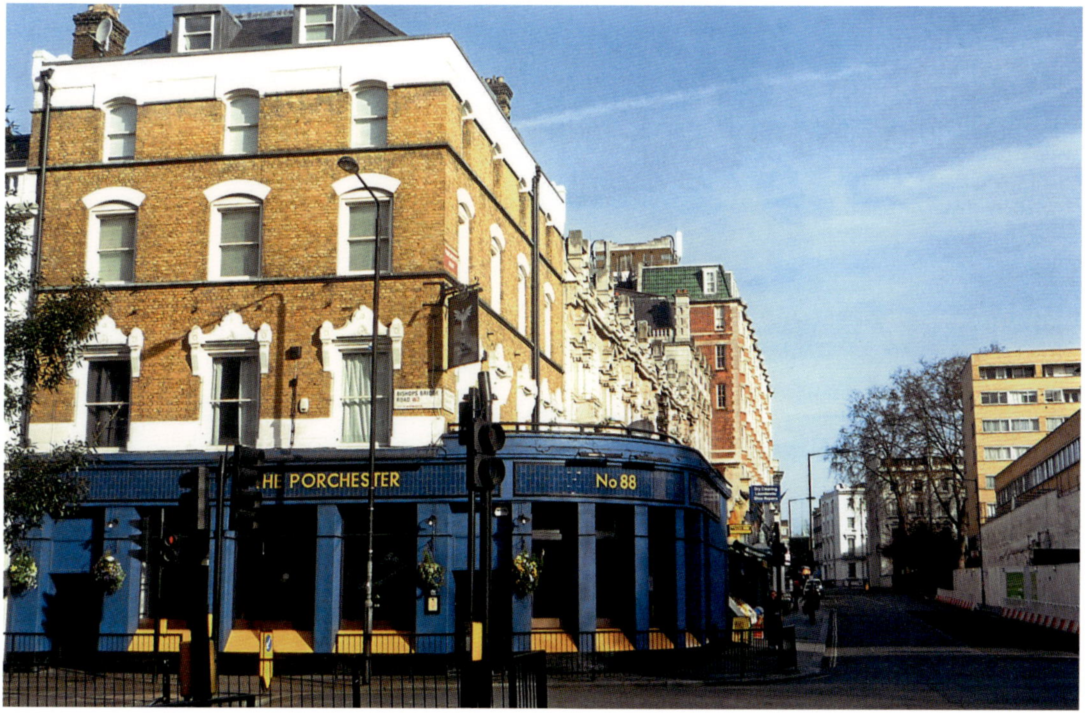

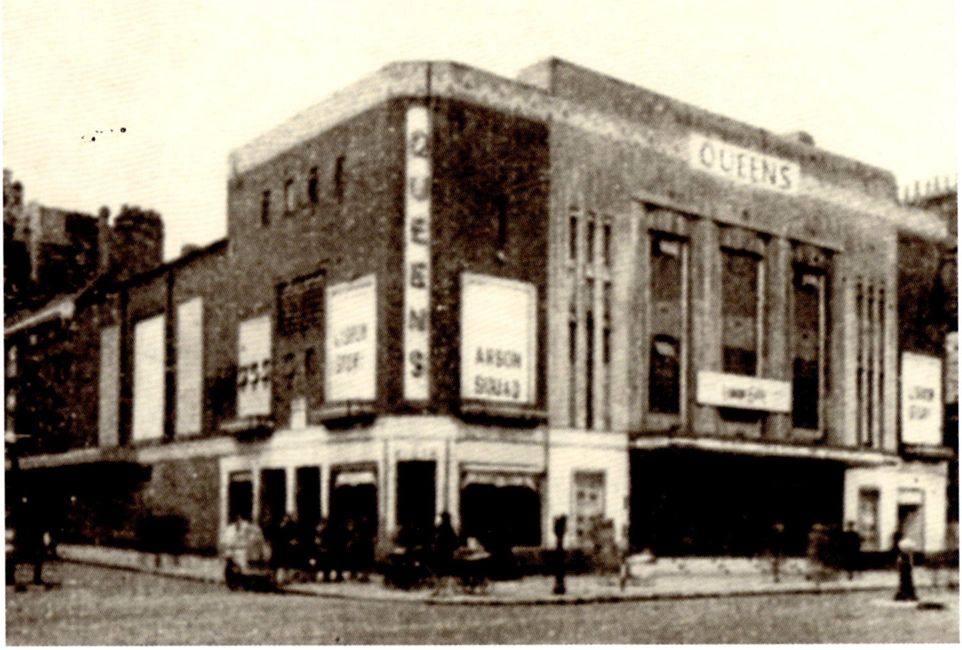

The Queens Cinema, Bishop's Bridge Road, *c.* 1955

The 1920s and 1930s saw the rise of the super-cinema in London, and among them was the Queens which replaced a row of old shops. Seating 1,417 movie-goers, the Queens boasted a superb façade in the, then, fashionable art deco style. As cinema attendances gradually dwindled in the face of television and bingo, the Queens closed. However, it has been reborn as the Queens Apartments, which respect the art deco design behind the beautifully restored façade.

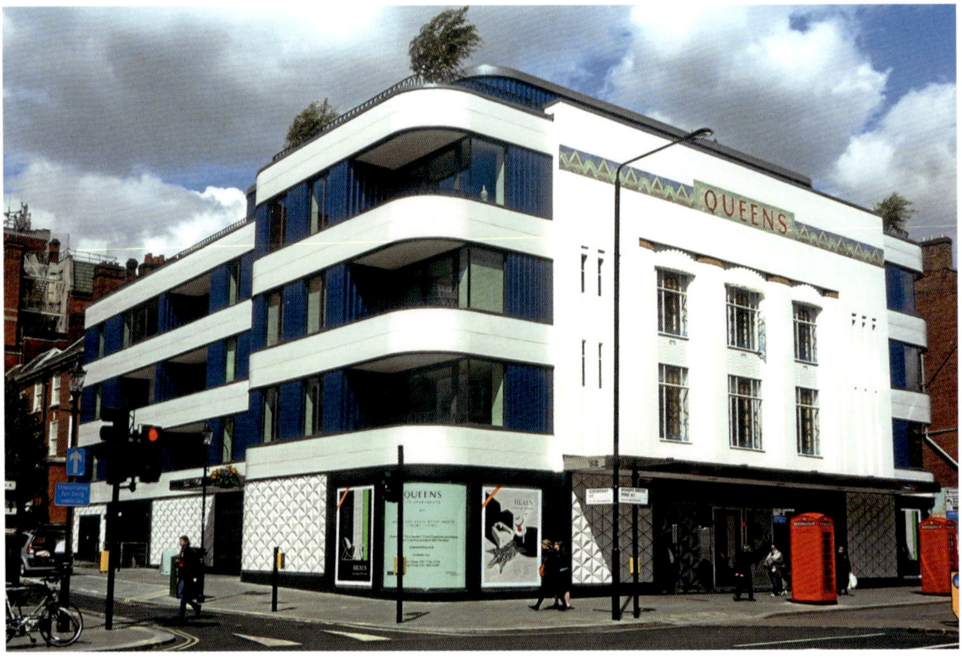

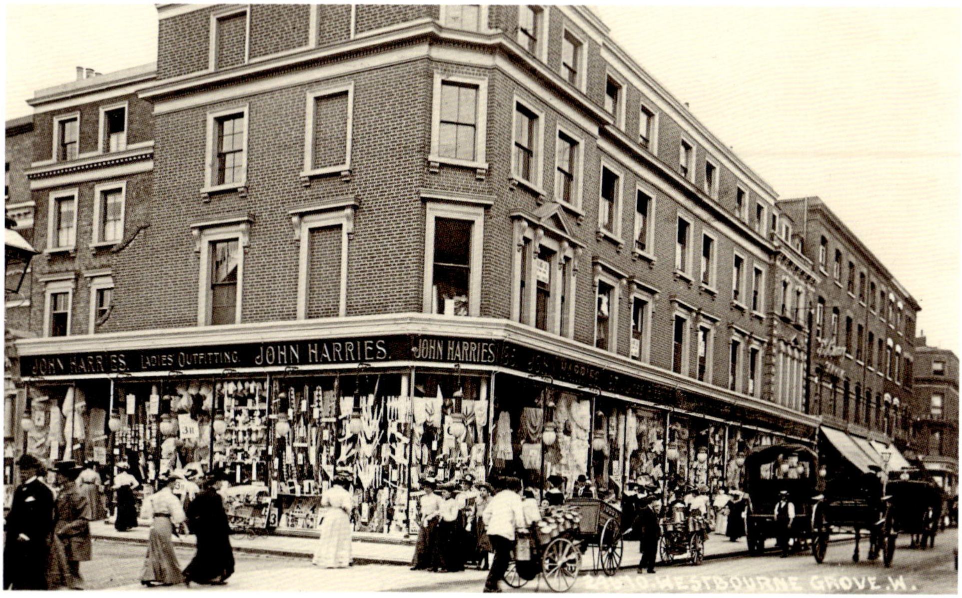

Westbourne Grove by Monmouth Road, *c.* 1908

Wesbourne Grove had pretensions of rivalling Oxford Street as a major London shopping destination, and in the Edwardian era a variety of large department stores sought the shoppers' guineas. Curiously, though, there were no grand purpose-built stores. Instead, many of the original small shops were knocked through to create spacious retailing floors. A classic enterprise was that of John Harries, ladies' outfitter, who created a single store out of Nos 97–103. As time passed, this large emporium dwindled away, and as is seen here the small individual shops returned.

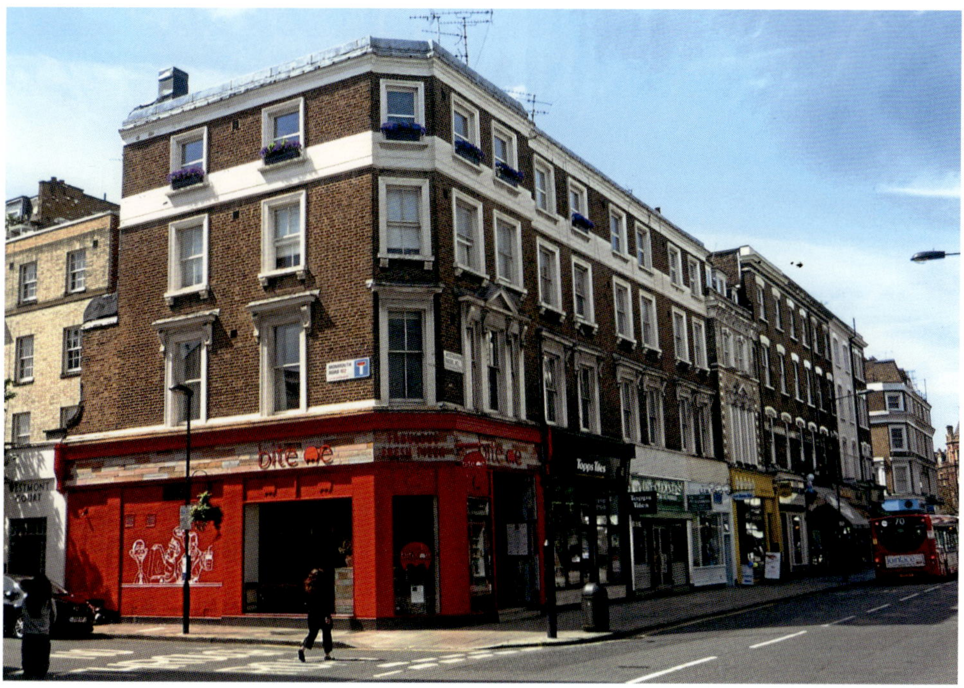

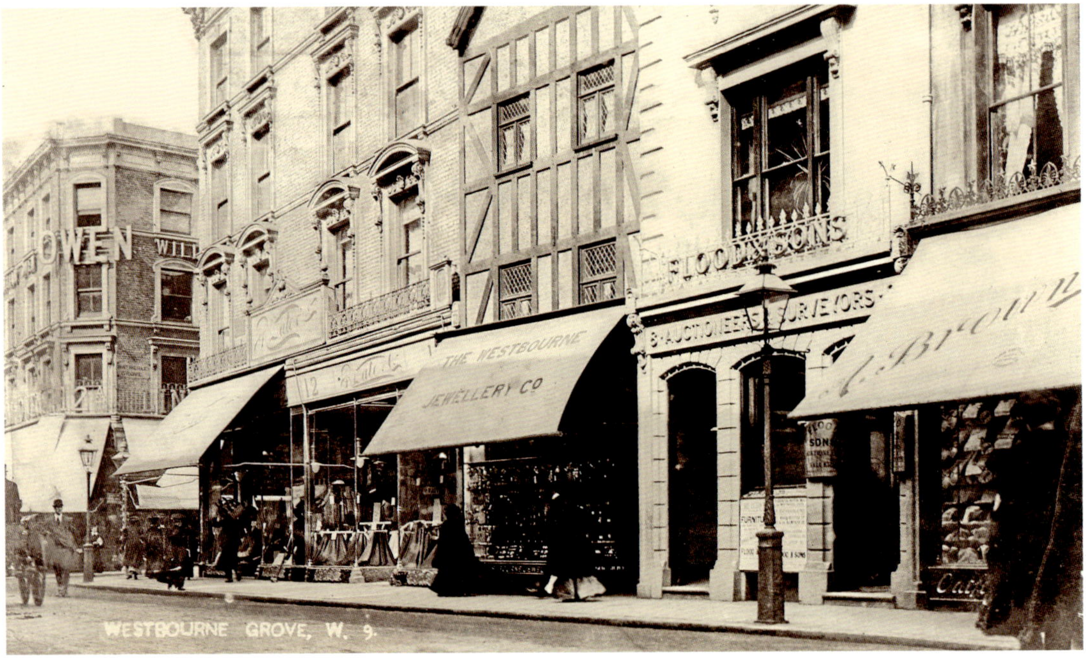

Westbourne Grove by Hatherley Grove, *c.* 1910

This part of the street always retained its small shops, but on the Hatherley Grove corner the draper William Owen ousted a row of them. While the architecture was solidly Victorian, the Westbourne Jewellery's Co. tried the Tudor look with nailed-on half timbering and leaded windows. It has now lost its original gable.

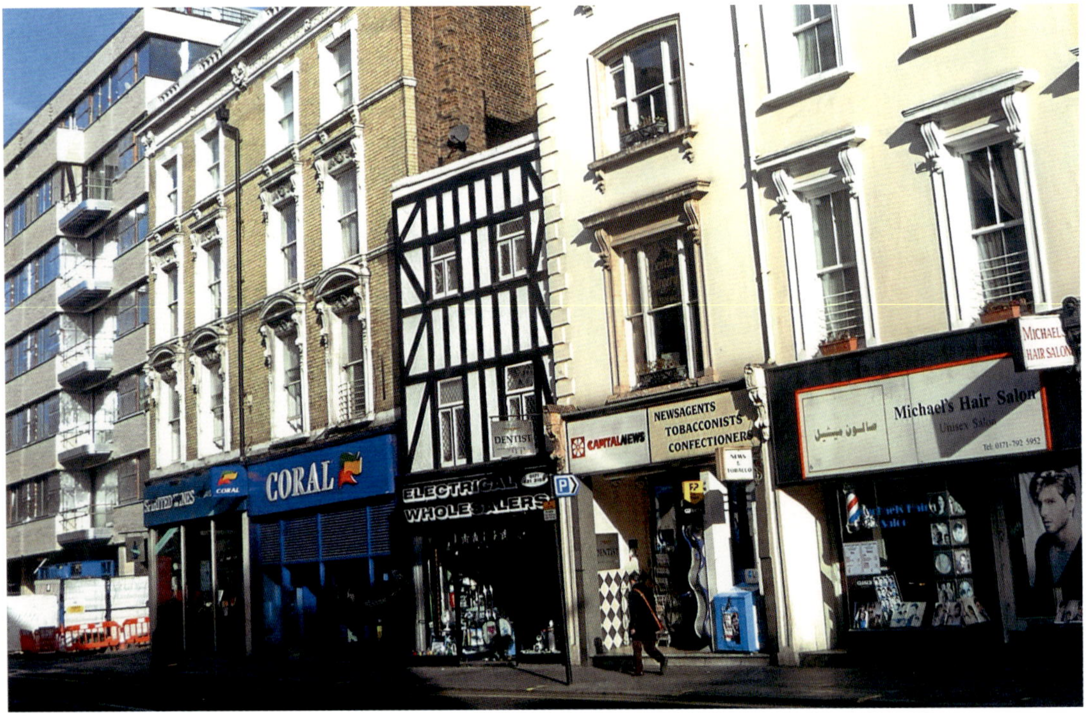

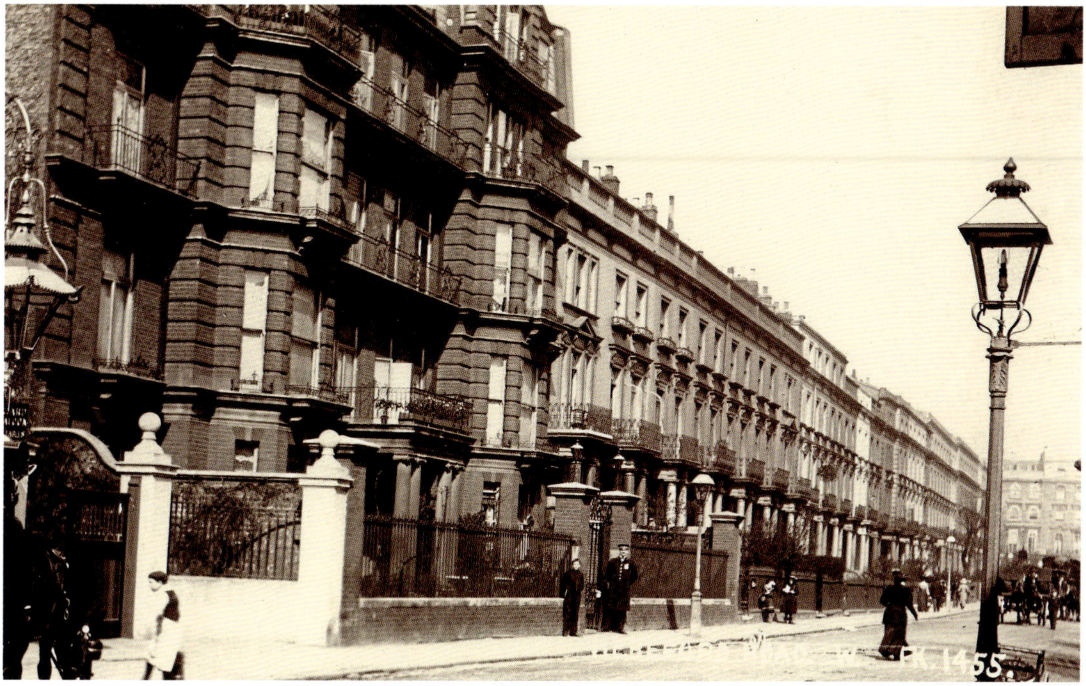

Hereford Road from Westbourne Grove, *c.* 1904

This remains a well-preserved street of mansion flats and residential terraces, the earliest of them are from the 1850s. We see the street in its Edwardian days above, when the street was lit by gas; the hanging lamp on the Princess Royal pub (to the left of the bottom image) still gives a reminder of those days.

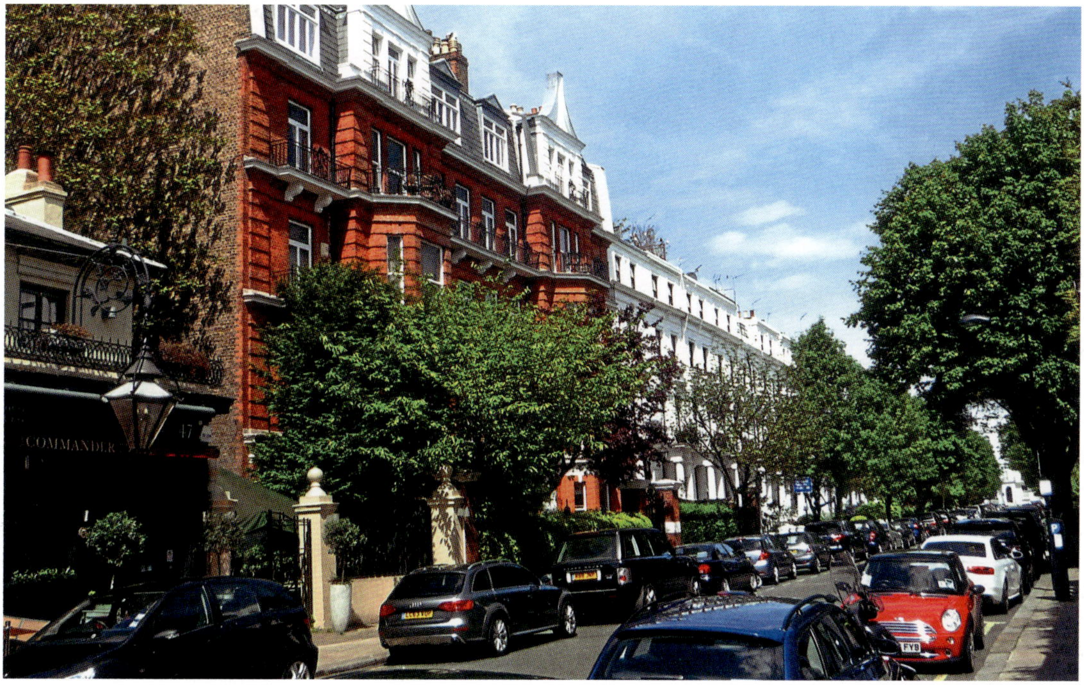

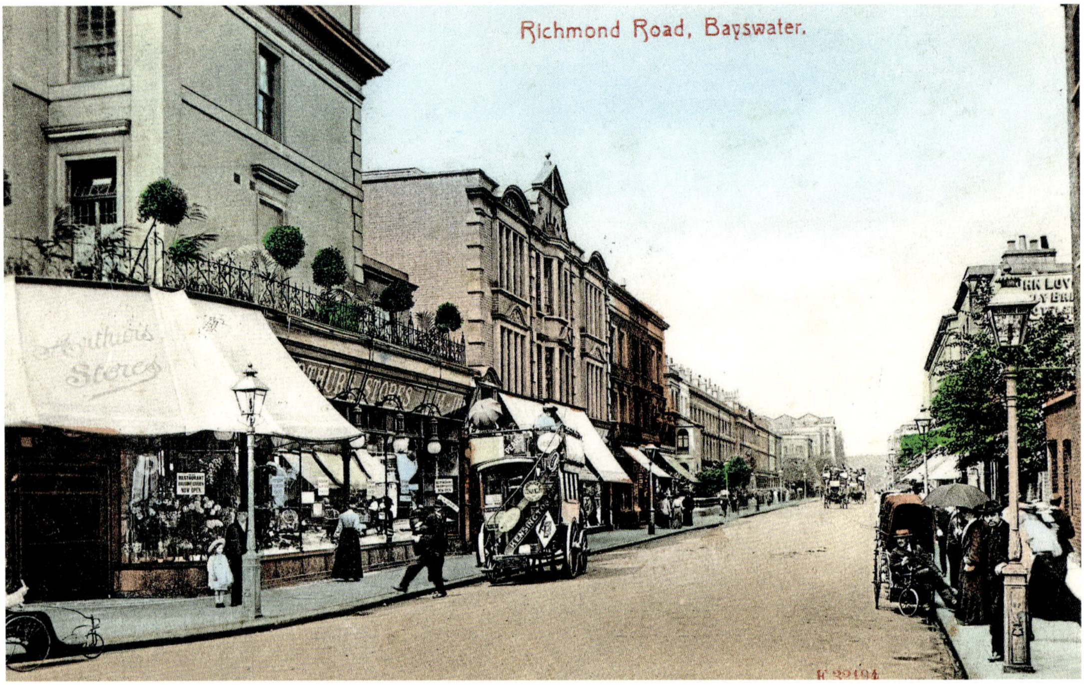

Richmond Road (Chepstow Road) from Westbourne Grove, *c.* 1905
Much of this street retains its original housing, apart from the group on the left where Arthur's Stores was housed in what was once a grand Regency villa. This was one of several 'Richmond Roads' in London to be given a new name in the 1930s.

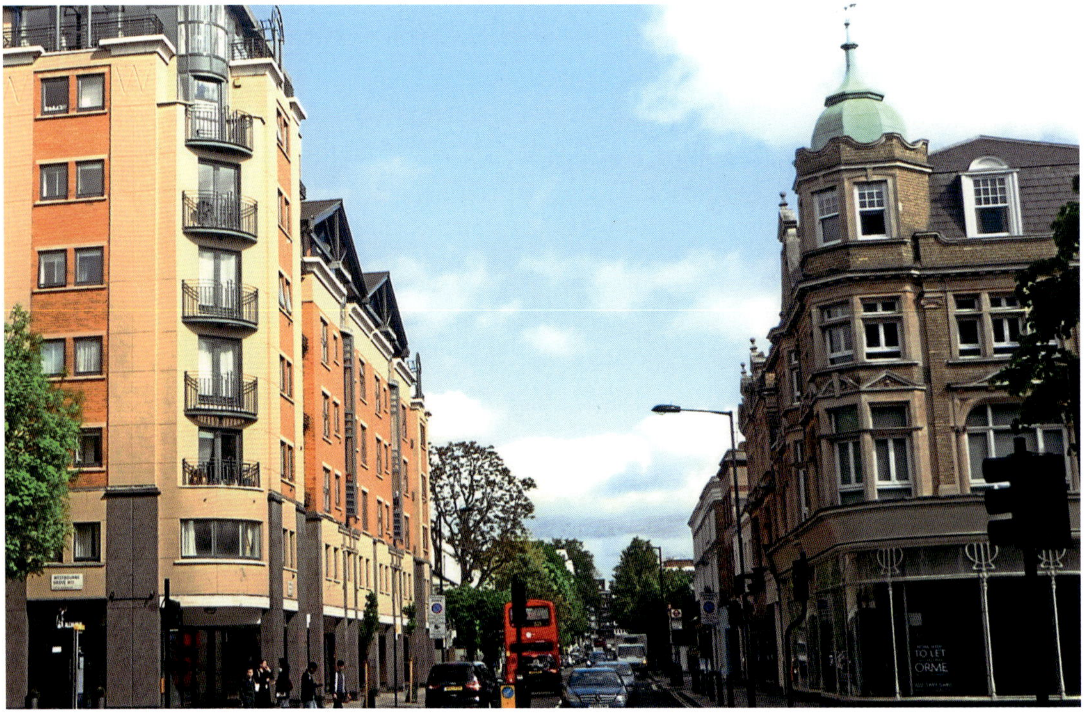

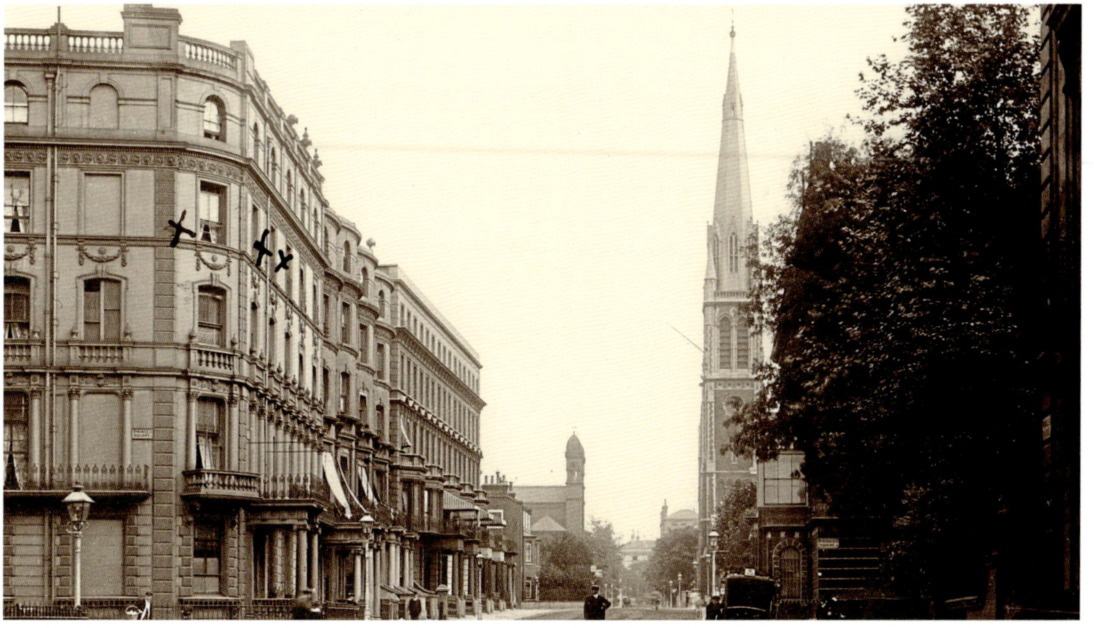

St Petersburg Place from Prince's Square, *c.* 1906

The slender spire of St Matthew's Bayswater (1881–82) looks out over a classic Bayswater townscape, which in Prince's Square included a group of tall houses with bowed fronts that were characteristic of the neighbourhood. The outline of the New West End Synagogue (1877–79) is visible in the early image, but in this street of mixed faiths, St Sophia's (known as the Greek Orthodox Cathedral from 1932) is just out of sight.

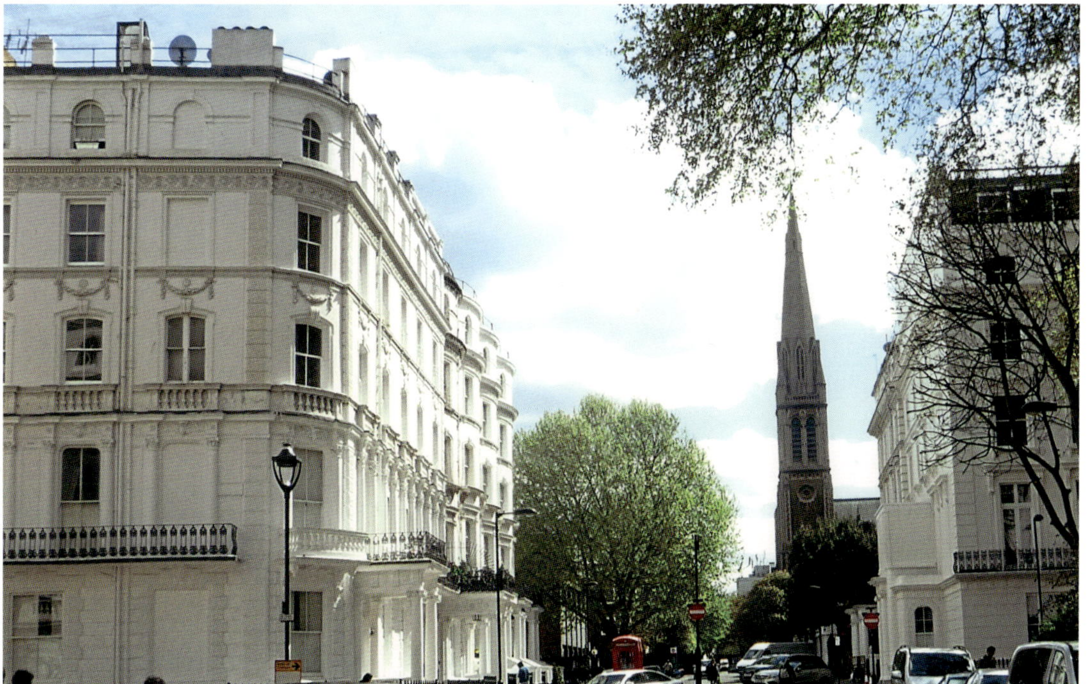

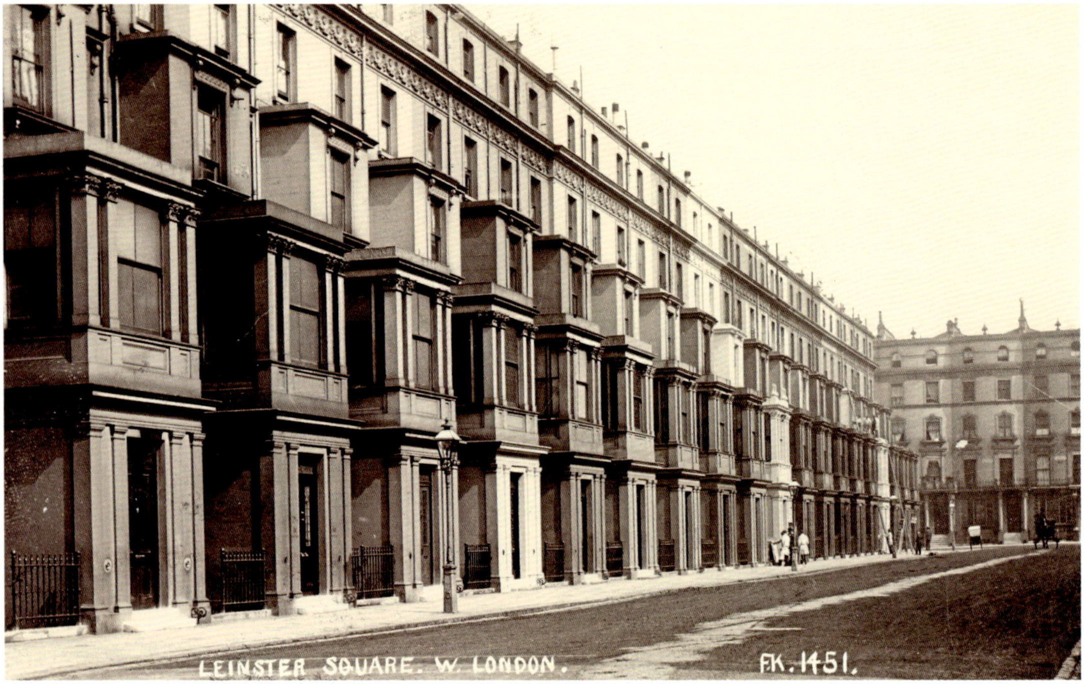

Leinster Square, *c.* 1905

These are some of the curious 'back-to-front' houses that are unique to Notting Hill and Bayswater. What we see here are actually the fronts of the houses, while the 'back' has a more imposing façade overlooking leafy communal gardens. The houses and hotels that some of them contain have been well preserved, and there are new saplings to soften the urban image.

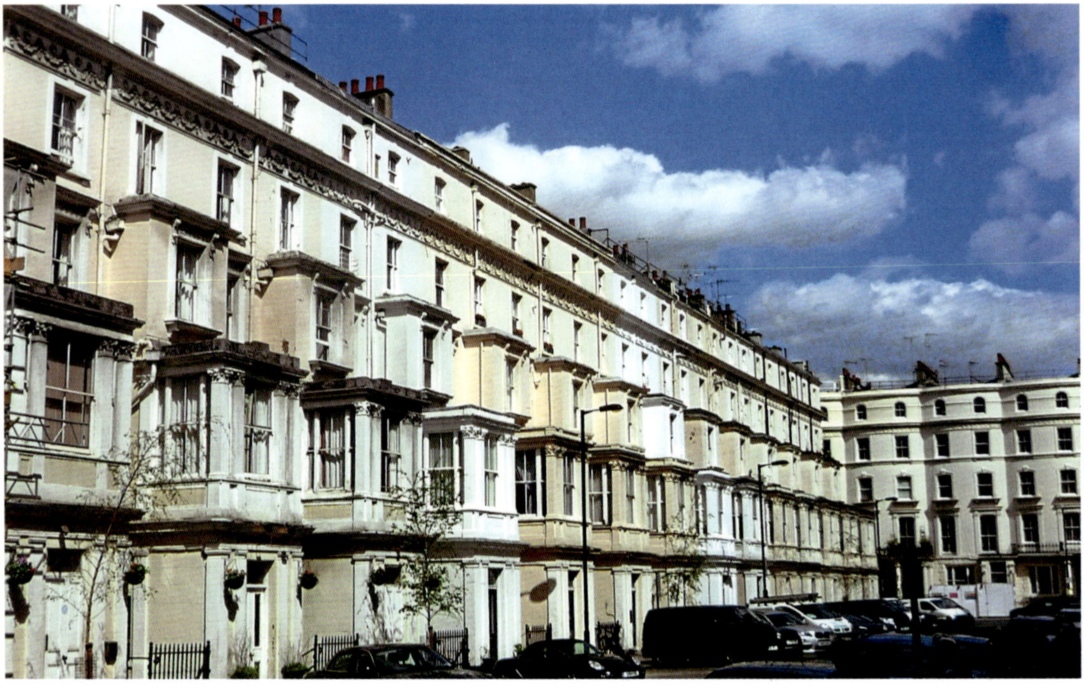

Holy Trinity Church, Bishop's Road, *c.* 1870

A spectacular local landmark for over a century, this fine Gothic Revival church was designed by Thomas Cundy and built between 1843 and 1846. The church closed in 1971 with its subsequent demolition in stages, beginning with the spire in 1972 and with the entire process completed in 1984. Holy Trinity flats arose on the site in 1986.

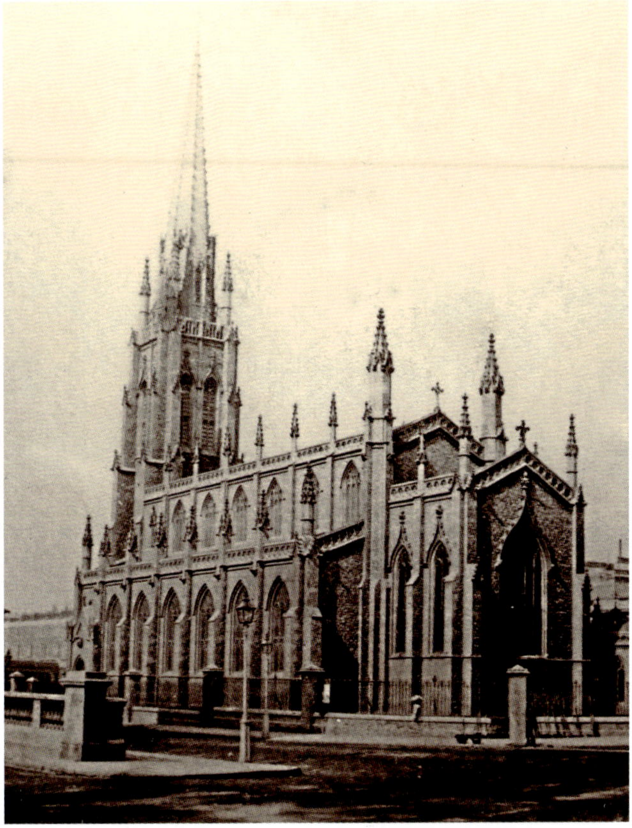

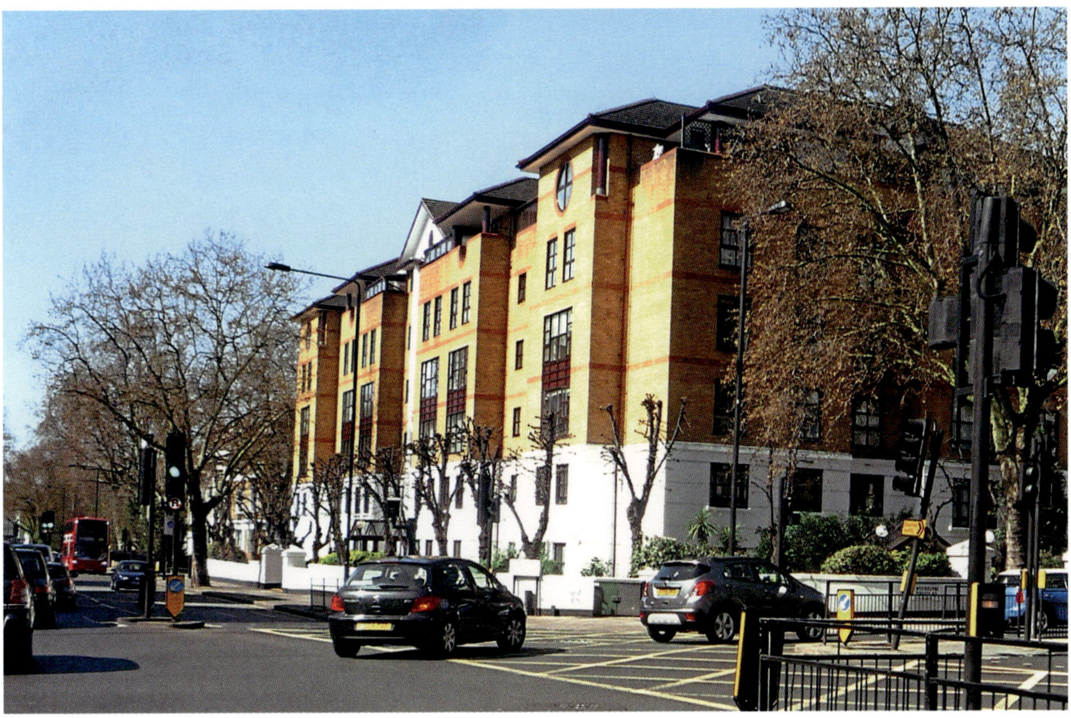

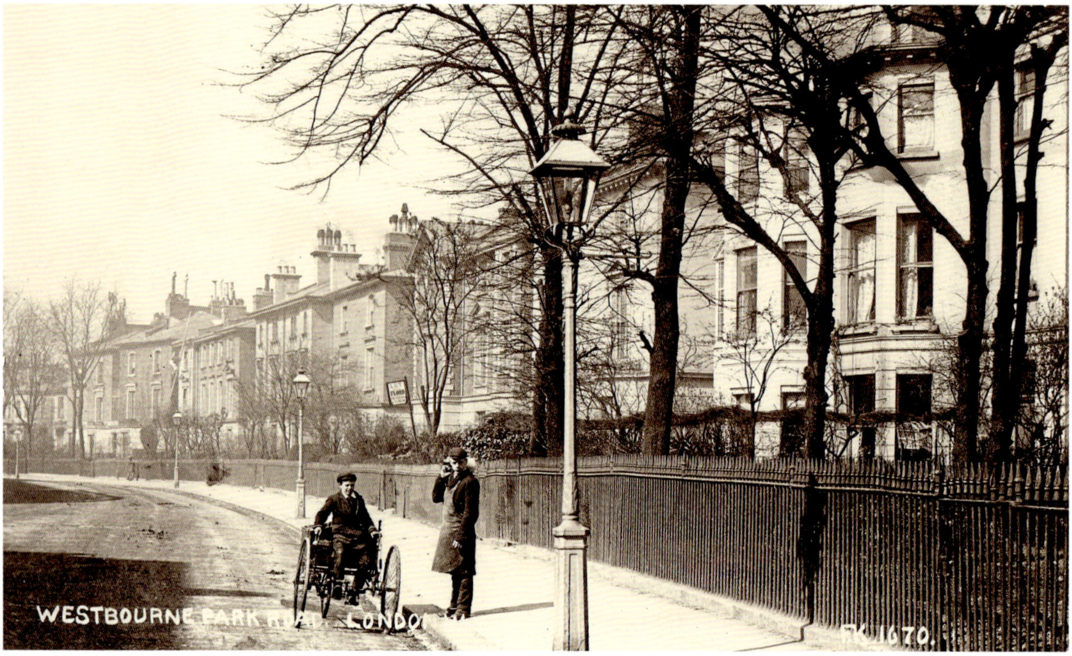

Westbourne Park Road, *c.* 1905

Here the large semi-detached villas have a more spacious layout and the curving nature of the street, with its generous greenery, contrasts with the more formal vistas of much of this area. Modern rebuilding has respected the scale of the surviving originals. In the above image a delivery boy from a local bakery, complete with tricycle, takes a break by the gas lamp.

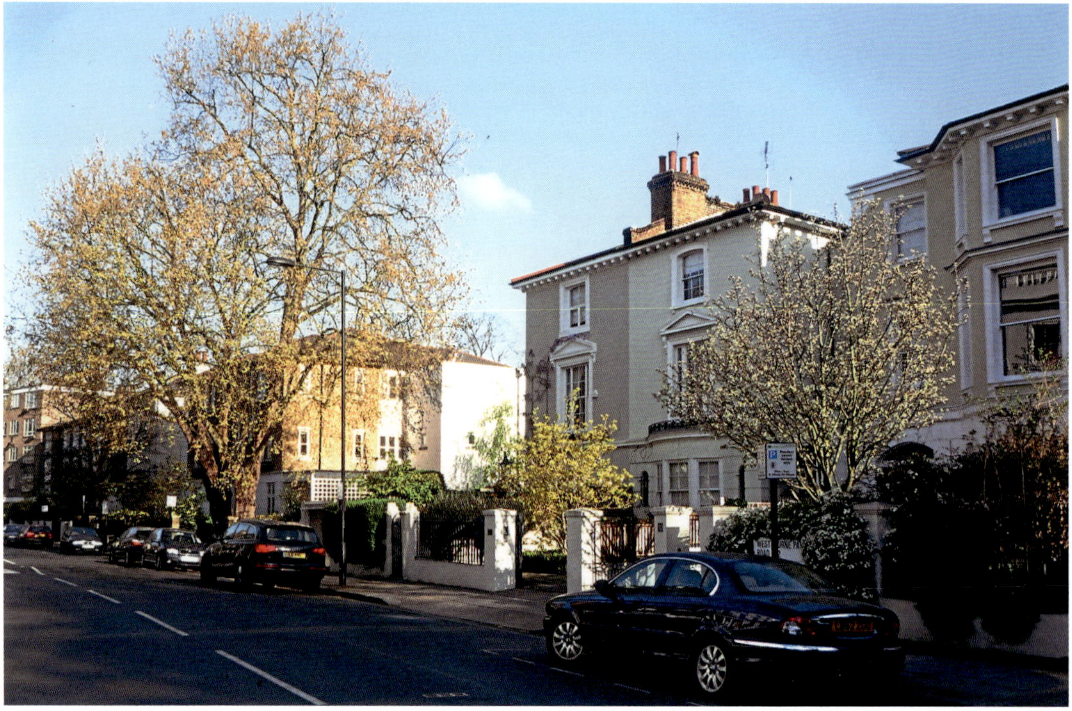

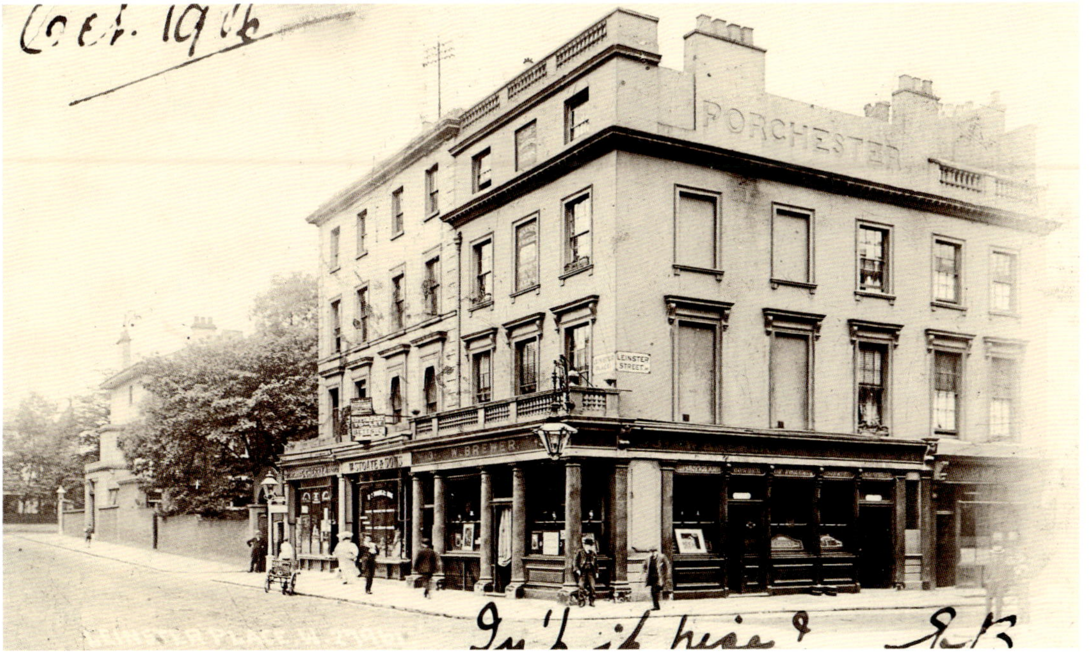

Leinster Place by Leinster Street (Leinster Gardens), *c.* 1906

Some 17 acres of old Bayswater was given a new look in the post-war years with the development of the Hallfield Estate. Building took place in two phases – the first was between 1951–55 and the second from 1955 to '58, resulting in fifteen blocks of much admired modernist housing. The old neighbourhoods had the usual Bayswater mixture of residential terraces, shops and pubs (the Porchester pub is visible on the corner above).

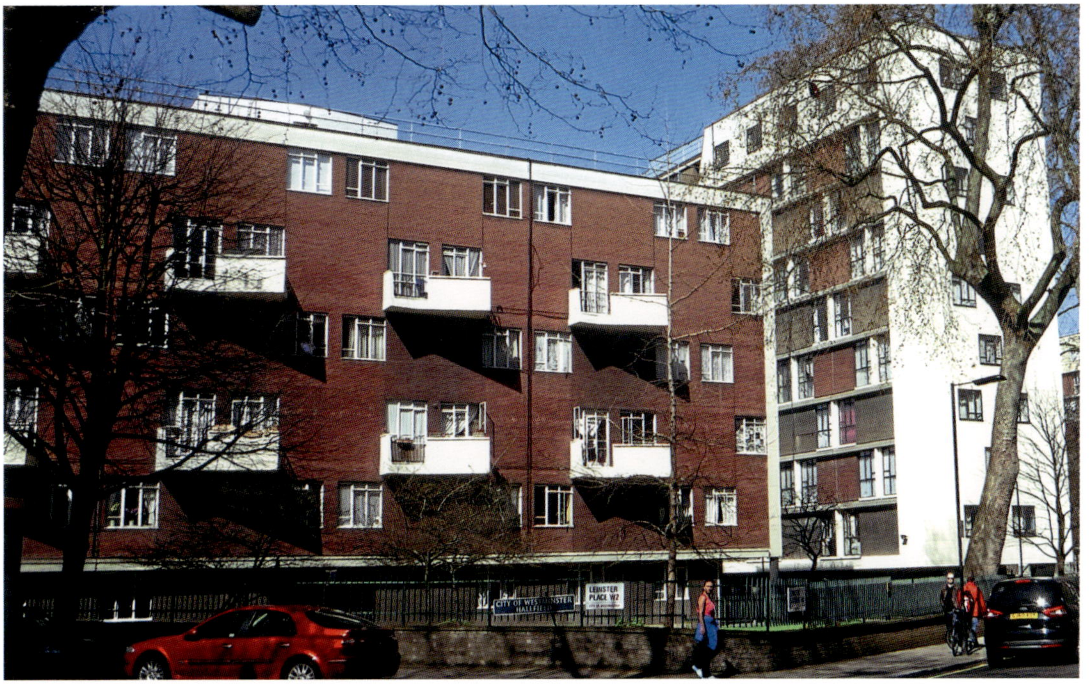

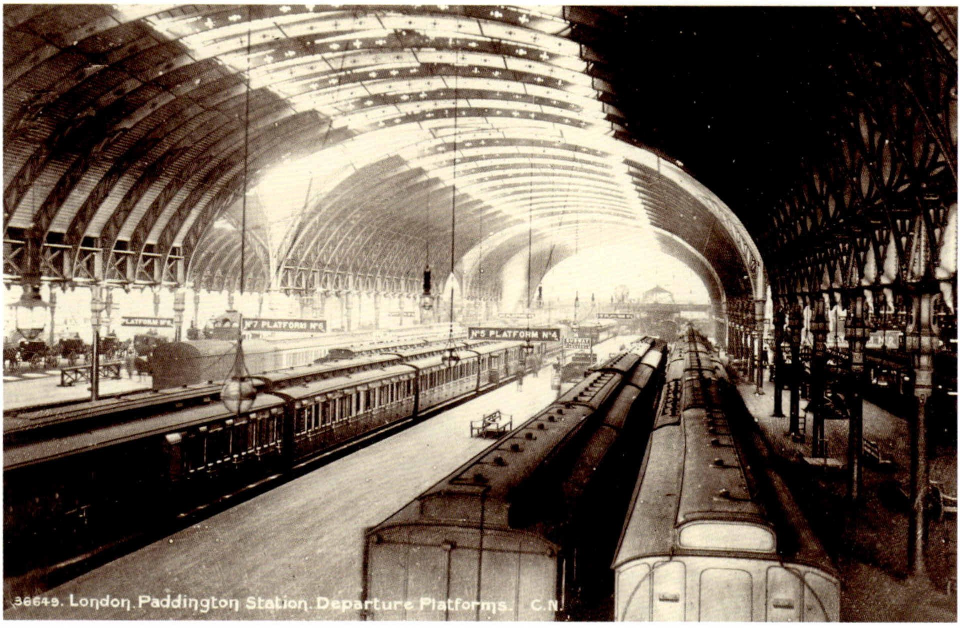

Paddington Station, *c.* 1910

The first station here opened in 1838 and was made of wood, but the grand London terminus we know today opened in 1851 and was built to the designs of Isambard Kingdom Brunel, the GWR engineer. The station is noted for its spectacular train sheds with roofs including some three acres of glass. Although the age of steam has long passed, the station continues to evolve and will soon be connected to an entirely new railway, Crossrail.

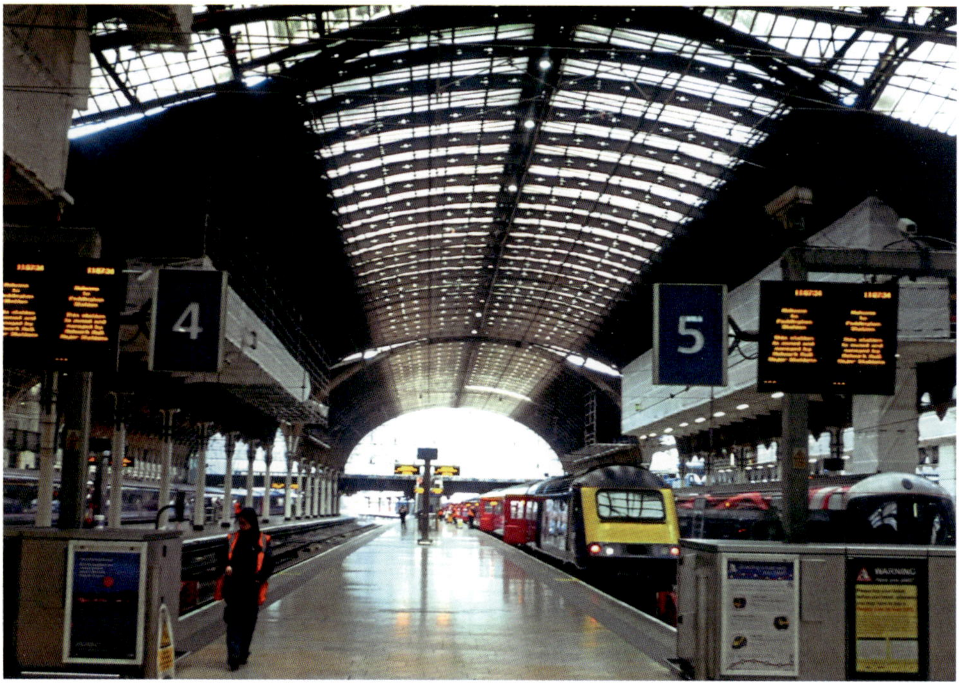

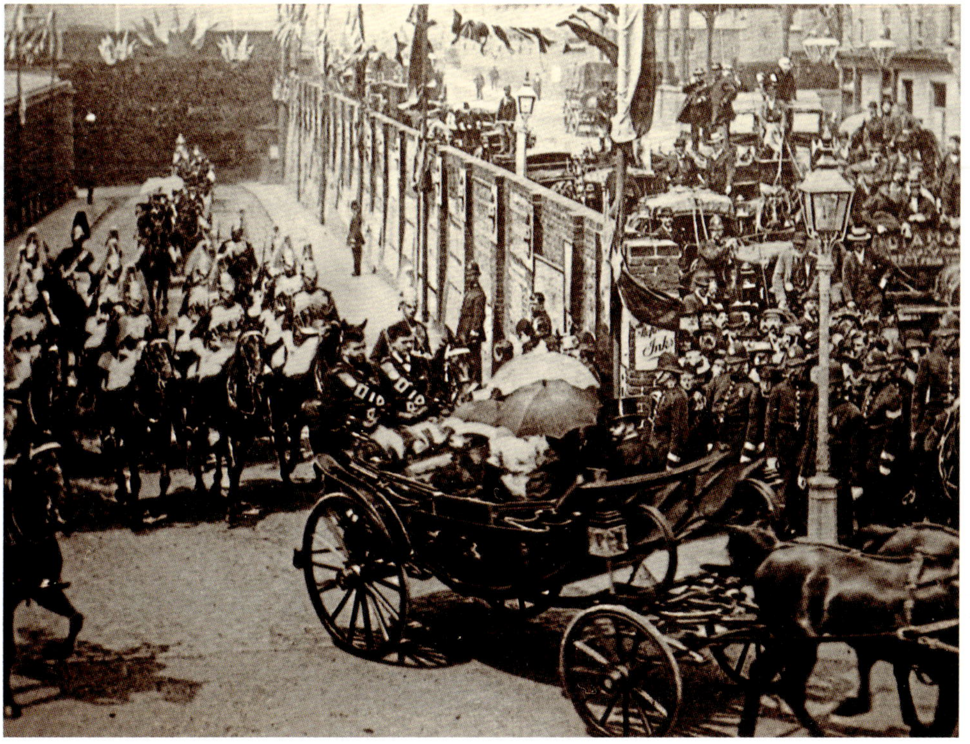

Queen Victoria's Diamond Jubilee, Paddington Station, from Praed Street, 1897
Paddington station has long witnessed scenes of royal pageantry as members of the Royal Family avail themselves of the Royal Train running to Windsor and elsewhere. Queen Victoria made her first journey to the old station in 1842. The scene here catches Her Majesty and a military escort as they depart for Buckingham Palace on the occasion of the Queen's Diamond Jubilee.

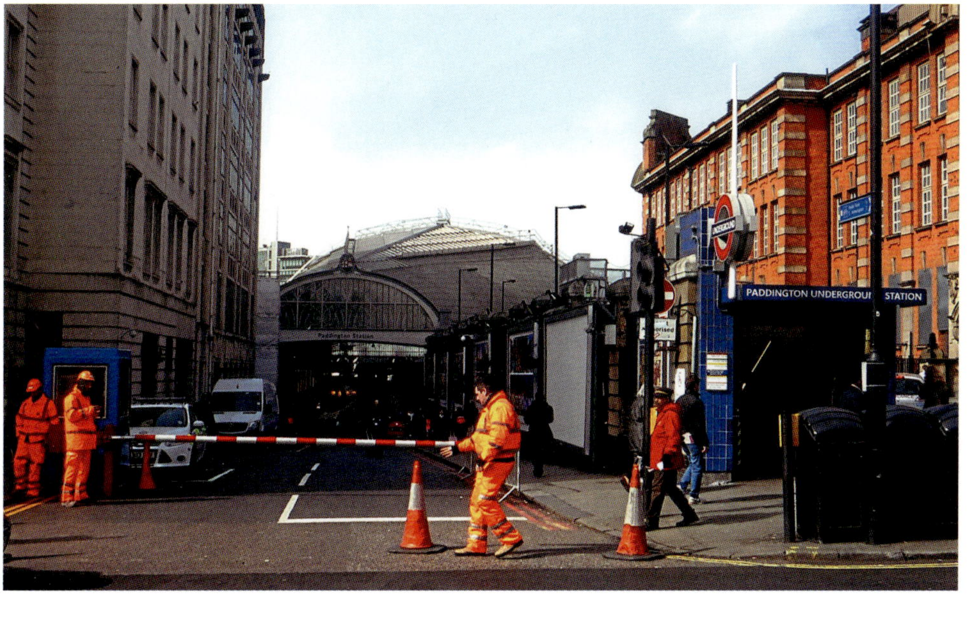

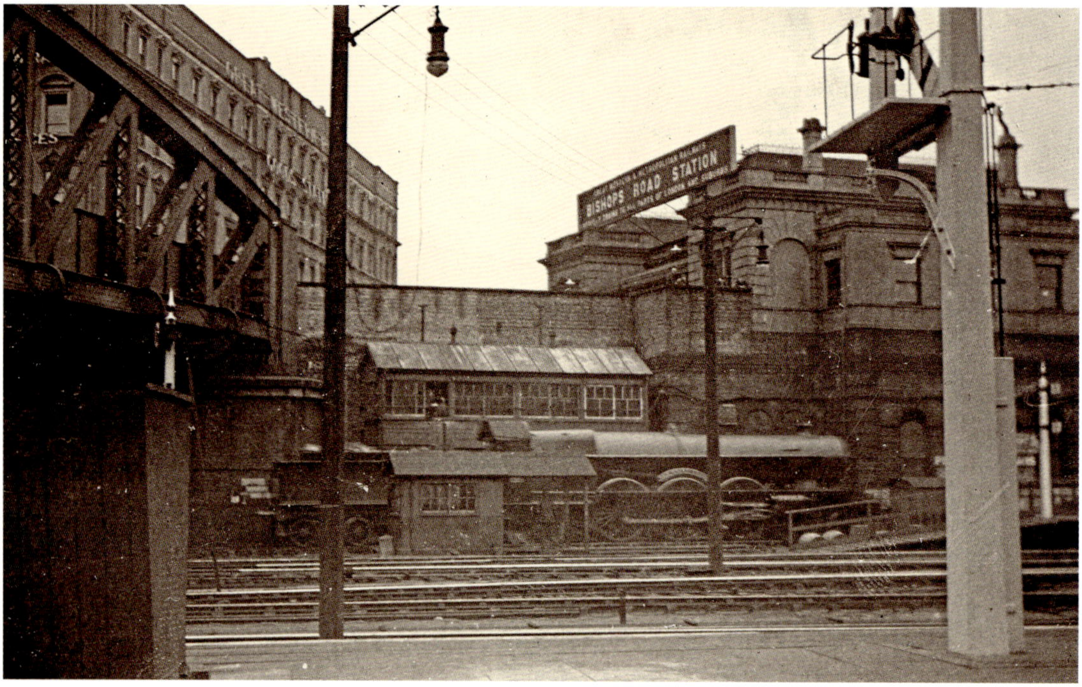

Bishop's Road (Paddington) Station, 1923

The above image shows an unusually angled view of a historic Underground station. It was the original terminus in 1863 of the world's first subterranean railway, the Metropolitan Railway. Bishop's Road was attached to the GWR Paddington terminus, but the buildings seen above were removed in the late 1920s. The modern image shows how the location has been revitalised with a new station and a canal-side path leading to Paddington Basin.

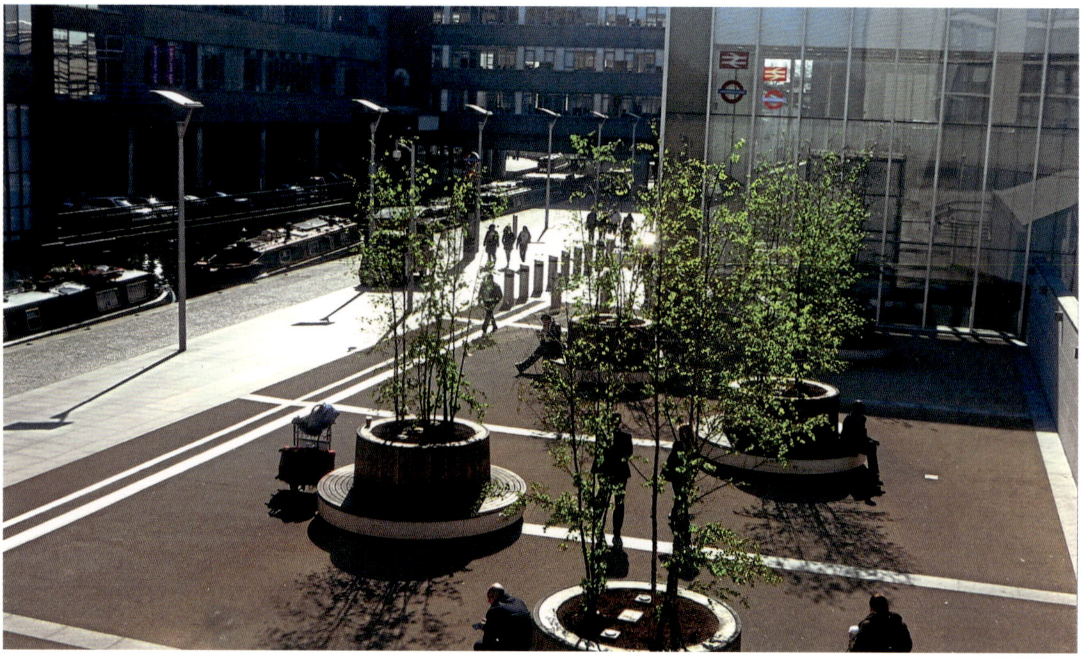

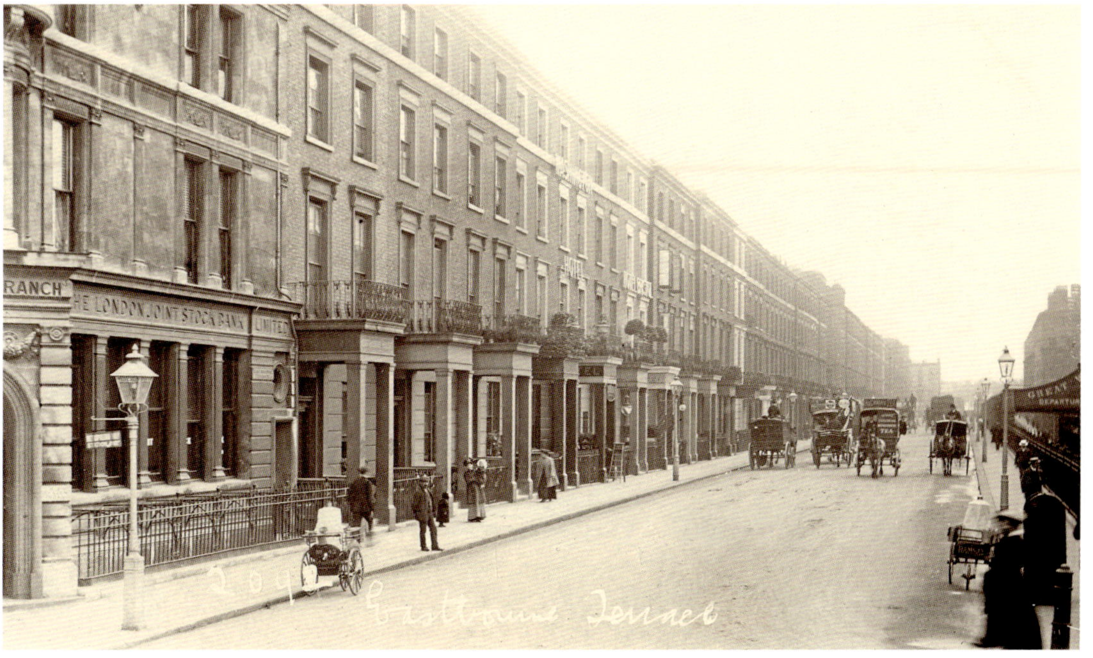

Eastbourne Terrace from Praed Street, *c.* 1905

Dowdy terraces faced the side of Paddington station where a ramp gave access for carriages, taxis and charabancs. Post-war changes in the 1960s created vast office block eyesores, but their appearance has been improved in recent years. The modern view shows part of the construction works for Crossrail.

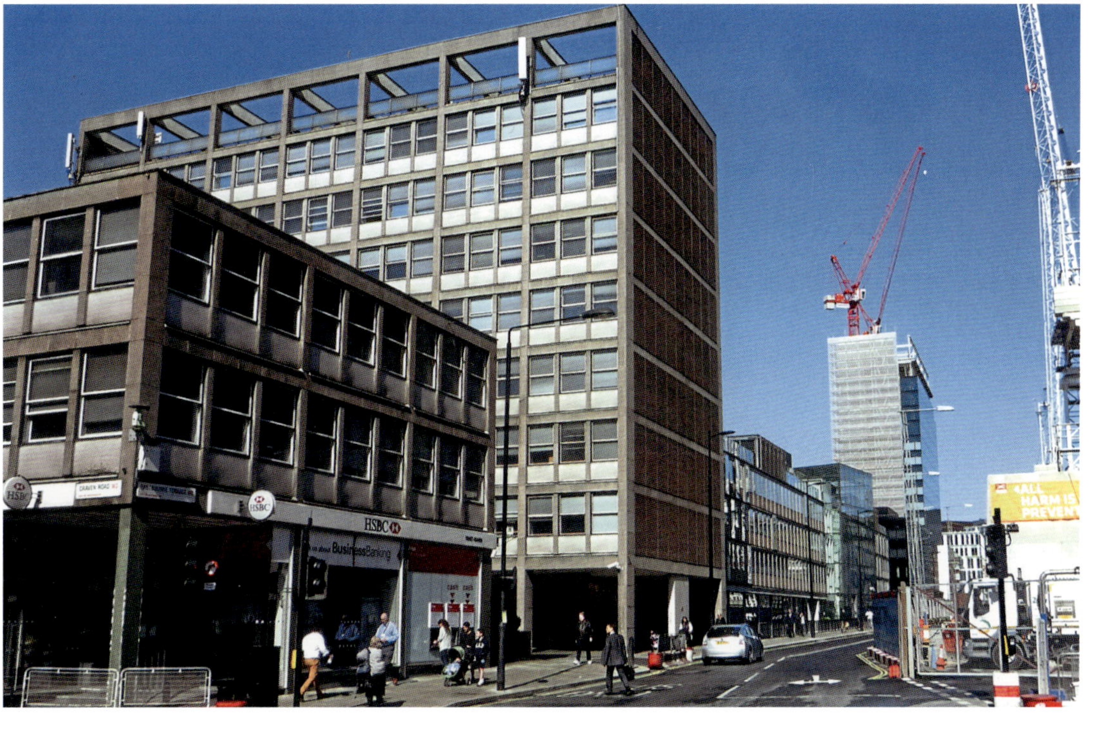

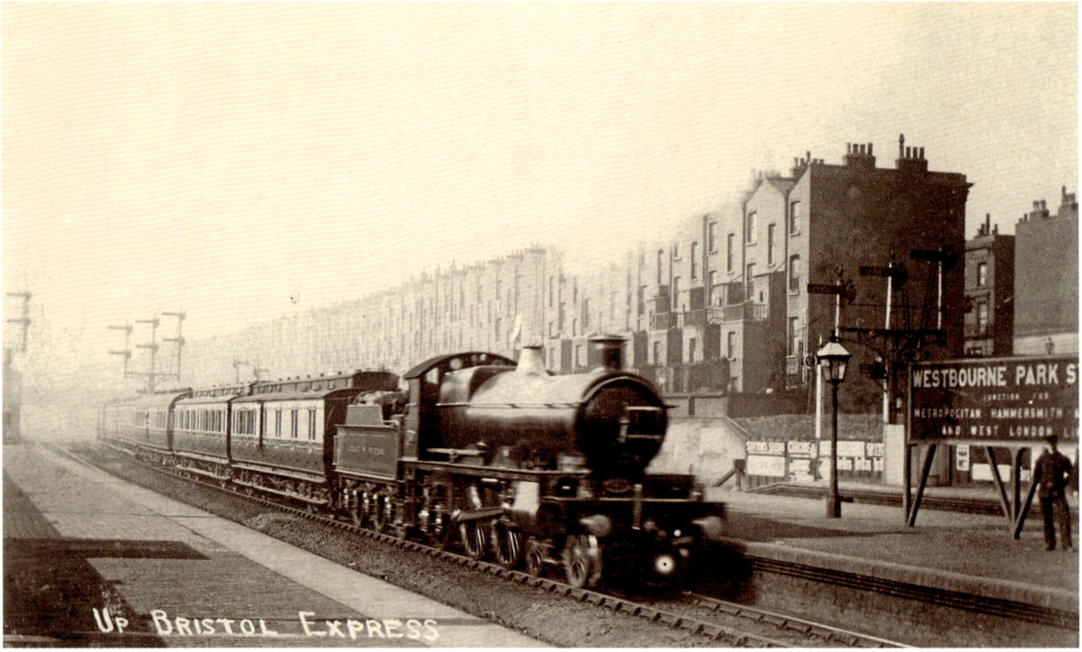

Westbourne Park Station, *c.* 1908

The station opened in 1866 and served travellers on the GWR and Metropolitan Railways. The main-line route ceased calling here from 1992, but the image looks back to its heyday with the Bristol Express speeding towards its Paddington terminus. New building along the lines and the elevated Westway motorway have obscured much of what is seen in the earlier view.

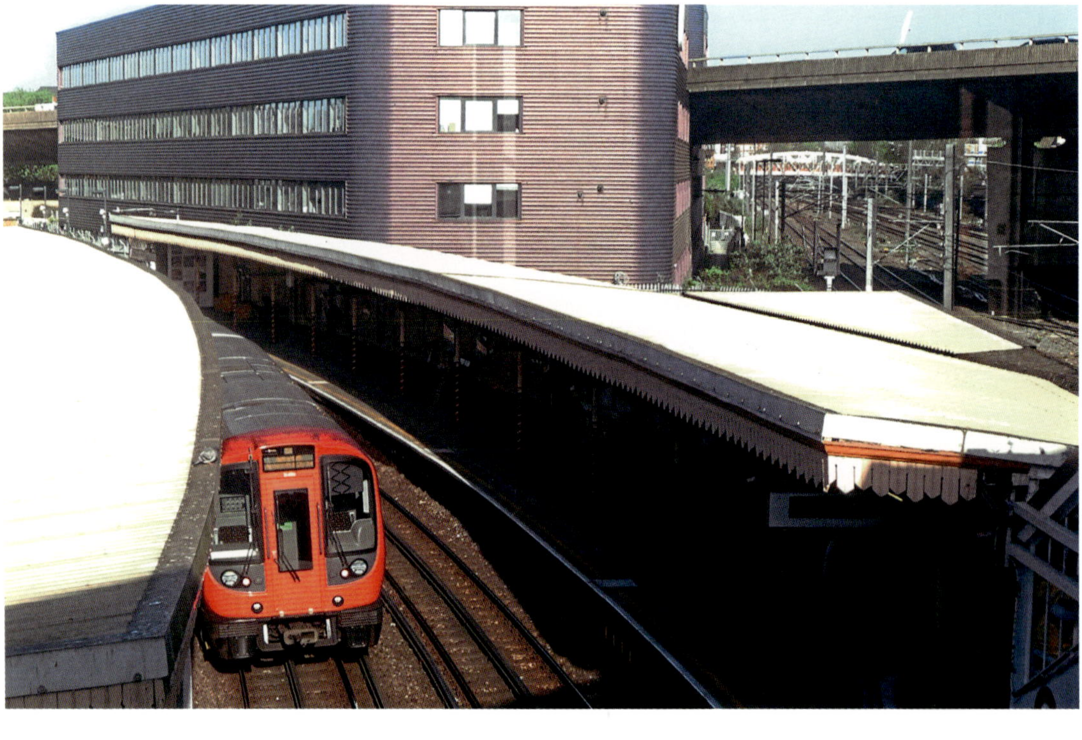

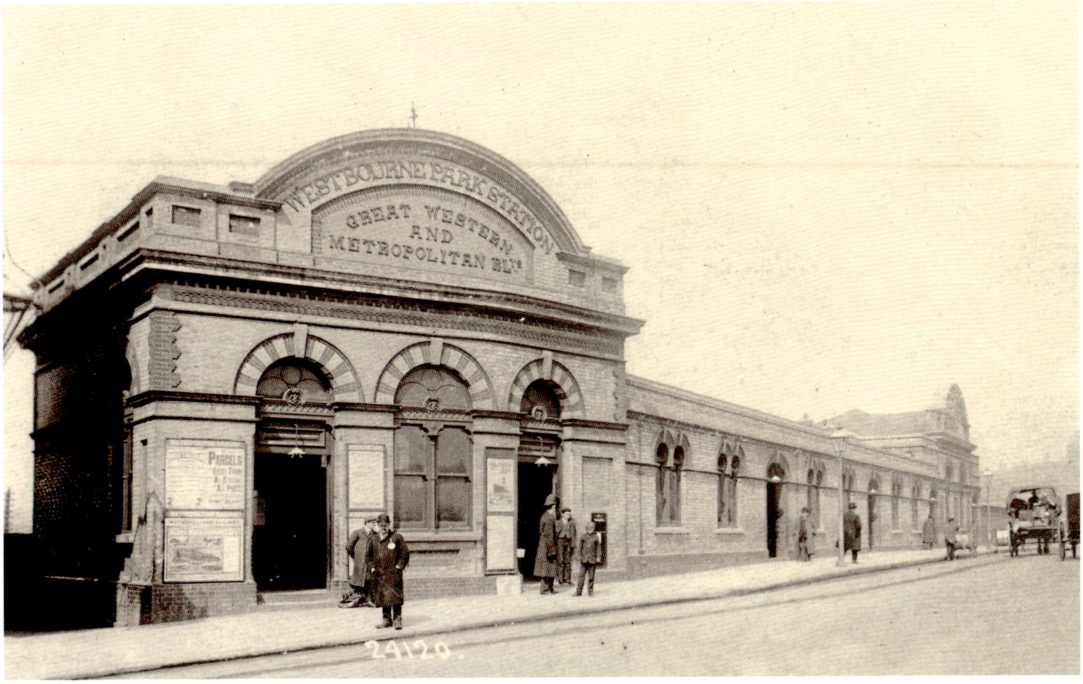

Westbourne Park Station, *c.* 1906
The street frontage revealed the now lost original lettering, but otherwise the station remains in a fine state of preservation apart from a few modern disfigurements. The street façade was among the longest on the Underground.

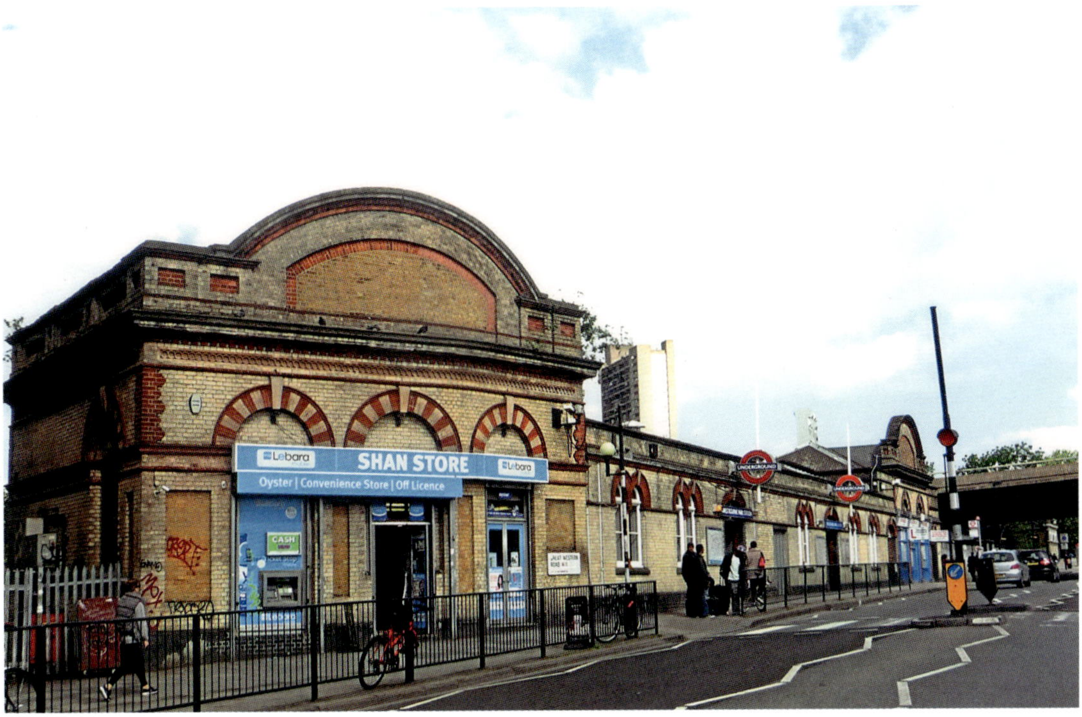

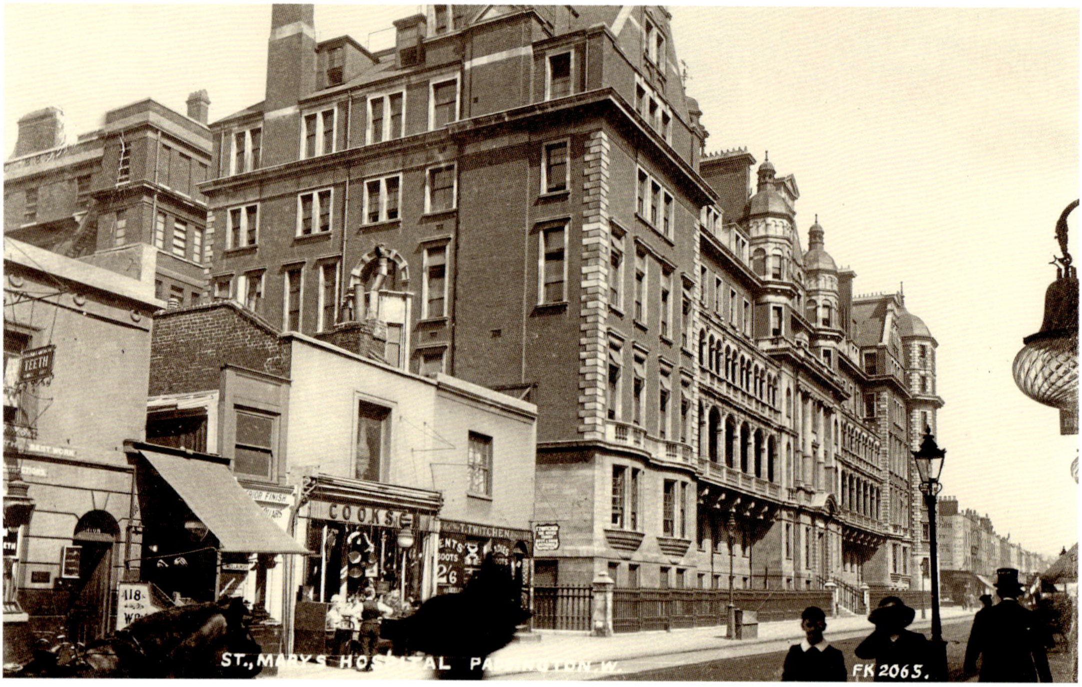

Praed Street, *c.* 1905

This major road links Edgware Road with Paddington station. With its shops and hotels, it typifies a neighbourhood in the vicinity of a great railway terminus. The street's architecture was modest, as is seen here above, but rising impressively in the midst of it is St Mary's Hospital's Clarence Wing that opened in 1904 – the hospital itself was founded in 1845.

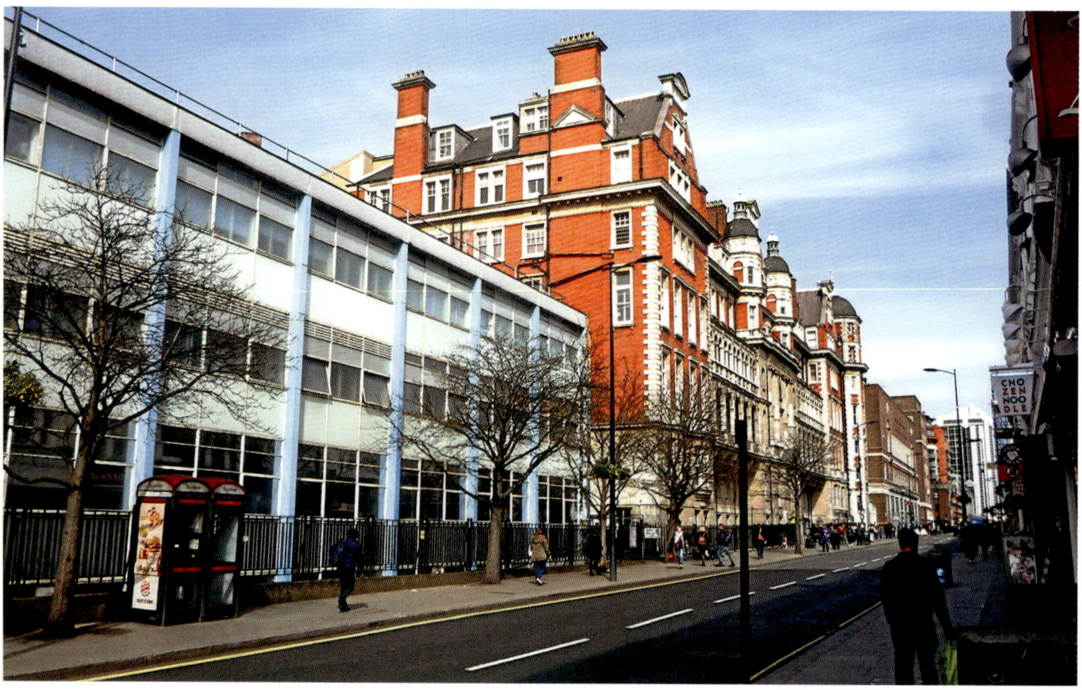

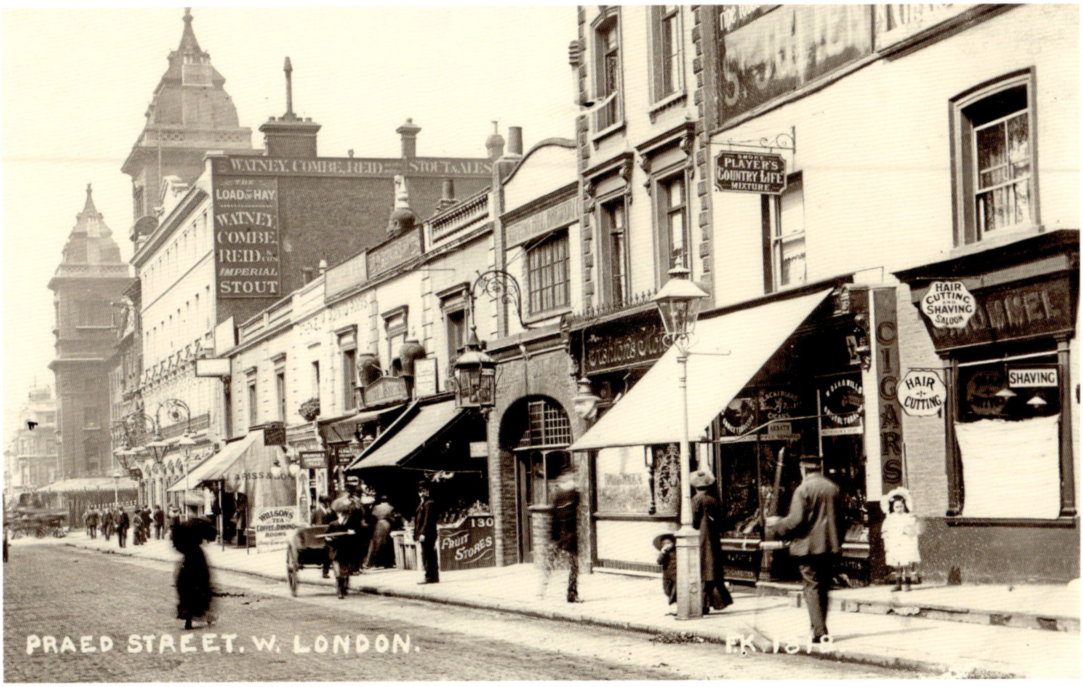

Praed Street, *c.* 1905

Modest shops, and a tiny beer shop with a fine lamp, lead on to the more opulent Load of Hay pub on the London Street corner. Further on, the twin pavilions of the Great Western Royal Hotel (1851–54) highlight the extravagance of the Victorian railway age.

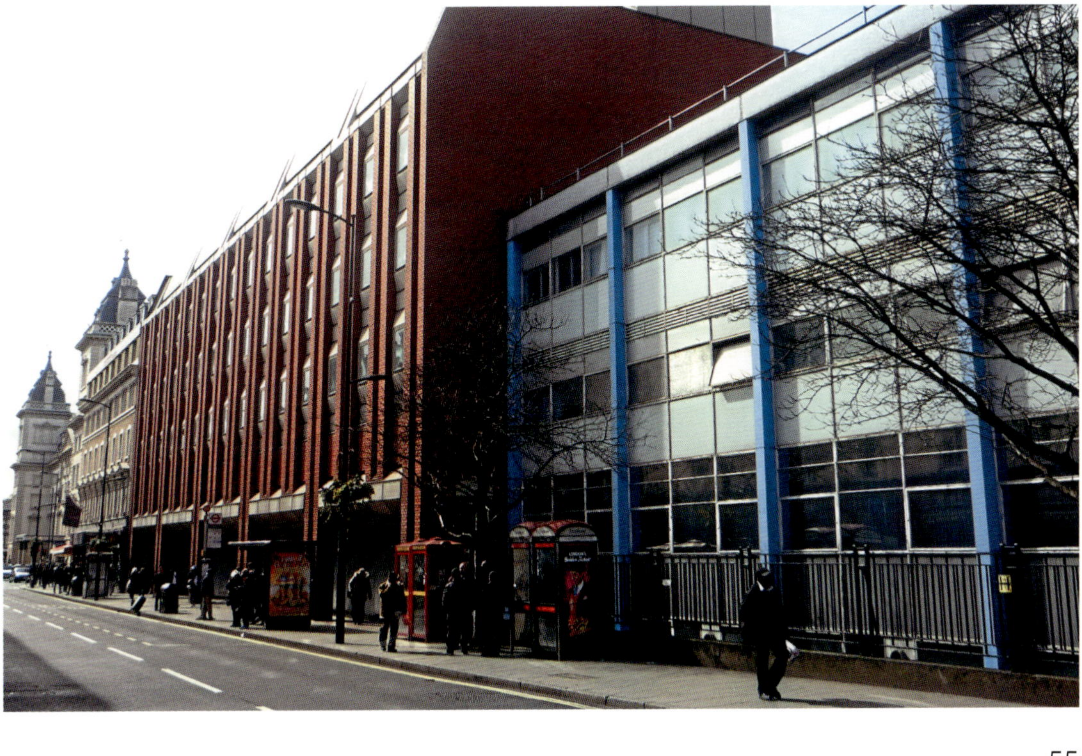

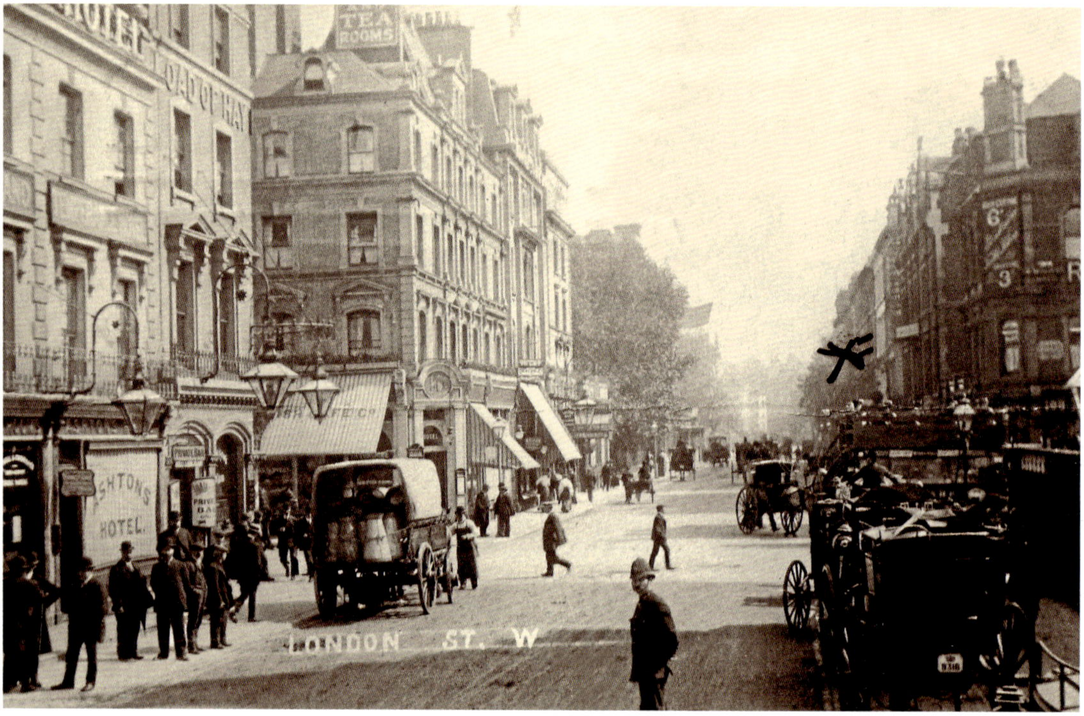

London Street from Praed Street, *c.* 1905

This street runs from the heart of Bayswater to Paddington station. It is lined with hotels and shops; the bustle of the train station has been well captured in the above image.

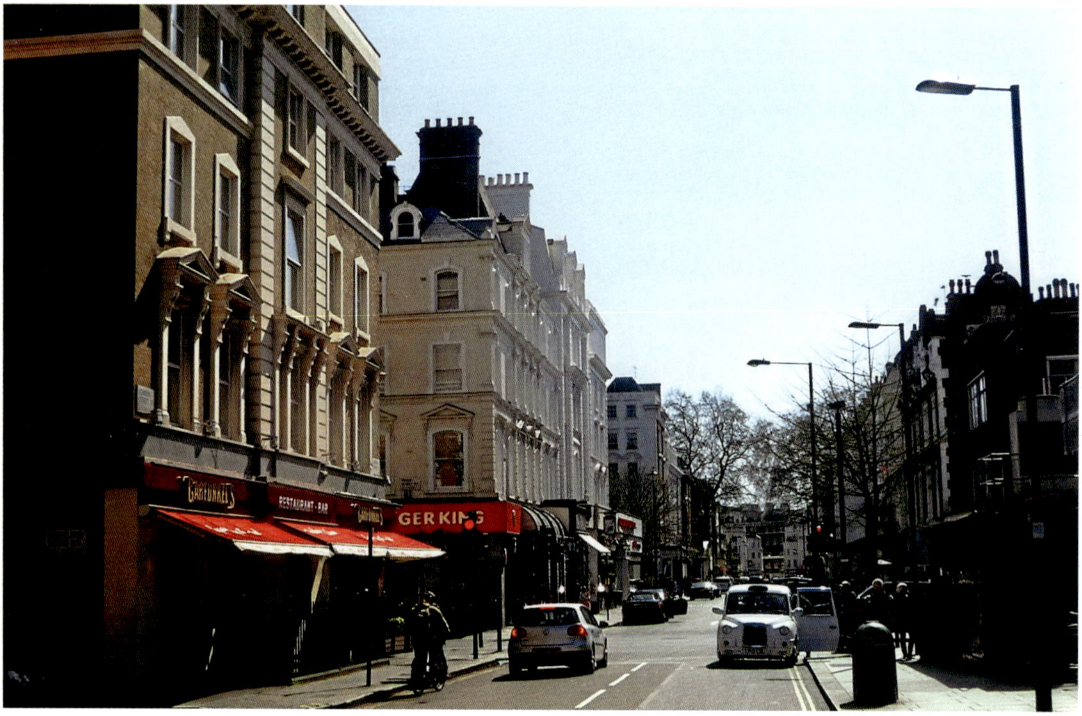

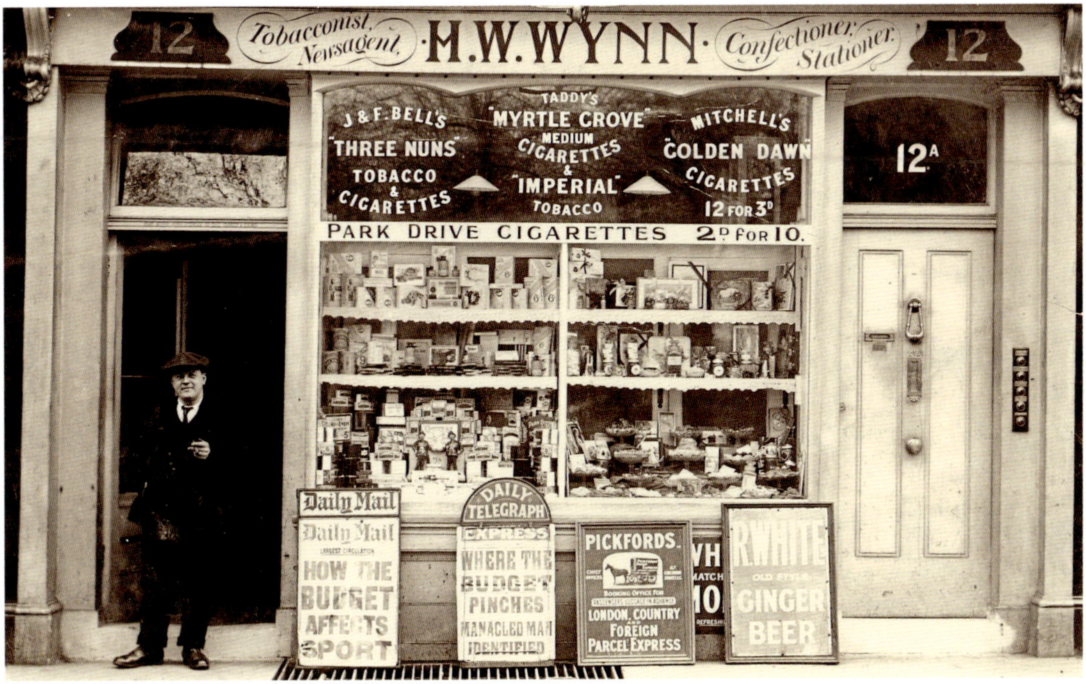

Henry Wynn, tobacconist, No. 12 London Street, *c.* 1911

Abundant advertising tells of long-forgotten tobacco products and the offer of '10 Park Drive cigarettes for *2d*' – looks a bargain if one discounts the health hazards. The Pickford's advertisement comes from the days when most of their delivery wagons were horse-drawn.

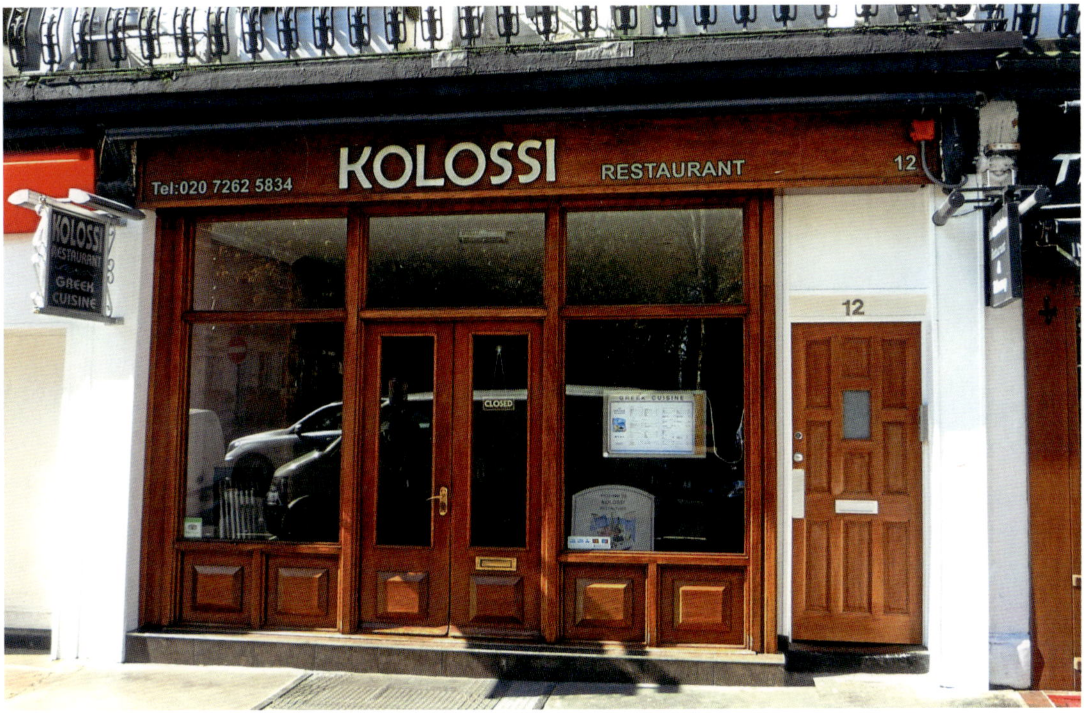

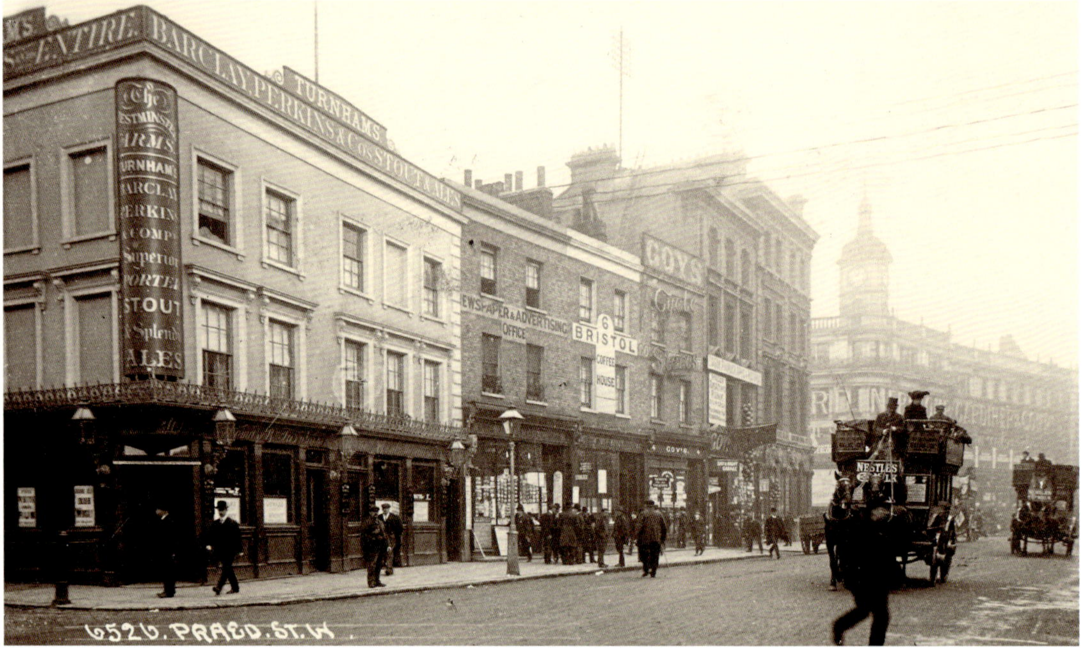

Praed Street by Irongate Wharf Road (Harbet Road) *c.* 1906
The building that formerly housed the Westminster Arms is still recognisable, despite the modernisation that has shorn it of many original features. The shops beyond included those of Whittingham's newspaper and advertising office, and Goy's cycle shop. The modern scene in the below image is dominated by the Hilton London Metropole Hotel, a 1986 extension of an earlier hotel in Harrow Road.

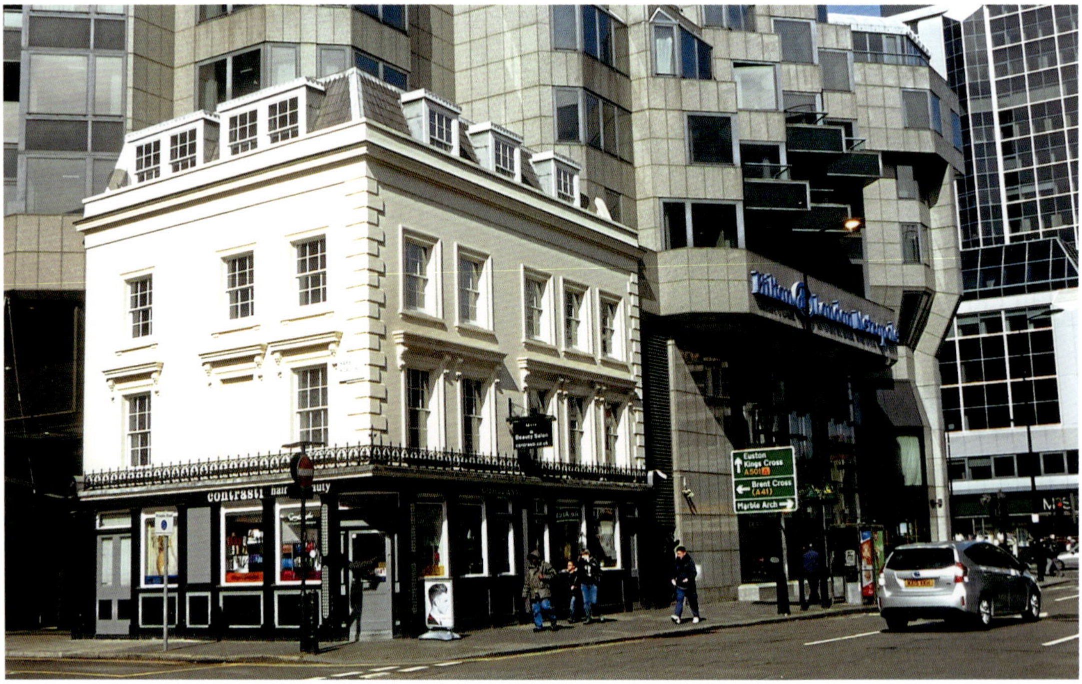

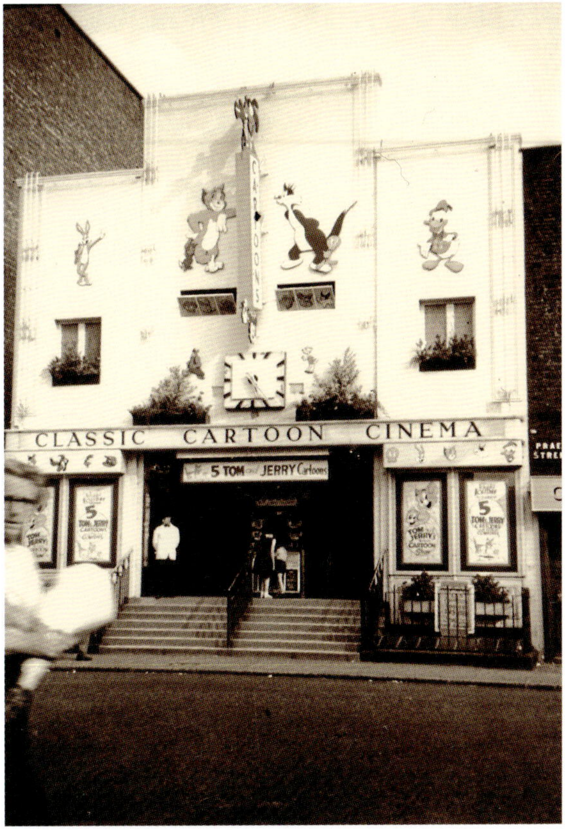

The Classic Cartoon Cinema, No. 5a, Praed Street, *c.* 1956

Built on the site of a Baptist chapel, this cinema opened around 1910 as the Universal Bioscope Theatre. This came during the first wave of British cinema building as the new craze for viewing 'moving pictures' took hold. Surviving the primitive conditions of the early years, the cinema flourished through the decades. It was known as the 'New Gaiety Cinema' in 1930 and featured billiard rooms in the basement. It also spent some years as a news theatre, which was a popular phenomenon before television brought the news into everyone's home. Later, it became the cartoon cinema we can see in the above image, where it is promoting a programme of five Tom & Jerry cartoons. In time these small specialist cinemas dwindled away; nothing now remains of this colourful slice of Paddington's history.

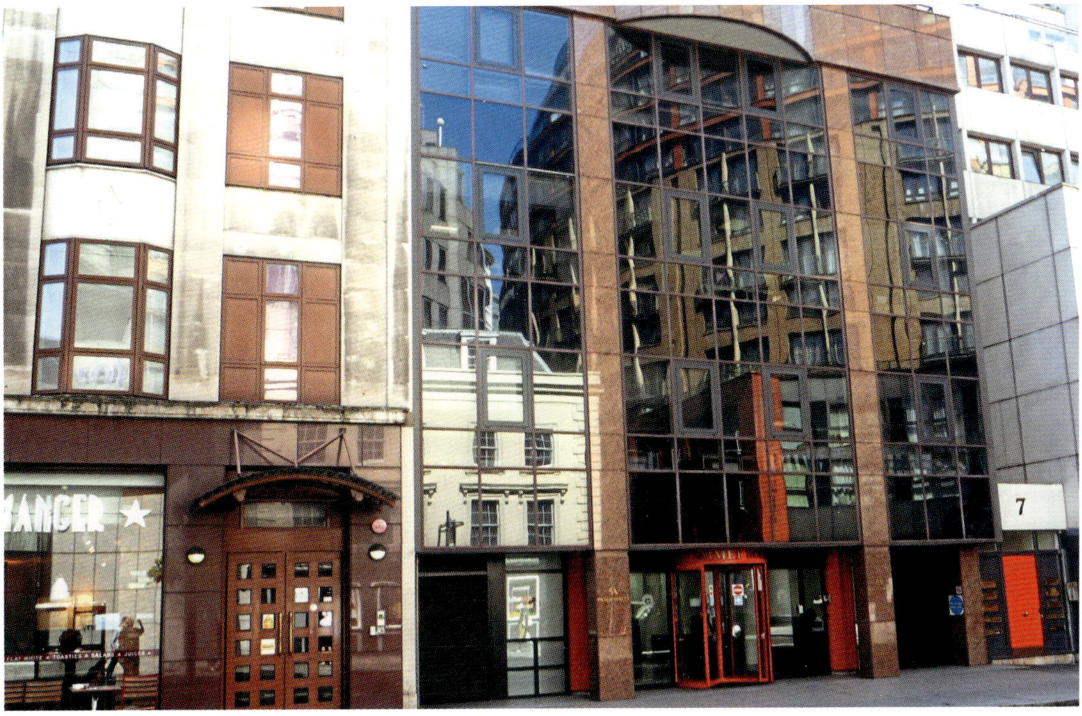

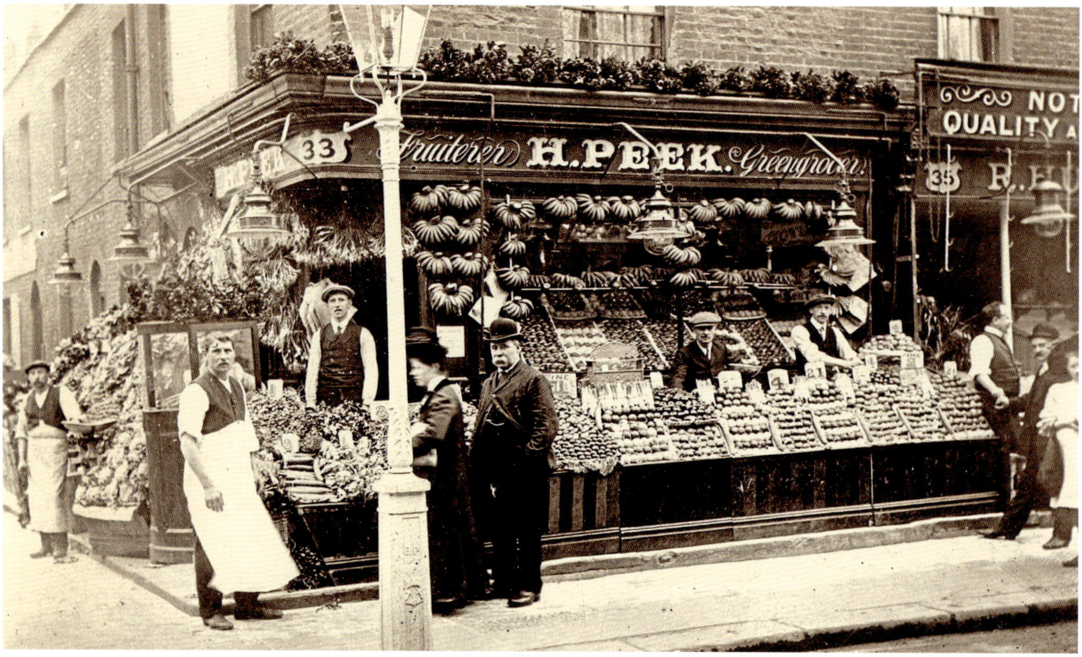

Henry Peek, Fruitier and Greengrocer, No. 33 Praed Street, *c.* 1908

An early start to the working day would have been needed here in order to display such an abundance of produce in such an attractive manner. To the left (above), Sale Place leads into a remarkable little area of modestly scaled streets containing small houses and cottages built in the 1820s for workers in the local canal system.

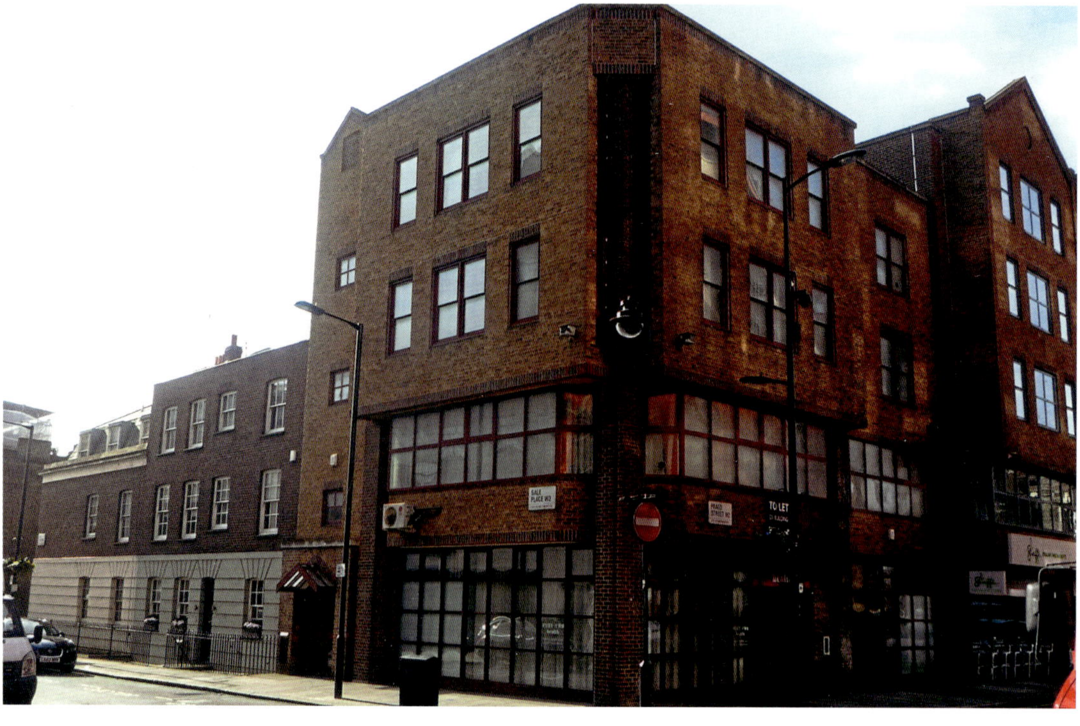

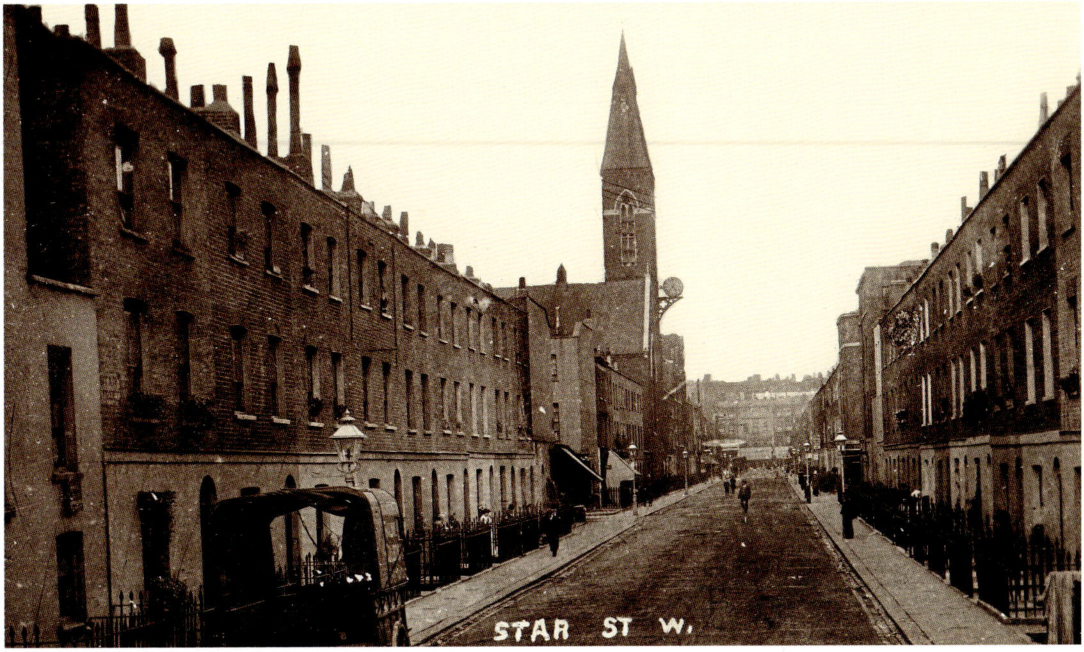

Star Street from Cambridge Place (Norfolk Place), c. 1905

The above image shows more of the old canal worker's houses that date from the 1820s. Post-war years brought drabness here, but gentrification has since turned the houses into highly desirable homes. While much of the street remains intact, a casualty was the church of St Michael & All Angels (built in the 1860s) that was war damaged and demolished in 1967, after which it was replaced by a nursery school and newly planted trees.

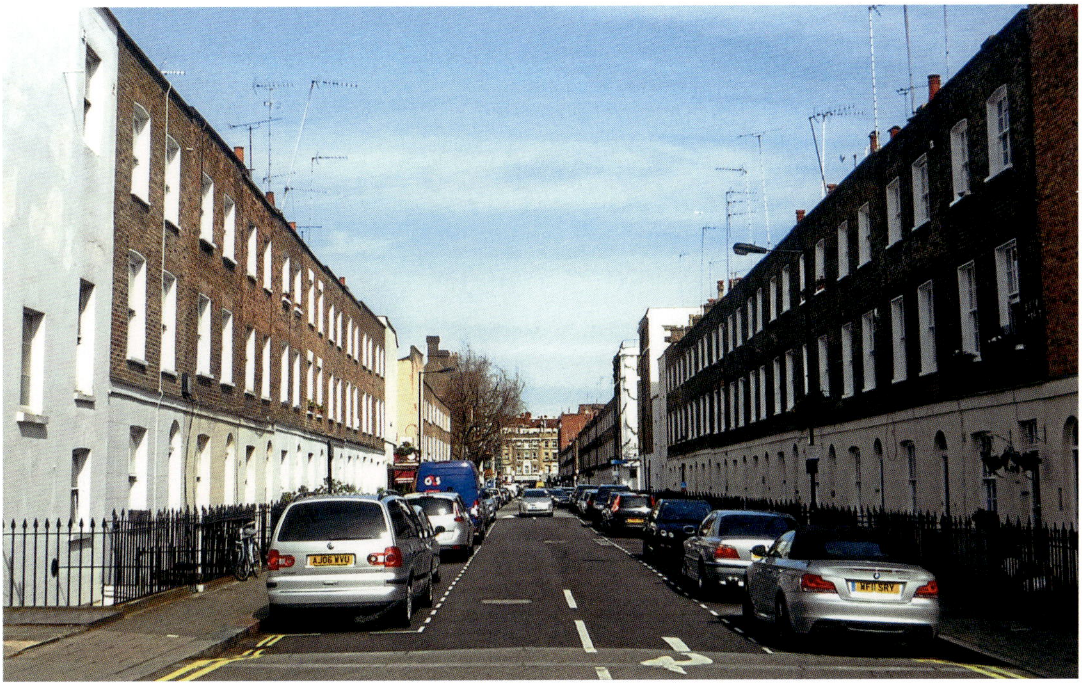

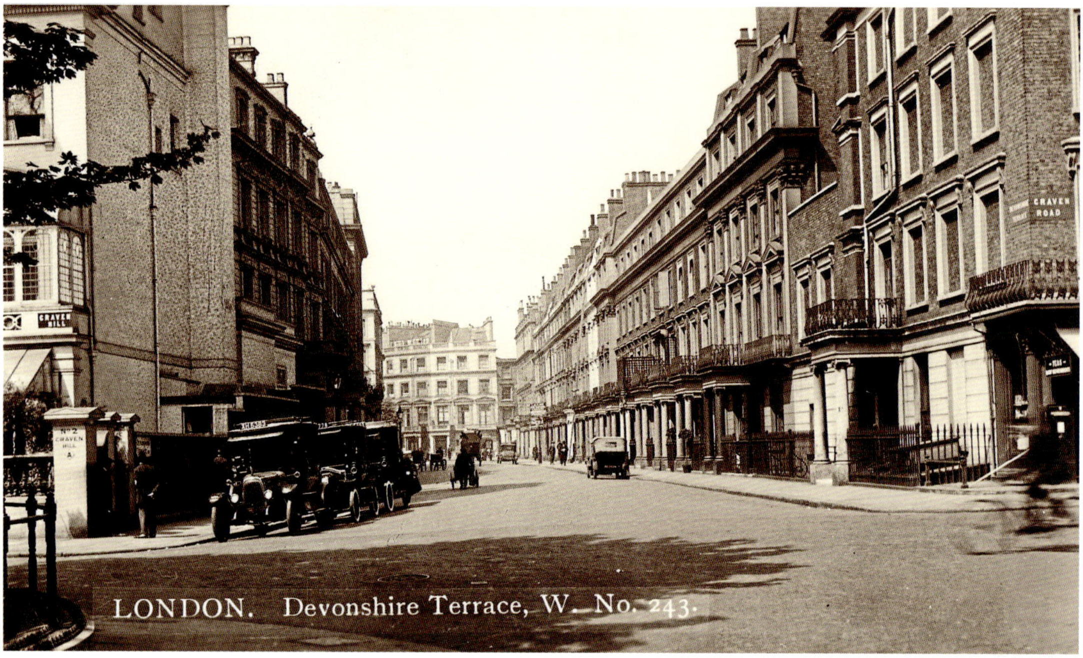

Devonshire Terrace from Craven Road, *c.* 1920

This is the unchanging face of one of Bayswater's classic streets. The main difference being the Italianate town houses that are now bright with new paint. A taxi rank by Craven Hill was usefully placed for the local hotels, while on the right of the above image, long-serving baker, Walter Chilton's shop, was entered through Corinthian columns adding grandeur to a modest enterprise.

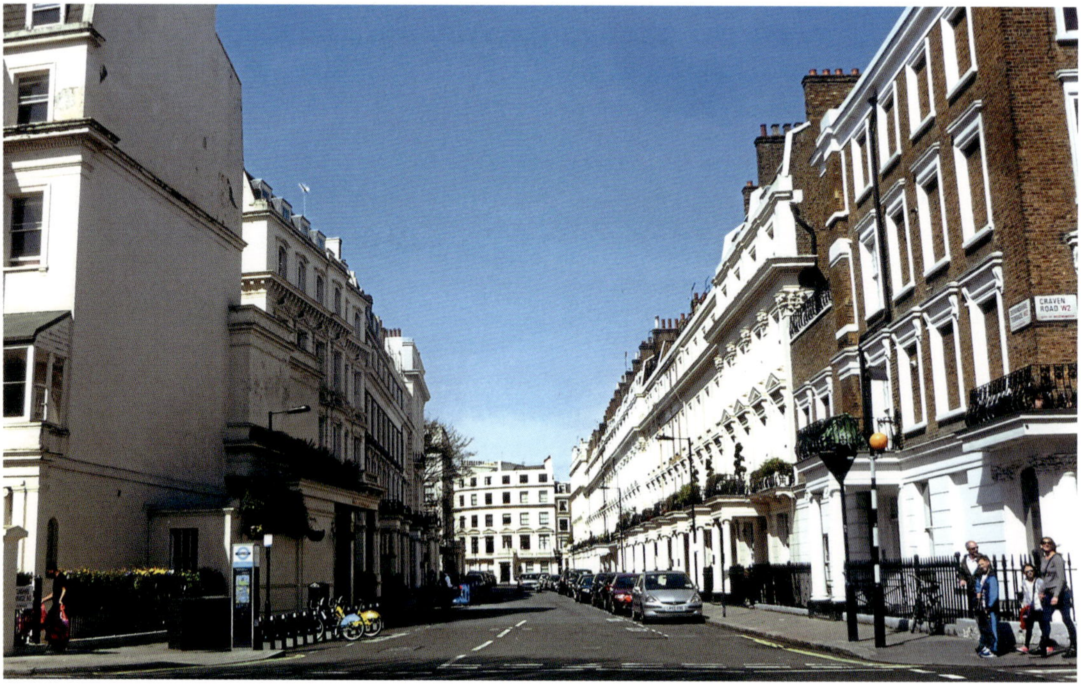

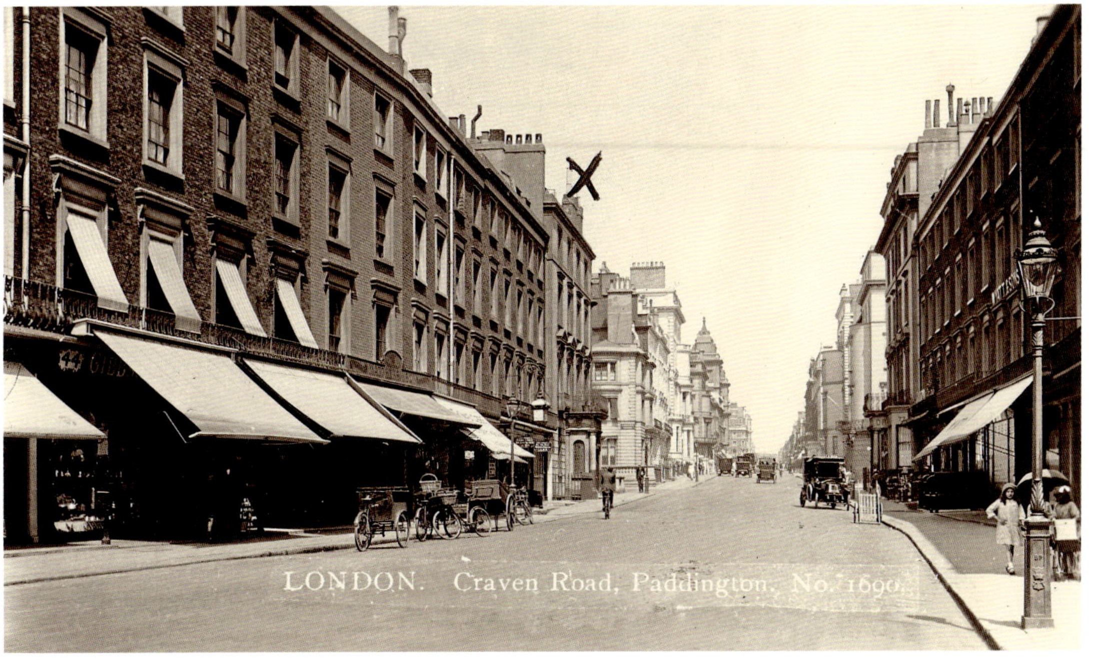

Craven Road from Devonshire Terrace, *c.* 1920

A Victorian street of shops that have living space above. A gathering of delivery vehicles, mostly cycle-based, marks the presence of Matthews & Sons butchers. In the residential section beyond, a blue plaque honours the 1940s radio comedian Tommy Handley who lived there.

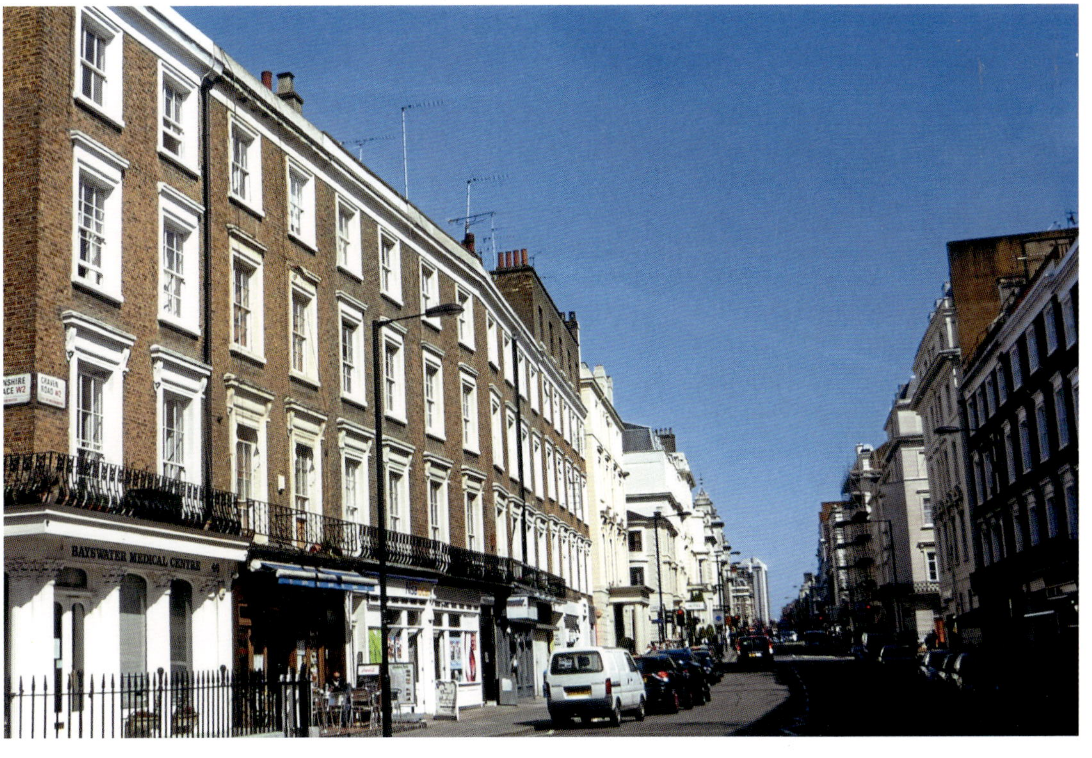

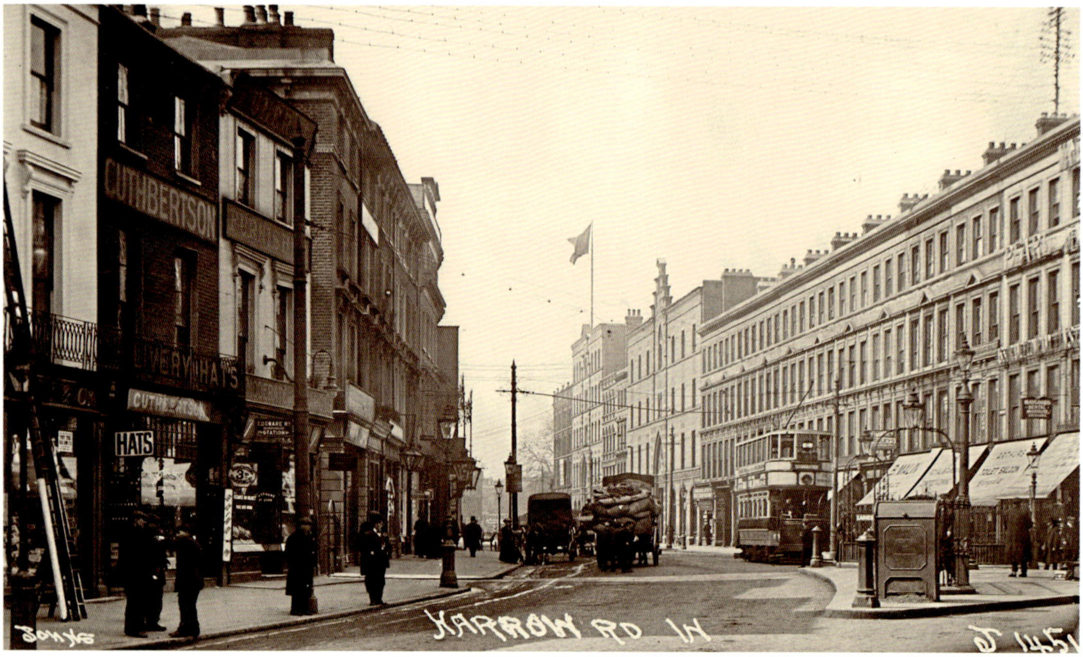

Harrow Road from Edgware Road (Marylebone Flyover), *c.* 1912

For centuries the ancient route to the hill-top town of Harrow ran through deep Middlesex countryside, until the nineteenth century when London's expansion caught up and brought transport innovations including canals, railways and a tramway. A commercial locality developed at the Edgware Road end, enduring until the 1960s when the building of the Westway motorway swept everything away. Marylebone Flyover opened in 1967 in advance of the rest of the motorway in 1970.

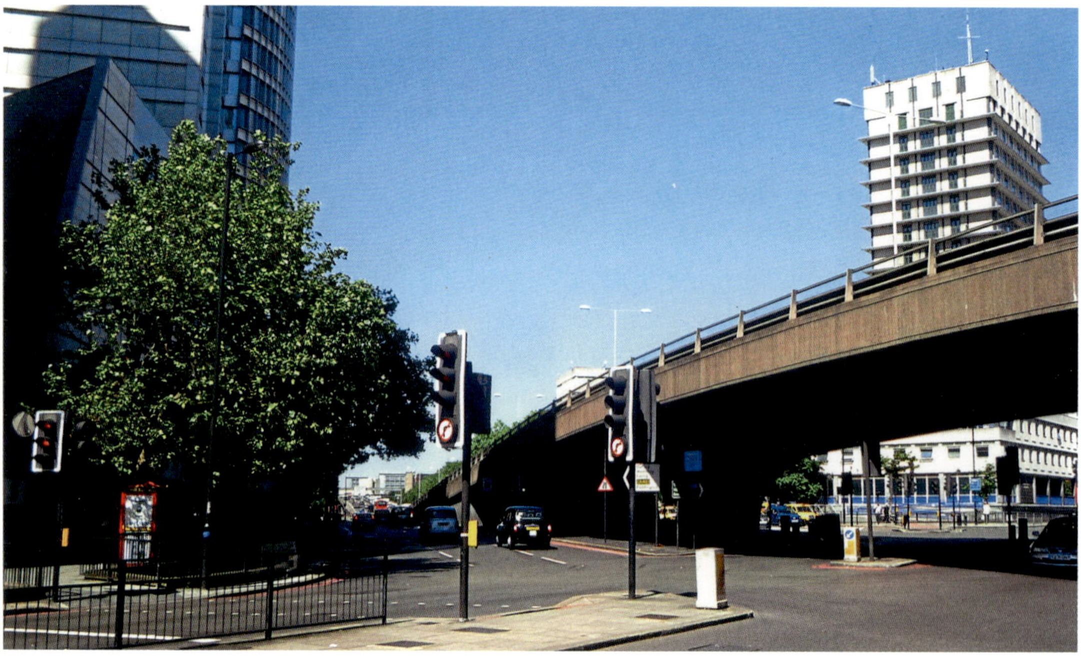

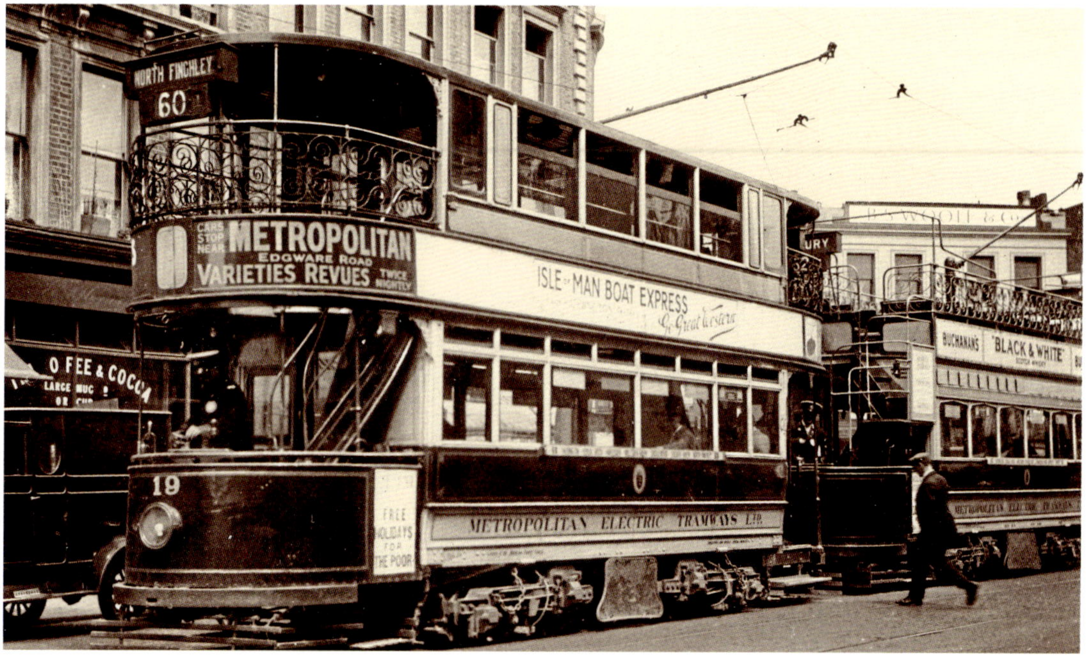

Harrow Road Tram Terminus by Edgware Road, 1927

Harrow Road's first horse-drawn tram service began in 1888 with a route from Paddington's Lock Bridge to Harlesden. With electrification from 1910, the route was extended through Wembley to Sudbury, but due to opposition from Harrow School the trams never reached that town. At the London end, the route was also extended to a new terminus at Edgware Road as is seen here.

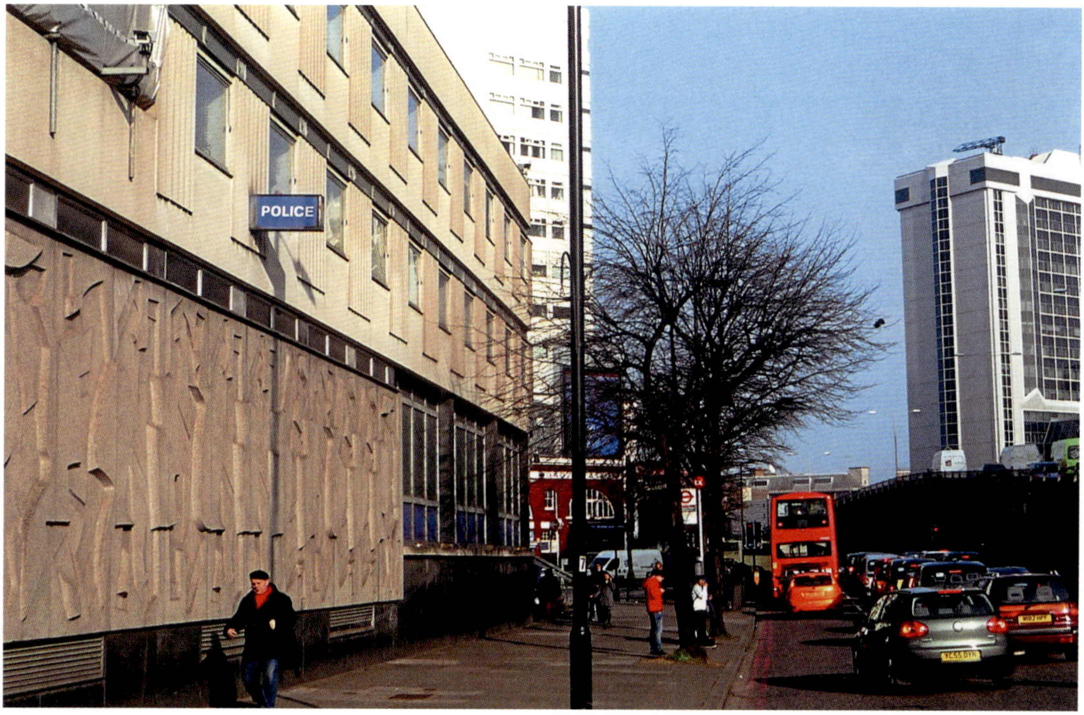

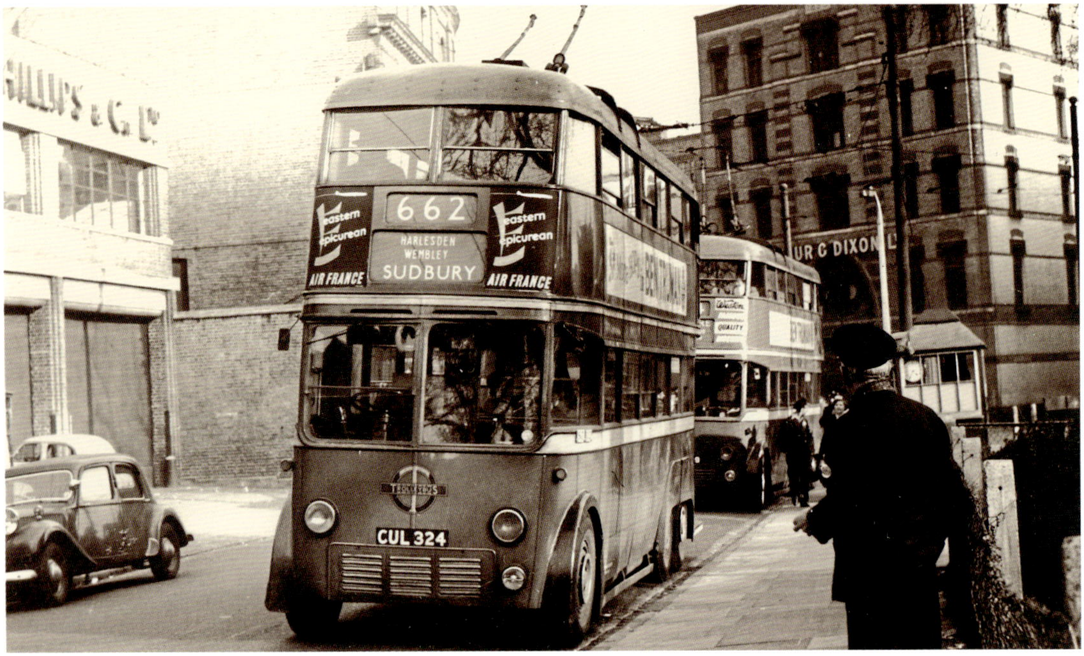

The Trolleybus Terminus, Paddington Green, *c.* 1955

Paddington's trams lasted until 1936 and were then replaced with trolleybuses that did not require tracks set into the road. The trolleybuses were swift and silent, but the old terminus at Edgware Road was unsuitable for them so a loop was created around Paddington Green enabling the trolleys to make their return trips along Harrow Road. These fine vehicles lasted until 1962. Lost commercial buildings in Harrow Road can be seen here in the above image.

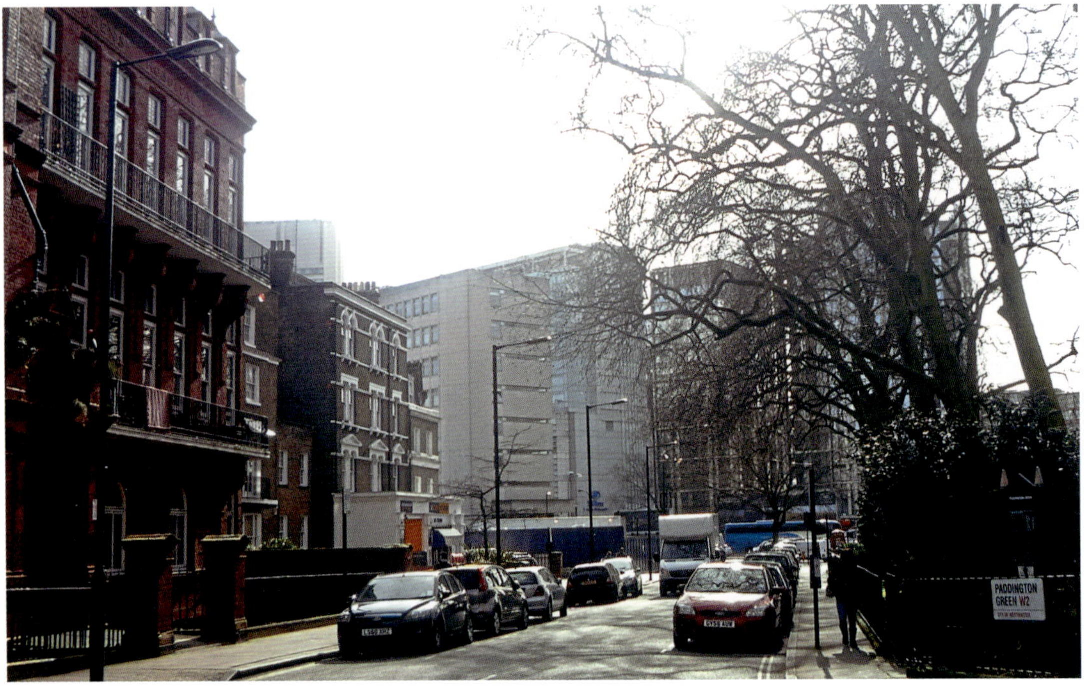

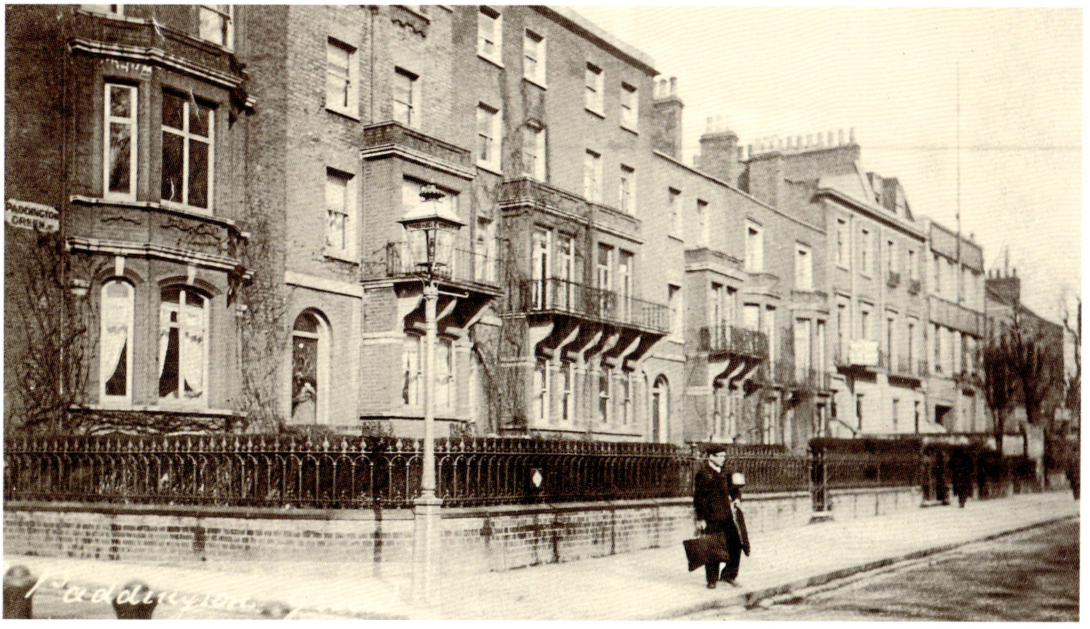

Paddington Green, *c.* 1905

Paddington Green was the centre of the old village of Paddington. It is home to St Mary's church whose origins can be traced back to 1222 when it was a chapel belonging to St Margaret's Westminster, the church we see today dates from 1788–91. Of the houses that looked out over the green, few examples remain. Those seen here form the site of the City of Westminster College, whose dramatic new building opened in 2011. It was designed by the Danish architects Schmidt Hammer Lassen and replaced a vintage 1960s building.

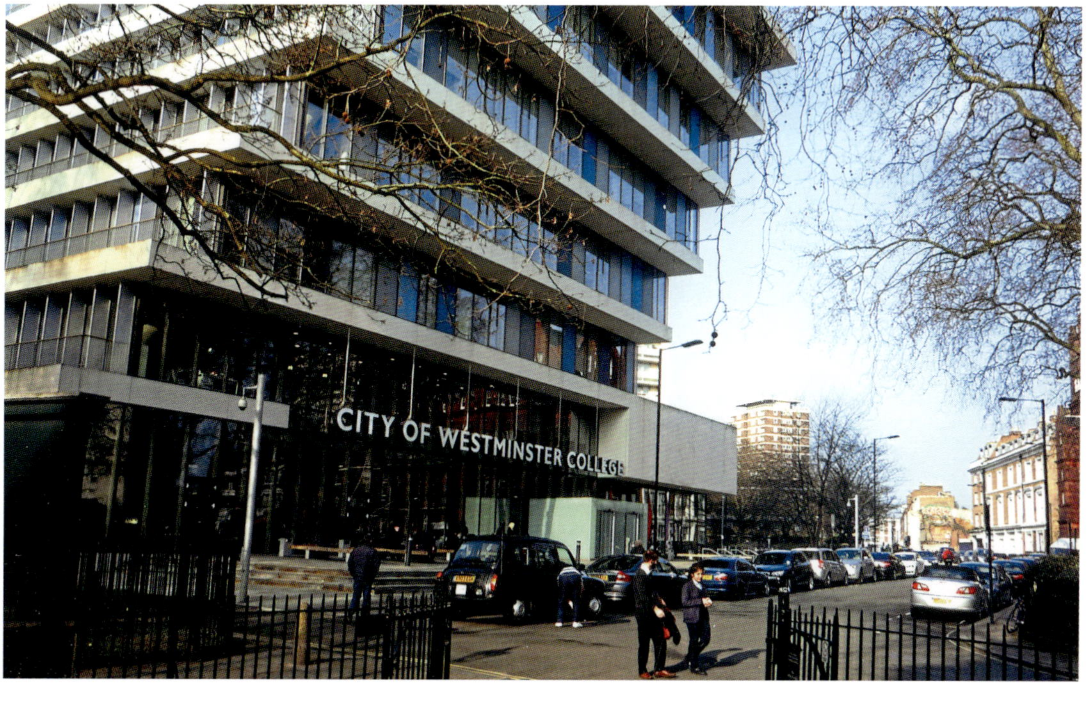

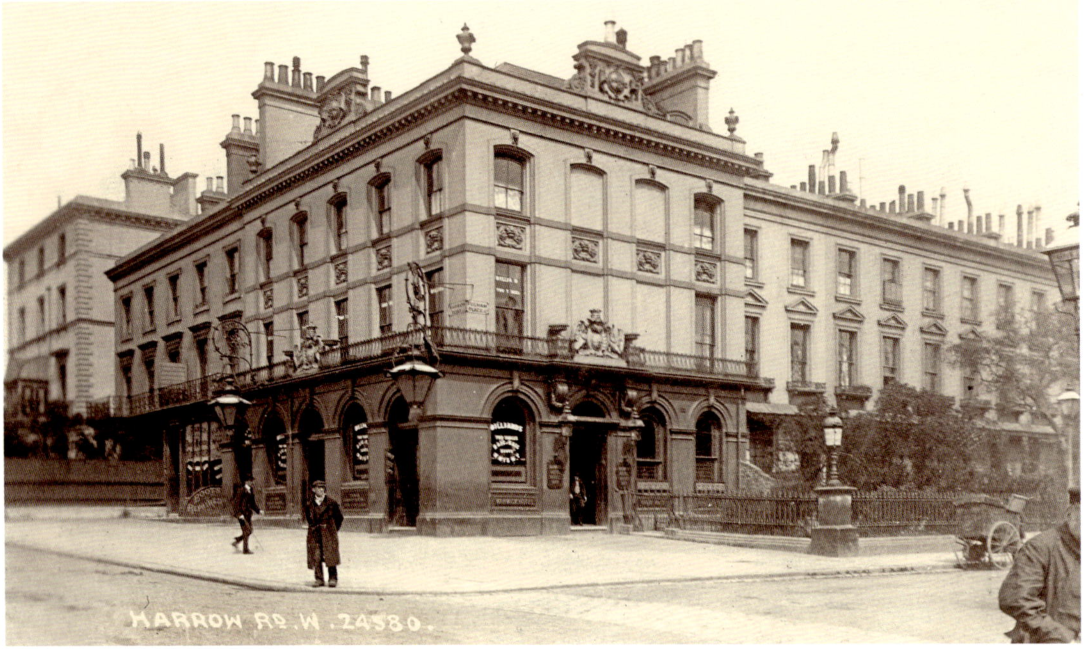

Harrow Road by Fulham Place, *c.* 1906

The Harrow Road area was distinguished by some remarkably handsome architecture before a different look was brought on by post-war decline, the construction of flats, and the realignment of the main road. However, a taste of former times can still be seen as the corner building in the below image was once the Warwick Hotel.

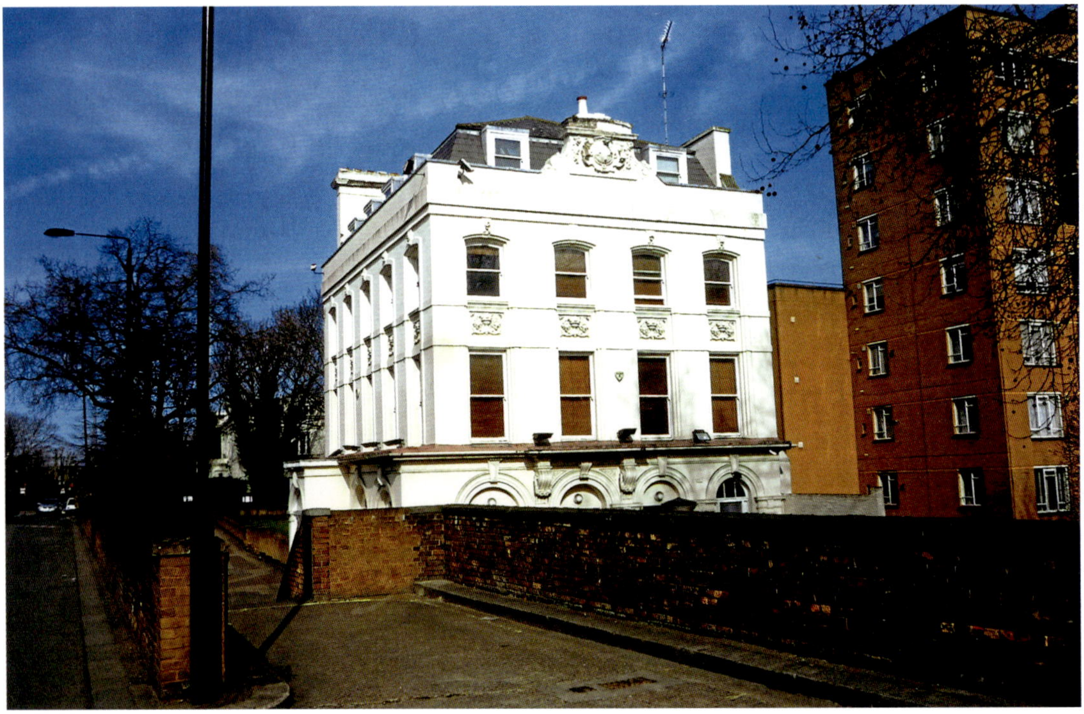

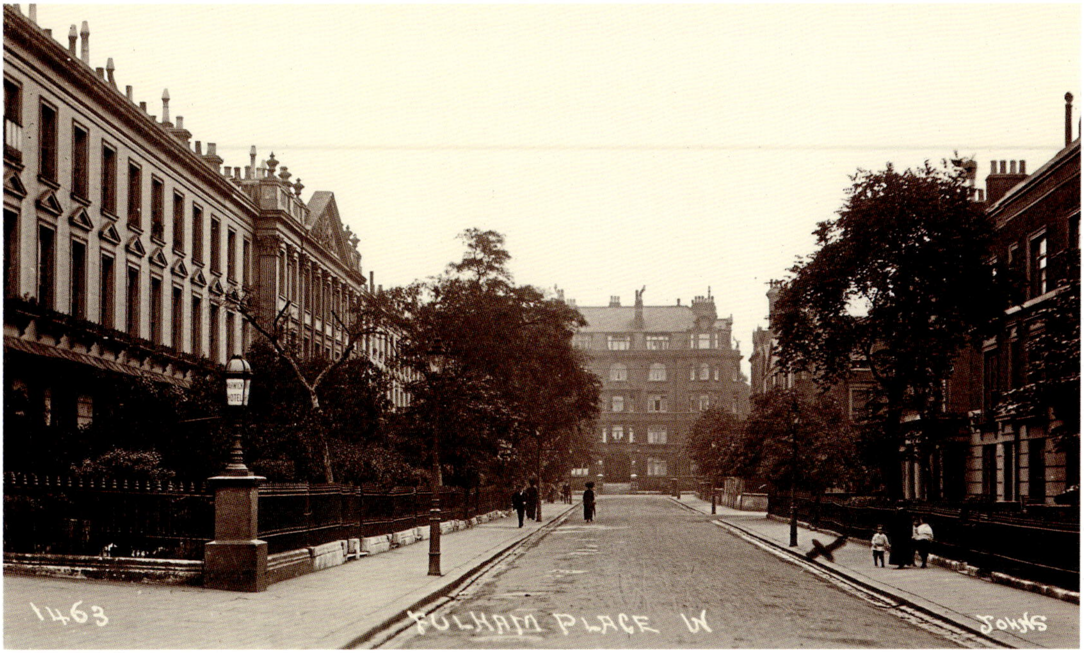

Fulham Place from Harrow Road, *c*. 1910

There is little today to remind us of the fine street as seen above with Victorian stucco-faced houses, but the background sight of St Mary's Mansions is common to both views. Although the name Fulham Place has been abolished, the course of the old street is easily spotted between blocks of post-war flats.

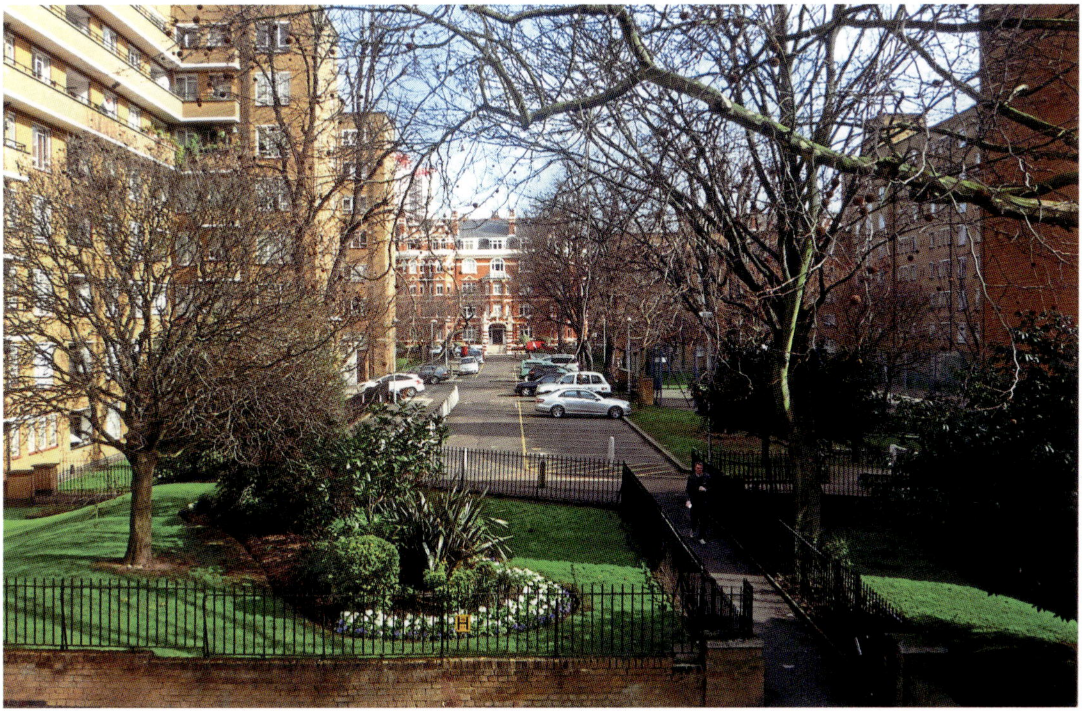

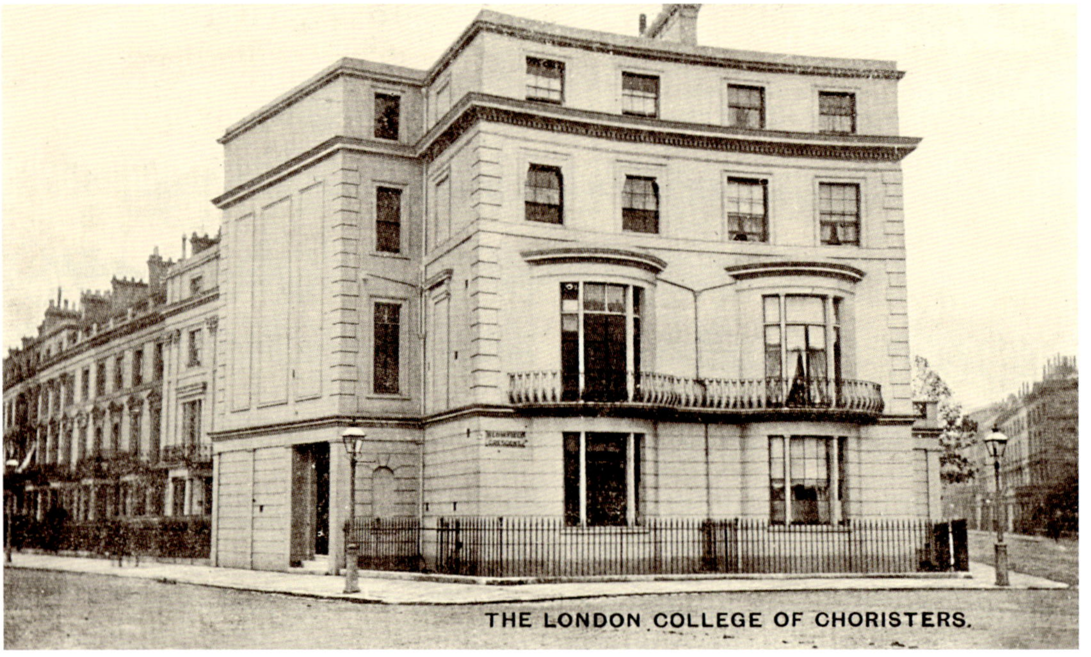

Blomfield Crescent, Harrow Road, *c.* 1906

Another lost street, Blomfield Crescent formerly existed at the point where Westbourne Terrace Road met Harrow Road. With only seven houses this was possibly London's smallest crescent, but its Regency architecture was much admired. The realignment of Harrow Road and construction of Westway wiped the old street from the map. In the photograph above you can see Harrow Road when No. 7 was home to the London College of Choristers in 1906.

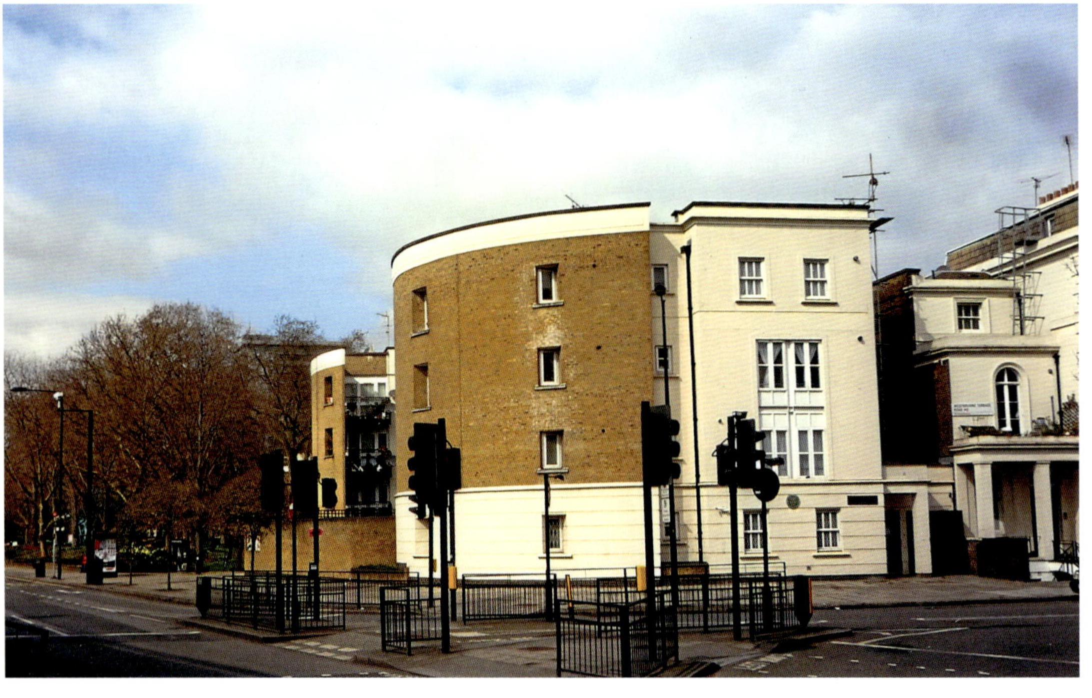

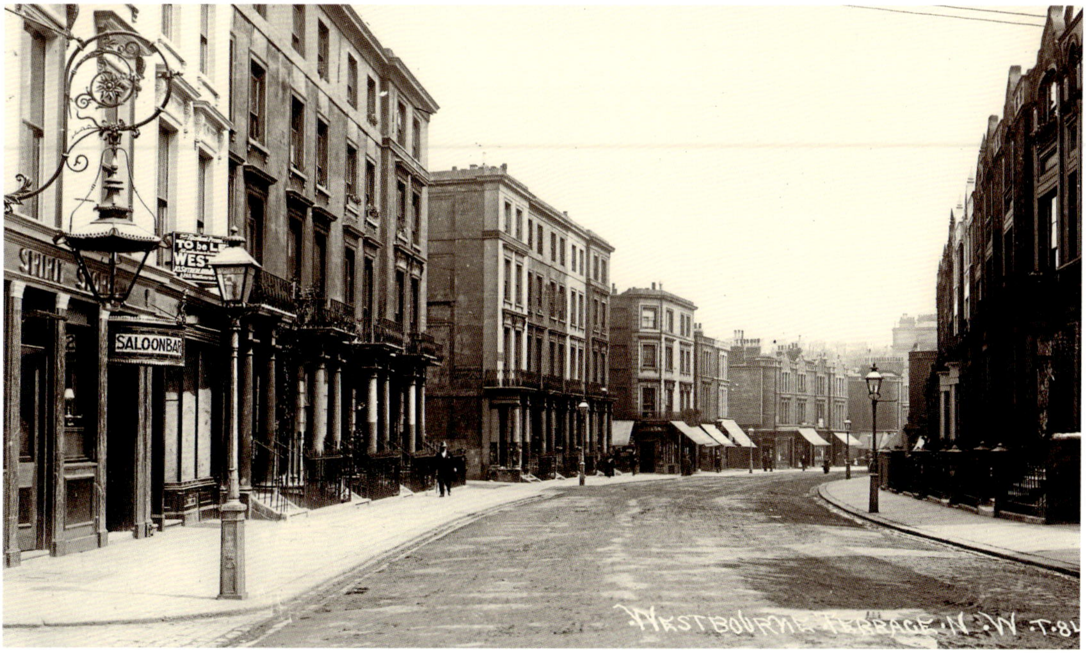

Westbourne Terrace North from Harrow Road, c. 1906

This was a principal street in a densely packed and populous district, running from Harrow Road to the canal. Post-war clearances preceded the attractive Warwick estate and a large area of open space called Westbourne Green. The above image shows the Oliver Arms by Oliver Mews, left, while further along, side streets included Hasborough, Stalham and Emily Streets.

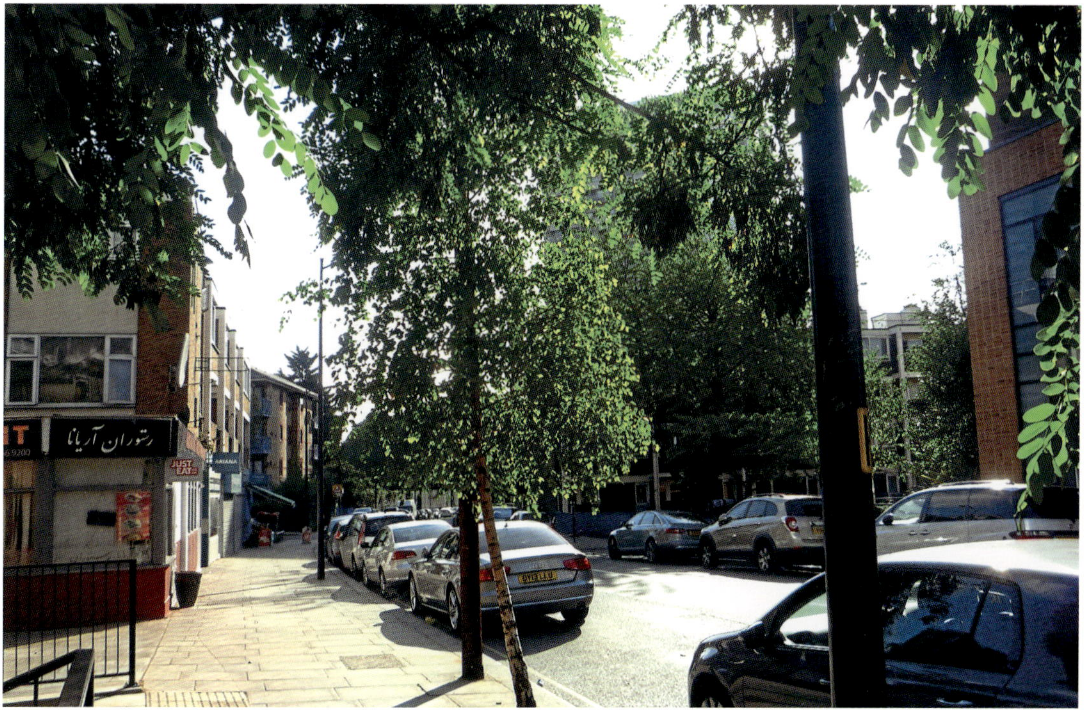

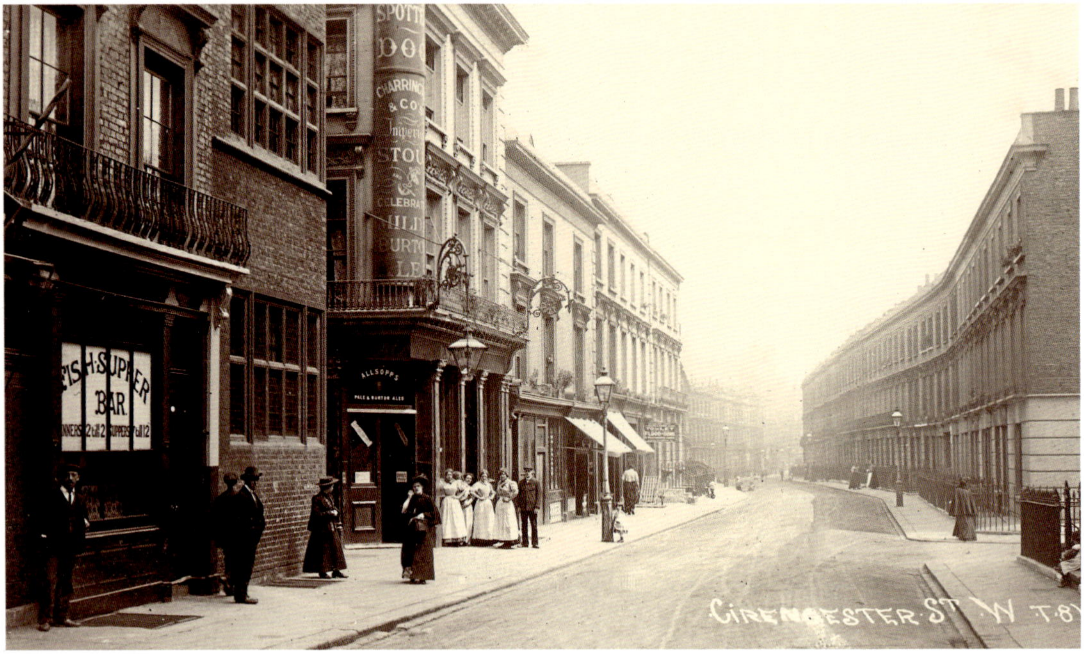

Cirencester Street from Harrow Road, *c.* 1906

This was another of the populous streets that lay between Harrow Road and the Grand Junction Canal. Terraced housing was crammed into restricted sites, a little of this remains today within the Warwick Estate. There is a glimpse here of the Spotted Dog pub (seen on the left above) whose staff have caught sight of the photographer. Woodchester Square is here now.

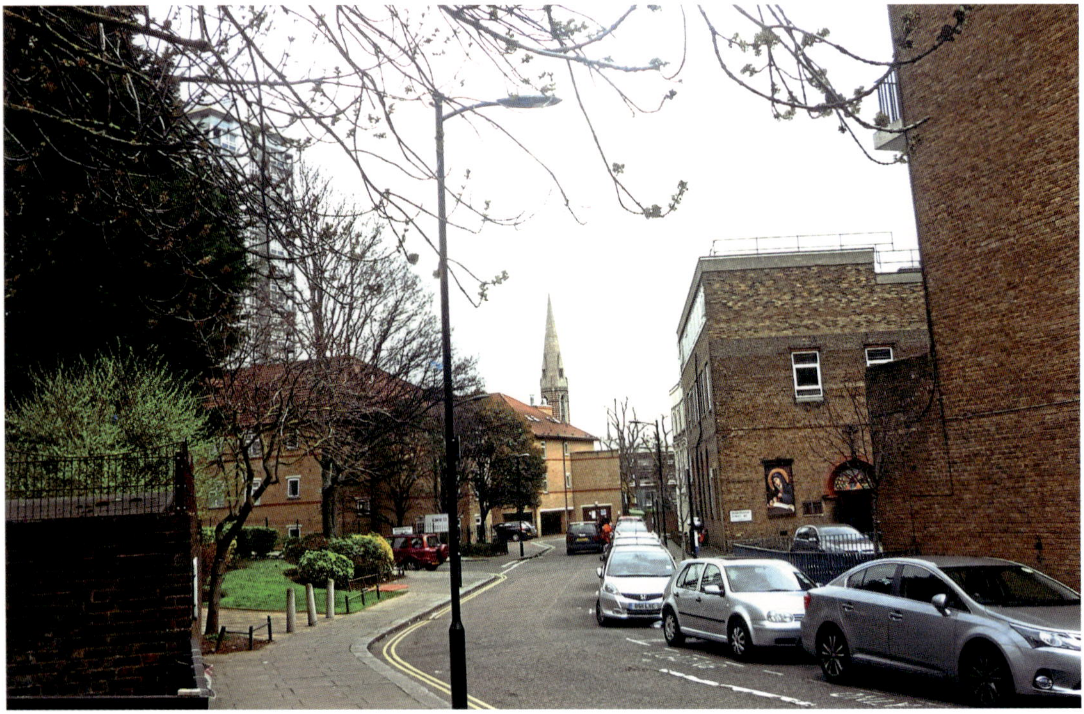

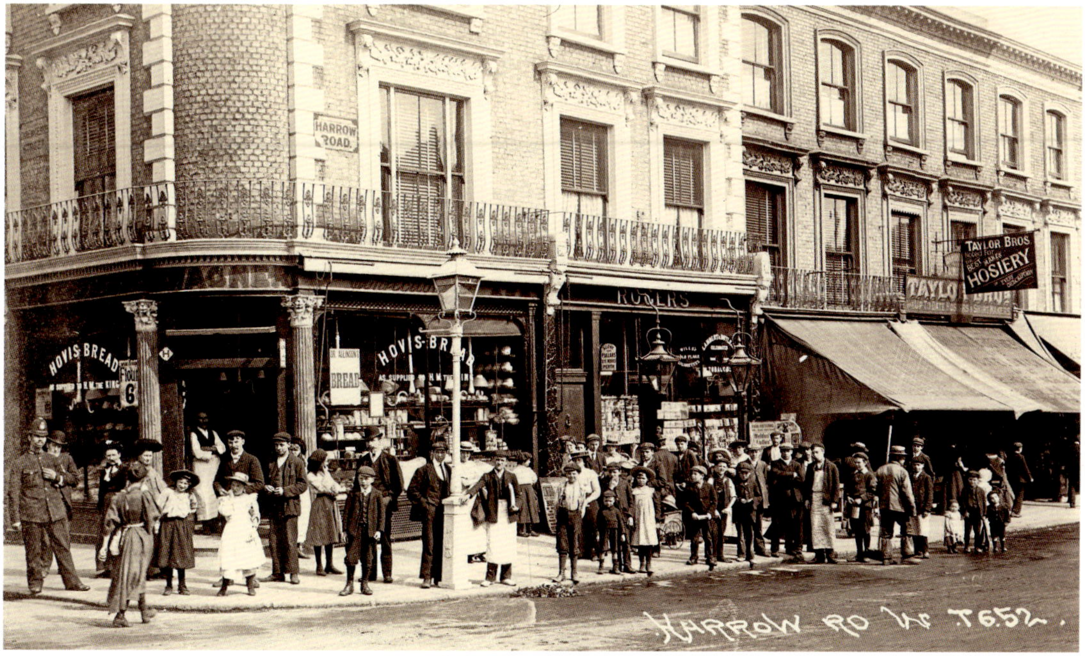

Harrow Road at Cirencester Street, *c.* 1906
This highlights the populous nature of the old neighbourhood before the area was transformed by the Warwick Estate. Philip Wagner's bread shop graced the corner with its pair of Corinthian columns – the still familiar Hovis and Allinson loaves were available within. Next door, Mrs Rosa Rogers' tobacco shop featured a fine pair of lamps that would have cast a cheery glow in the gas lit street.

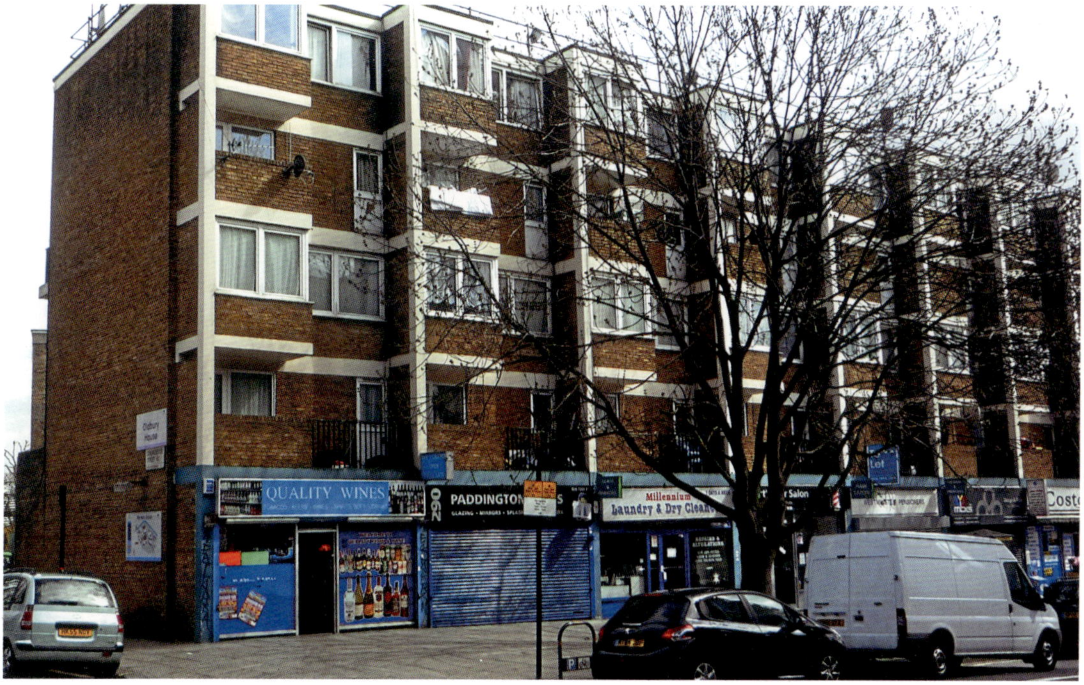

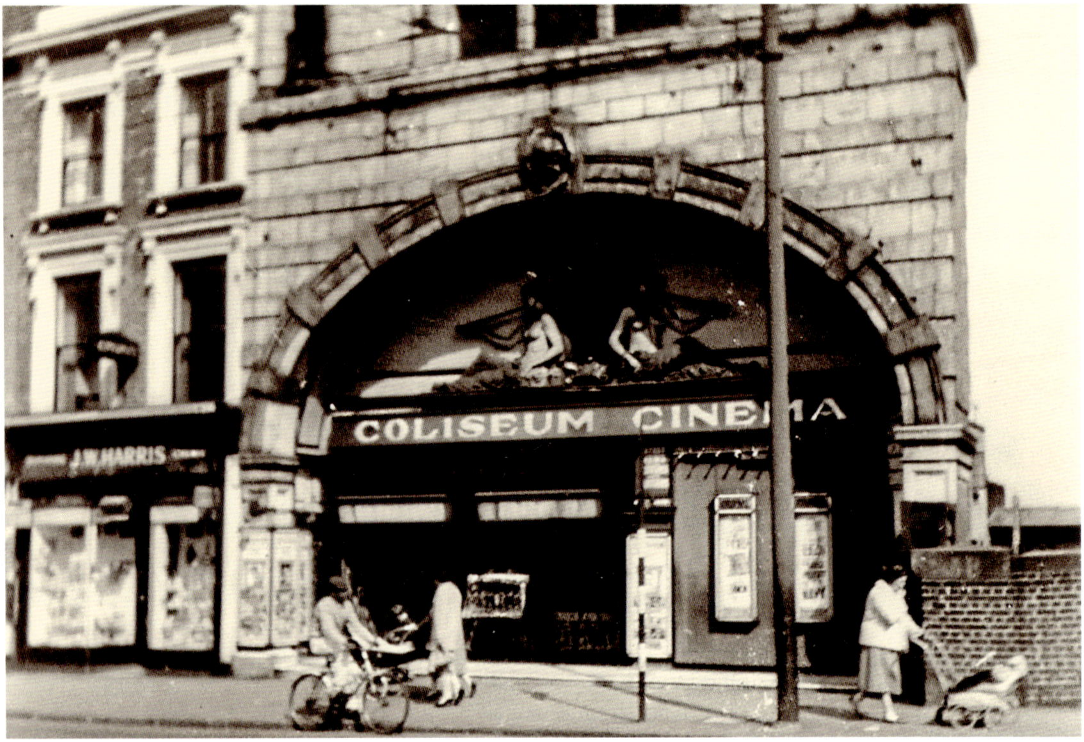

The Coliseum Cinema, Harrow Road by Lock Bridge, 1953

Grandly named but modestly scaled, the Coliseum was built in the late 1910s and achieved fame in 1949 when it featured in the film *The Blue Lamp,* much of which was shot on location around Harrow Road. This continues to revive nostalgic memories of the former police station, town hall and electric trolleybuses but the cinema was lost to an office block around 1962. The canal-side location behind the cinema was Amberley Wharves, where cargoes of timber were formerly handled.

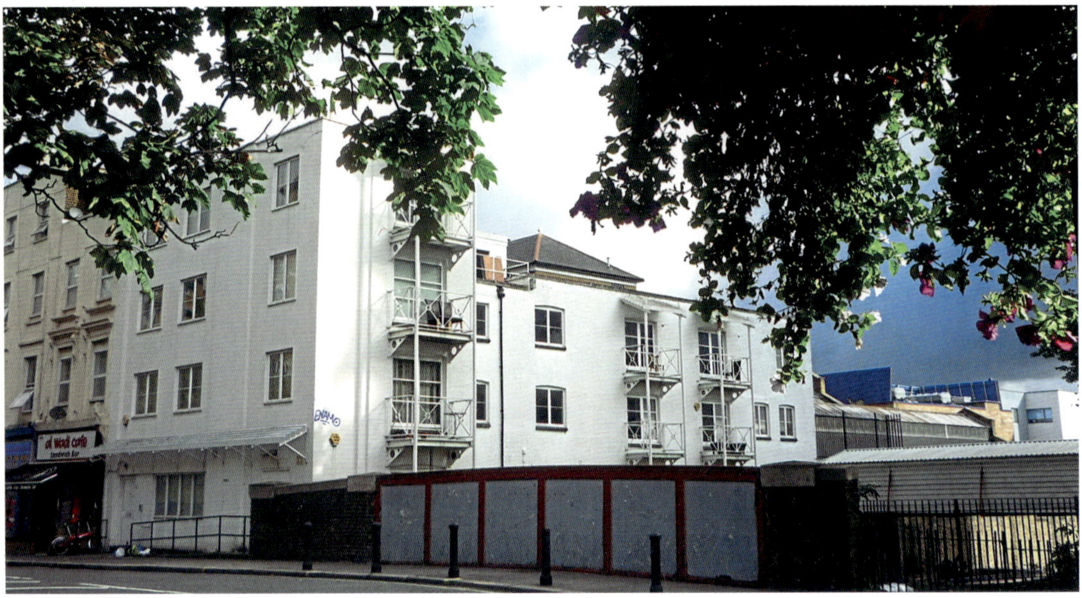

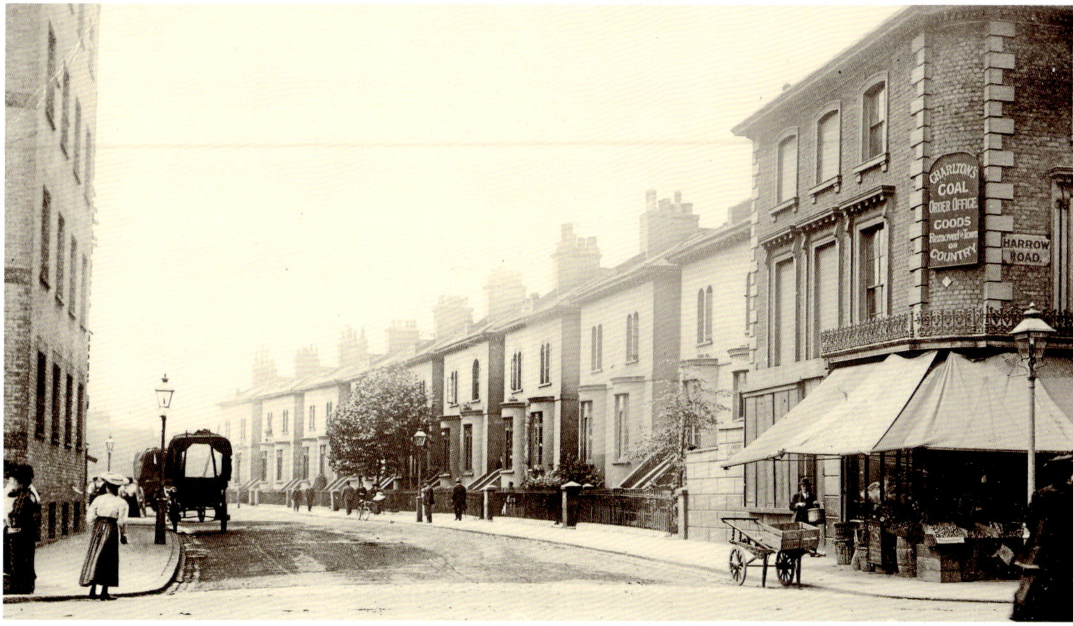

Marlborough Road (Torquay Street) from Harrow Road, *c.* 1906

The street was blessed with elegant Regency-style houses with bowed fronts, but when it all declined into post-war dereliction everything was swept away and replaced by the London County Council's Brindley Estate in the 1960s. In more enlightened times these fine houses might have been saved. We can see them above when their residents were served by George Charlton's, the greengrocer on the Harrow Road corner. Beds and mattresses were once made in the factory on the left of the image.

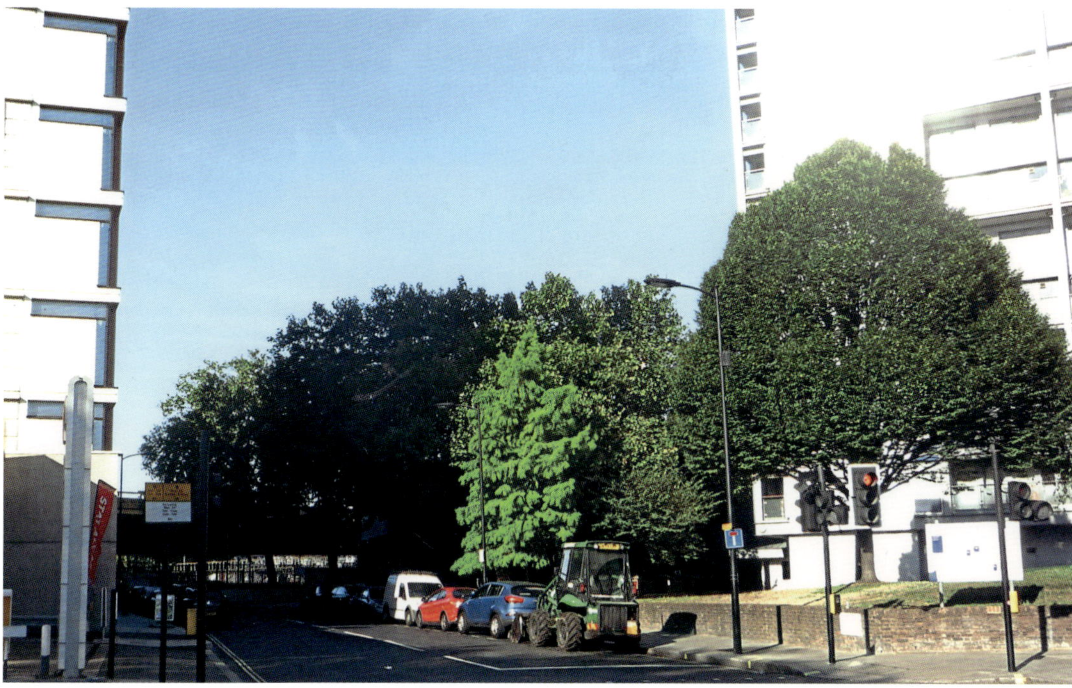

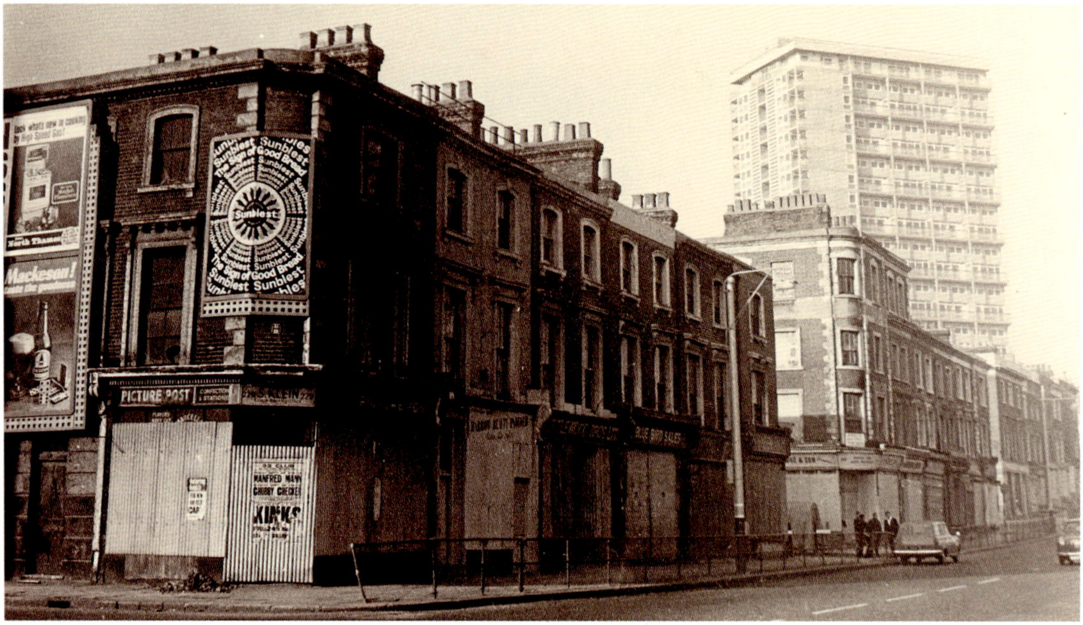

Harrow Road by Torquay Street, 1965

In the above image the last days of the old shopping terraces that formerly ran up to the Lock Bridge can be seen, as the new Brindley Estate rises in the distance. Although boarded up, the old shops still retained reminders of their former lives with adverts for 'Picture Post' on Samuel Klein's newspaper shop while posters for concerts by Manfred Mann, Chubby Checker and the Kinks adorn the old frontage. Westminster Academy in shades of green and yellow took part of the site in 2007.

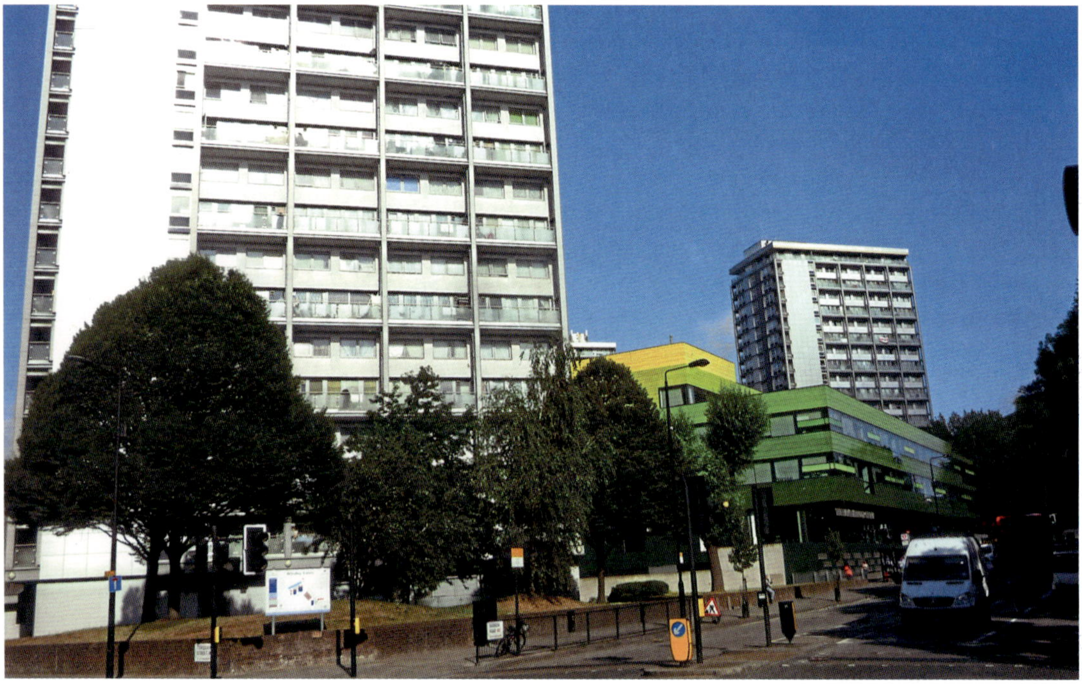

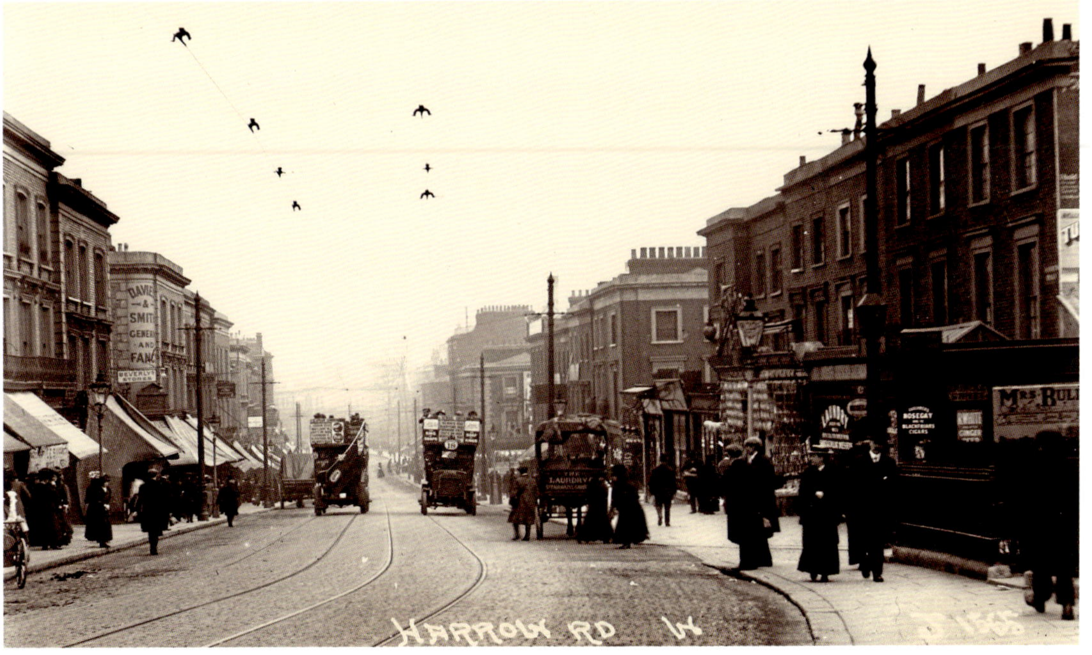

Harrow Road from Lock Bridge, *c.* 1912

This image shows more of the shopping terraces that once lined both sides of Harrow Road before the redevelopments of the 1960s. The electric tram tracks ran on towards the Edgware Road terminus, but the motor bus also served the Harrow Road in the form of route 18, one of the most enduring of the old routes of the London General Omnibus Company – it still runs today.

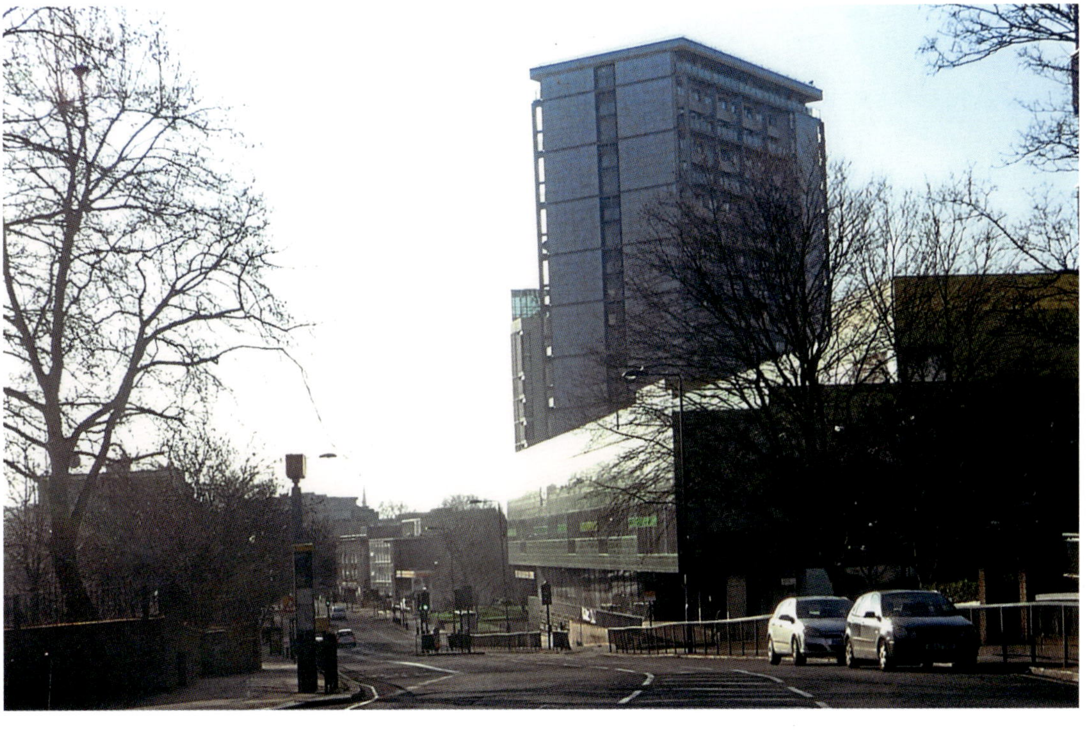

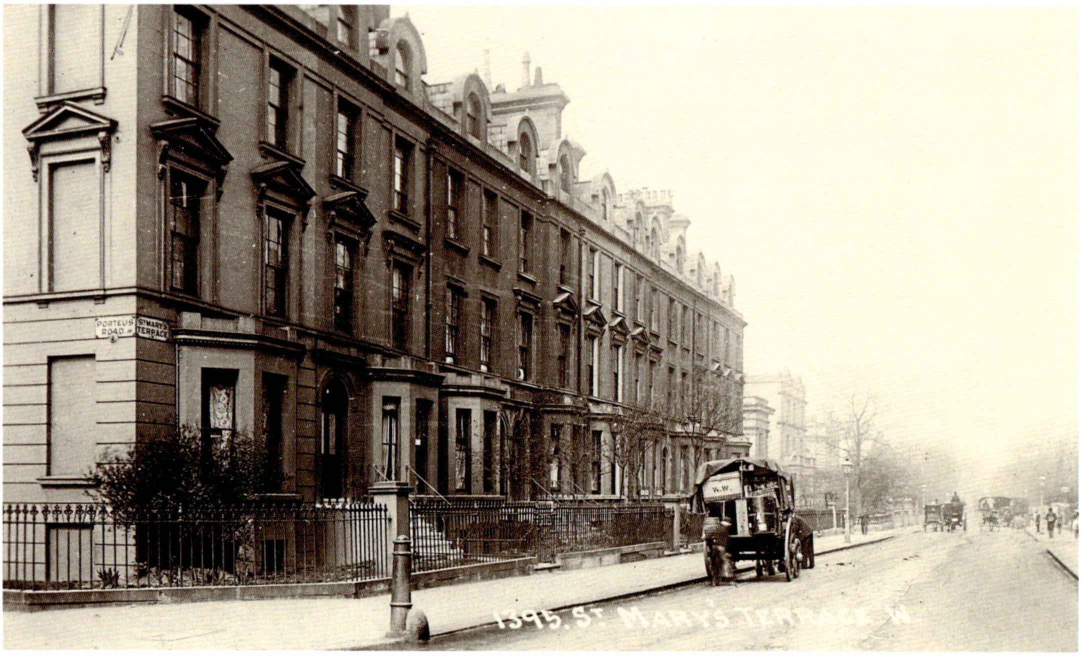

St Mary's Terrace by Porteus Road, *c.* 1906

With grand mansion flats on one side of the road (above, off-camera to the right) and modest terraces on the other, the street represented the contrasting fortunes of the area. While the mansions remain, the old terraces gave way to new blocks of flats as part of the reconstruction works immediately following the Second World War.

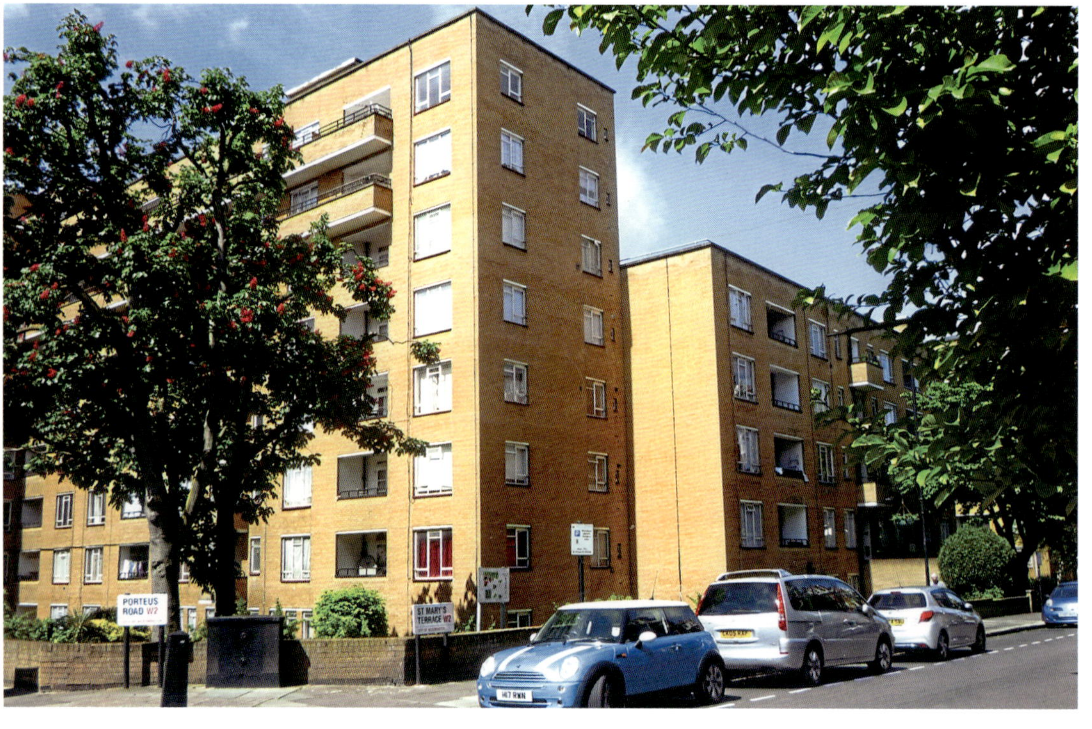

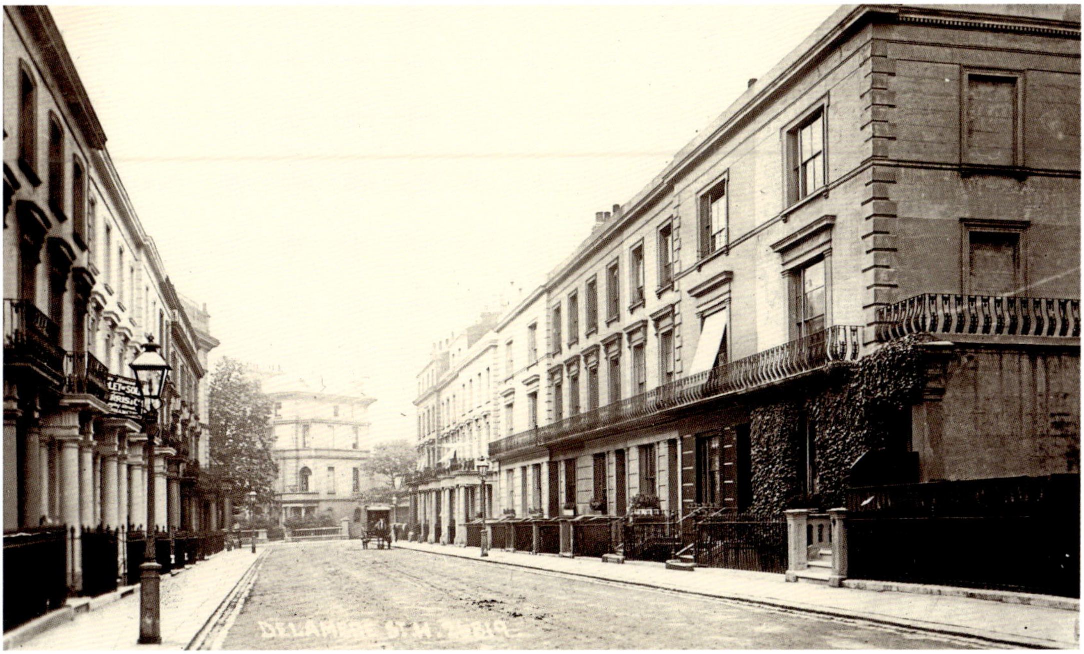

Delamere Street, *c.* 1906

The great post-war replacement of the aged housing to the north of Harrow Road left Delamere Street with only a fragment of its former self. The old street patterns were abolished in favour of new housing estates. In the above image there is a distant glimpse of the equally lost Westbourne Square.

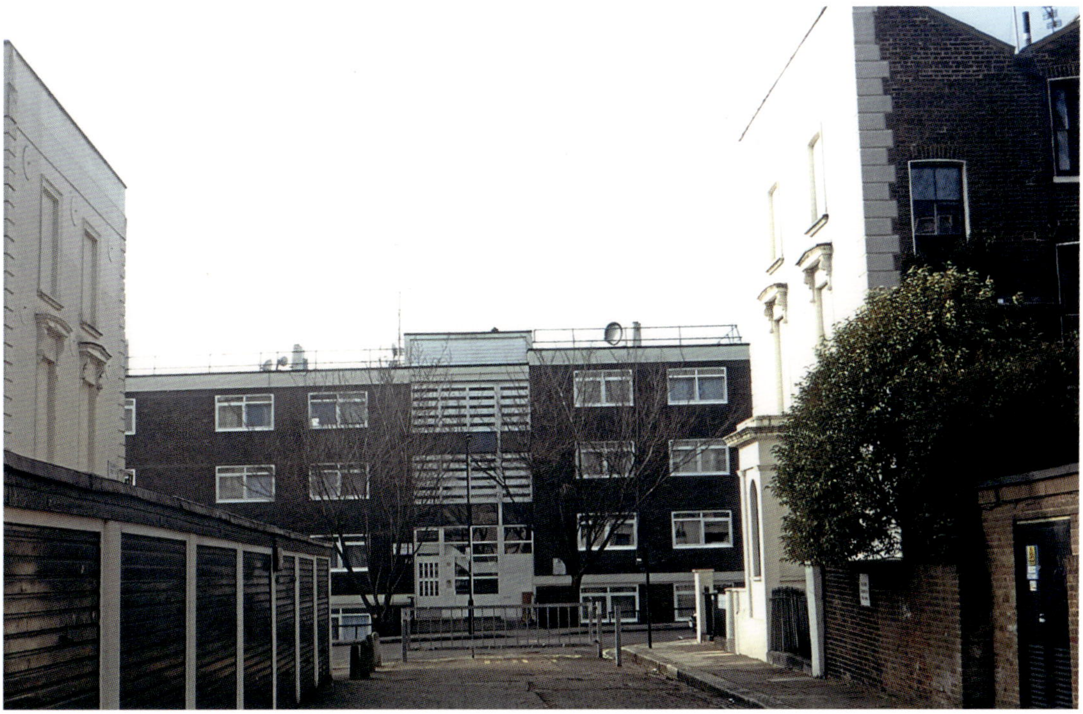

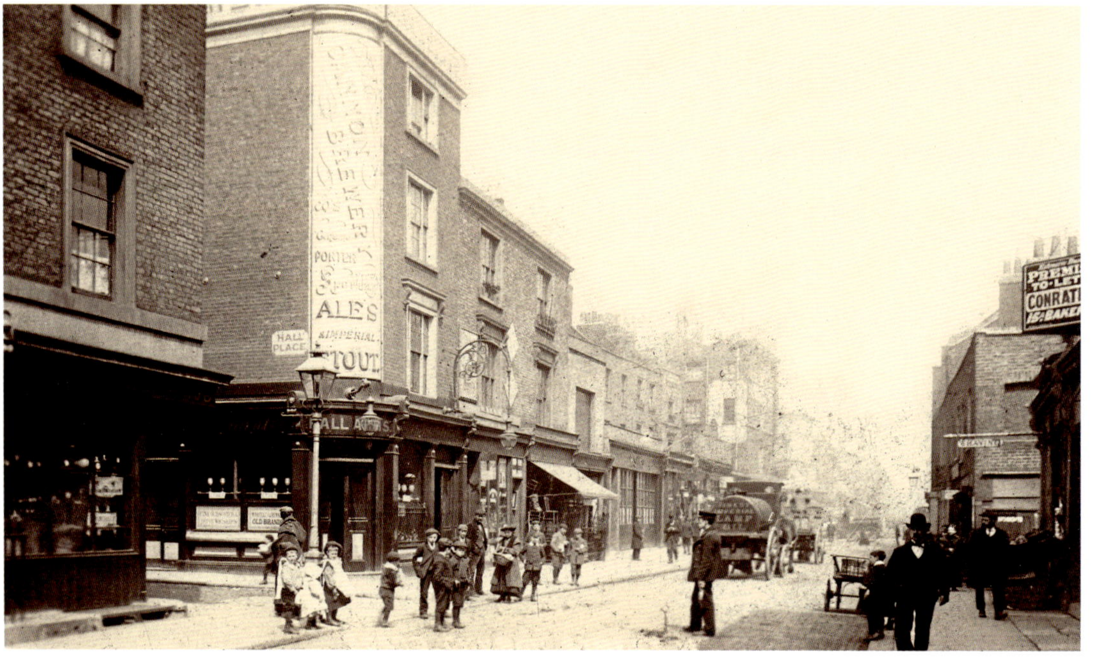

Church Street from Paddingon Green, *c.* 1905

This was the Edwardian face of an old rural route that crossed Edgware Road into Marylebone. The street is busy in the above image with shoppers, but almost everything seen here has now gone because the rebuilt New Hall Park brought high-rises and a leafier look. The side-turning of Hall Place is seen on the left above with the Hall Arms pub on the corner.

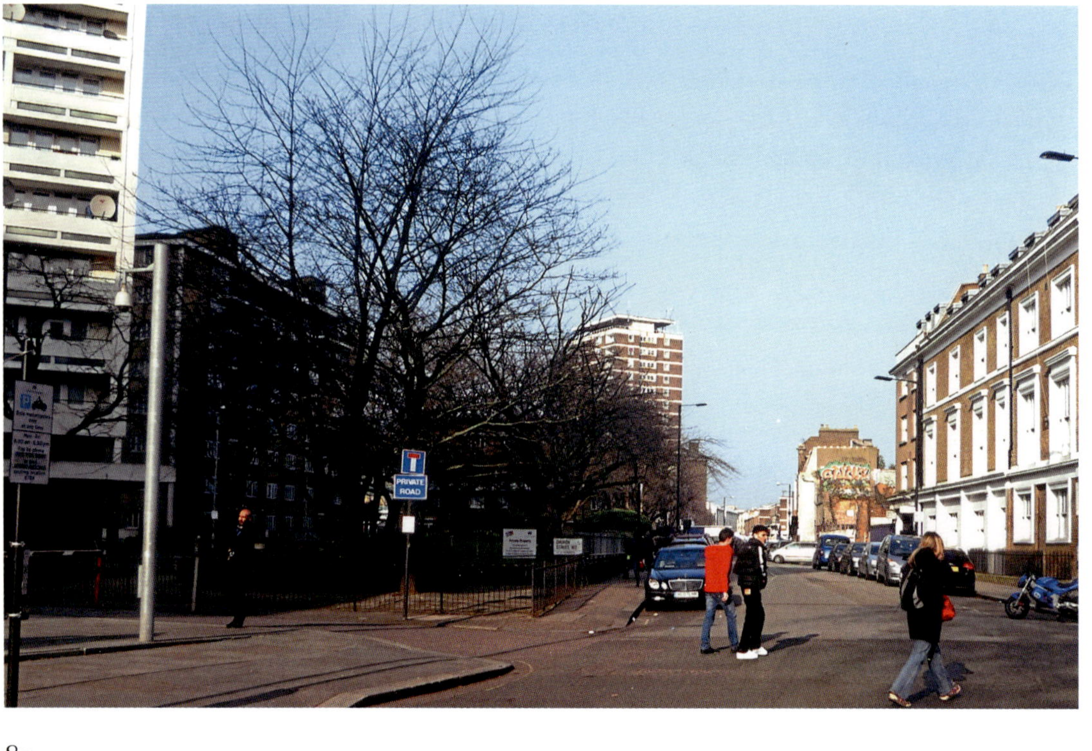

The Lord Collingwood, No. 93 Hall Place, *c.* 1906

In streets with modest properties, it was often the local pub that stood out due to grander architecture and a brightly shining lamp. The same is true above, where the Lord Collingwood sported a balustrade and a stuccoed front. Hall Place was part of Hall Park, an intensive development of formerly rural land in the 1850s. Conditions here were seriously overcrowded but most of it was replaced by the Hall Estate, a complex of high- and low-rise housing completed in 1973, but the old street pattern was lost. Hall Tower can be seen in the modern view below.

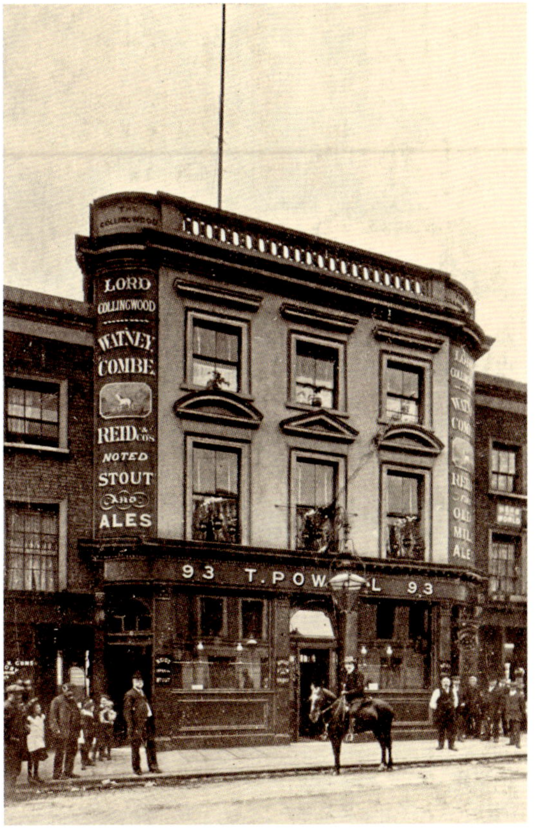

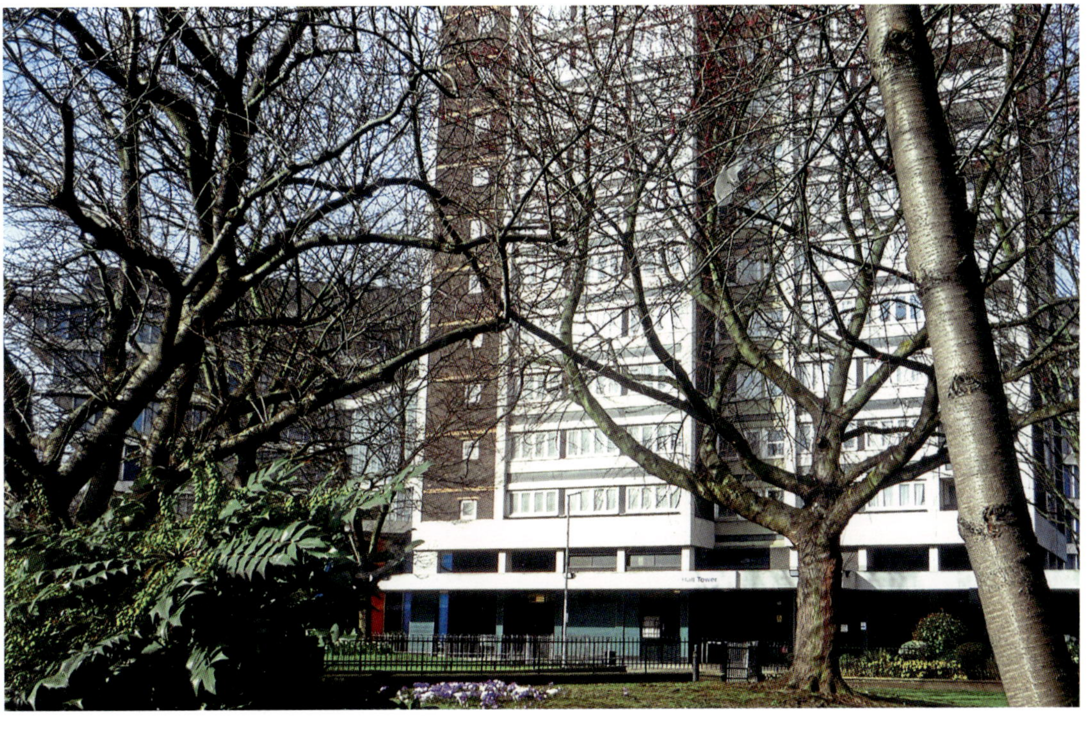

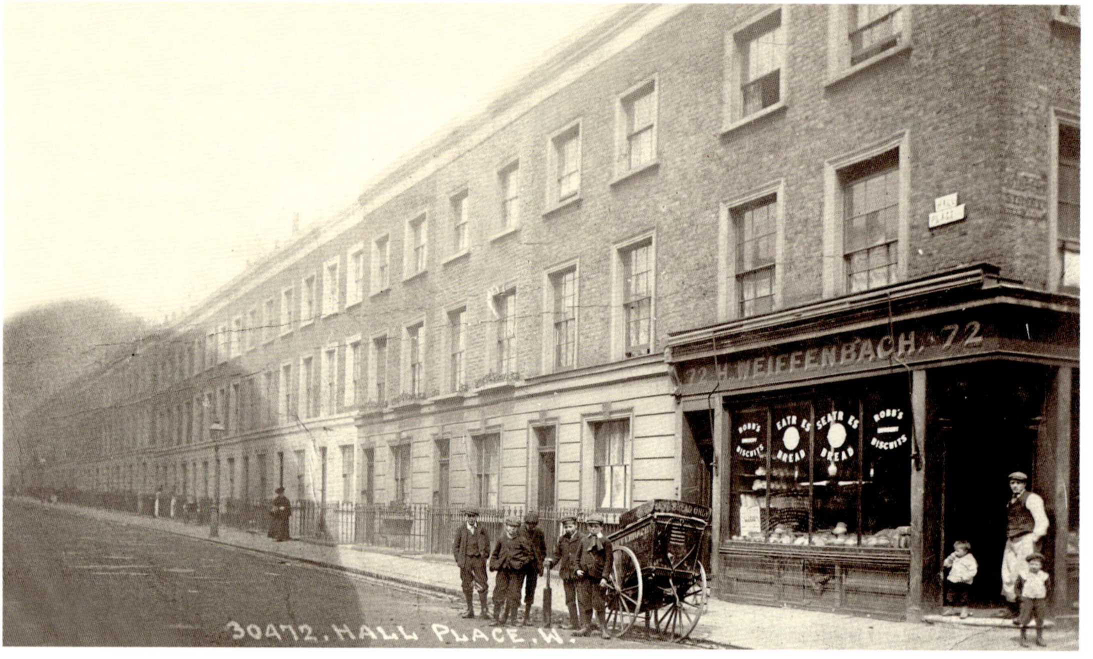

Hall Place by Cuthbert Street, *c.* 1906

The houses seen here were crammed together and it became a grim world of overcrowding and drabness. Appetising aromas from Ferdinand Wieffenbach's bakery by Cuthbert Street would have made a pleasing alternative to the less agreeable odours of coal smoke and dampness that permeated these crumbling tenements. The post-war slum clearance led to a far more agreeable environment.

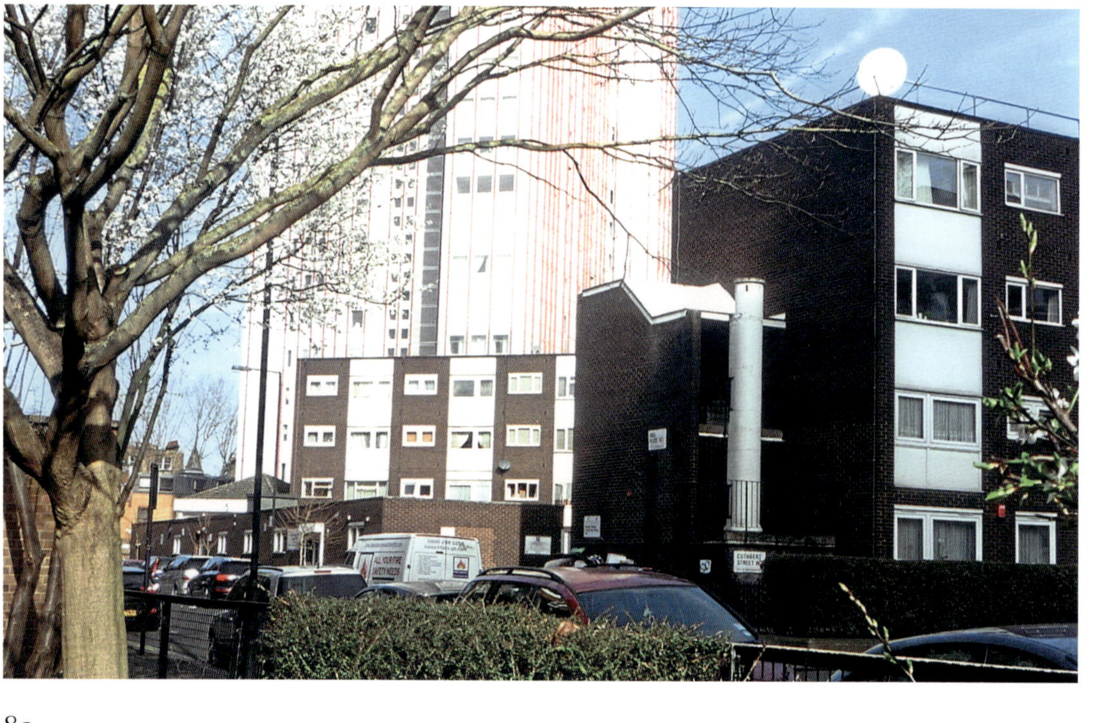

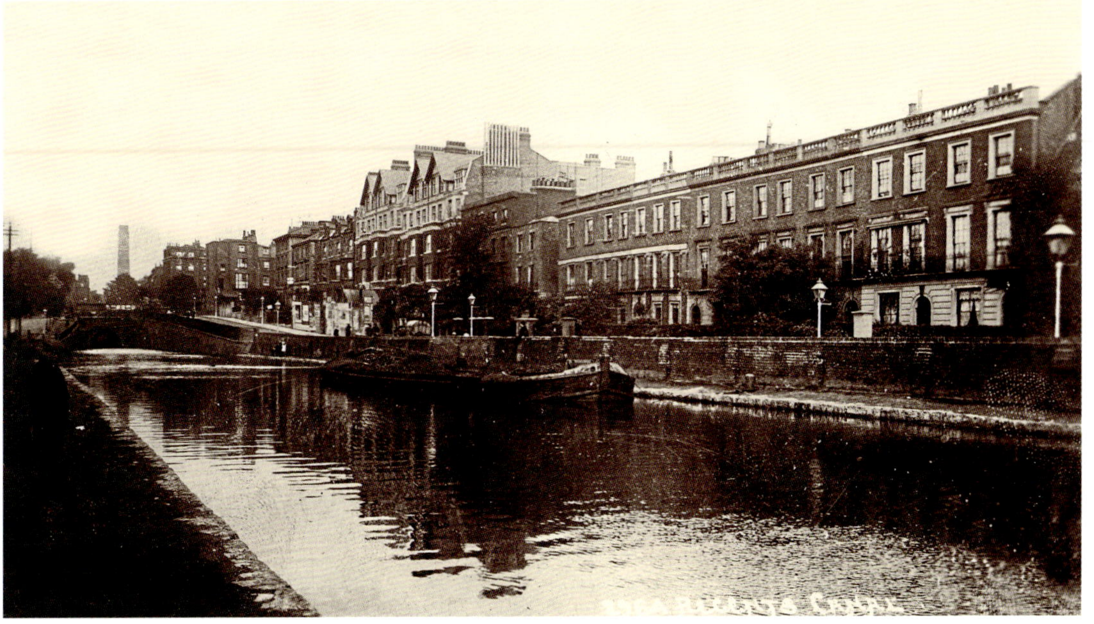

Regent's Canal from Blomfield Road (Little Venice), *c.* 1906

Paddington's 'water-world' of canals and commercial basins is part of an industrial past when canals linked parts of Great Britain with London, the Thames and the sea. The Grand Junction (now known as Grand Union) canal opened in 1801 and the Regent's canal, which extended the system from Paddington to Limehouse, in 1820. Regent's canal is partly overlooked by fine and highly desirable housing and in more recent times the waters have been colonised by a large community of houseboats, giving something of the atmosphere of an old Dutch city.

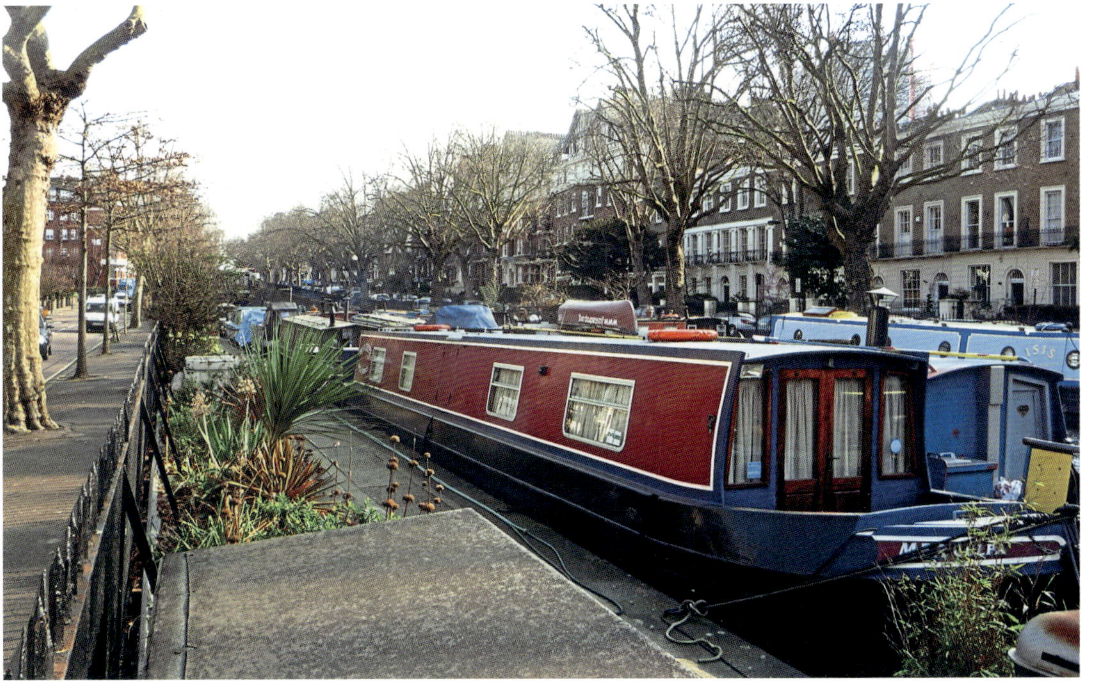

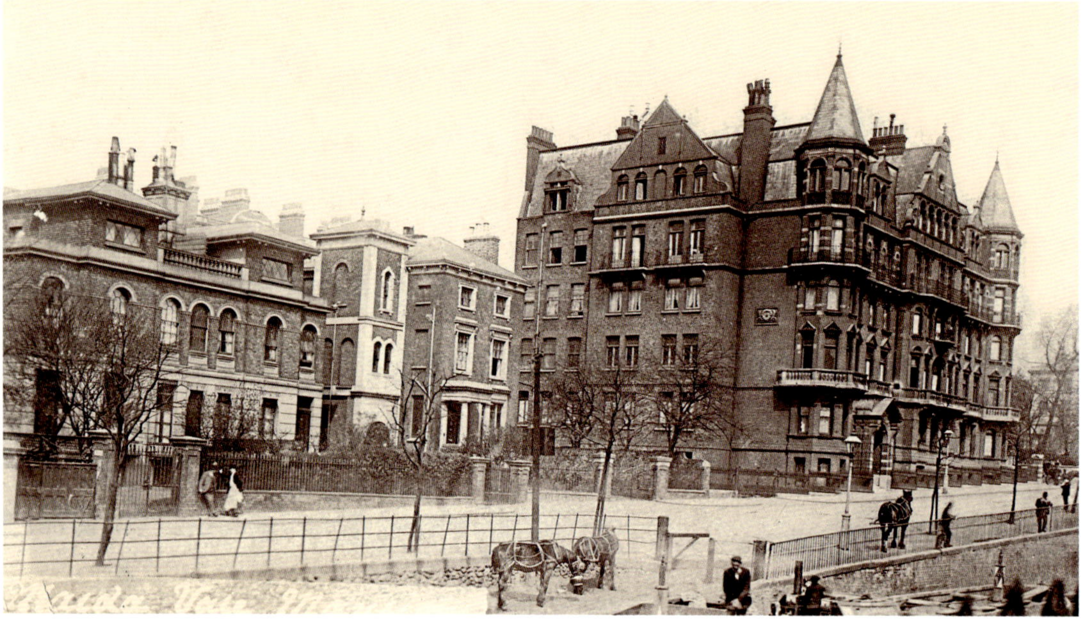

The Canal at Blomfield Road with Maida Vale Mansions, *c.* 1904

The image above captured some activity on the towpath; this was the point at which the horses towing the working boats were unhitched prior to a passage through the Maida Hill Tunnel. From here any unpowered boat had to be 'legged' through the tunnel, the bargee's legs and feet on the tunnel wall provided the propulsion. The towing horse was then led overland to the canal's next open section. Maida Vale Mansions were completed in 1892.

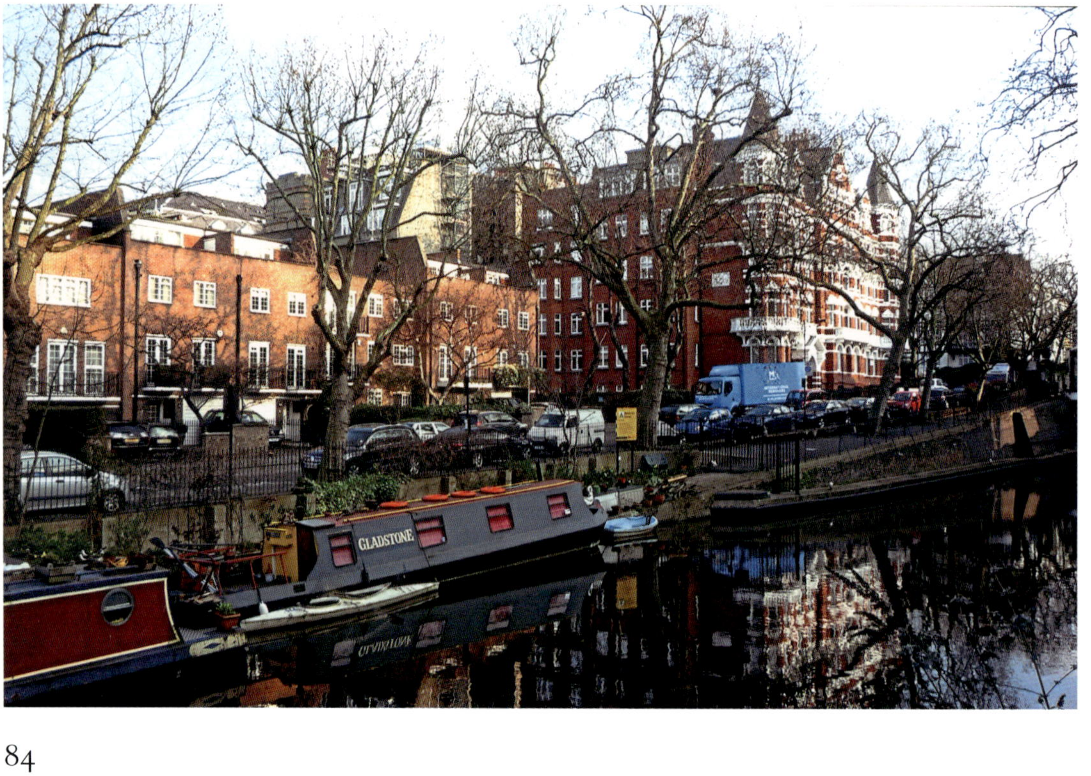

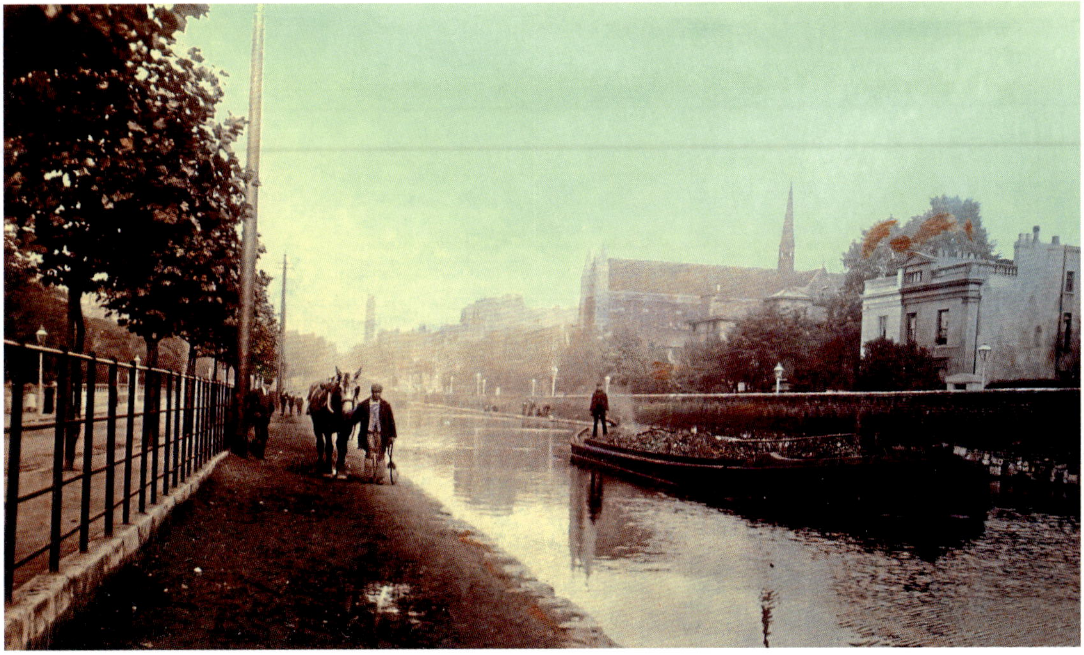

The Regent's Canal at Blomfield Road, *c.* 1905

This pair of images show the contrast of the working canal of old with its leisure and residential roles of the present day. Above, the towpath is seen fulfilling its original purpose, but today it is filled with the tiny gardens of the houseboat community. It is all overlooked by the Catholic Apostolic Church (1893) by J. L. Pearson.

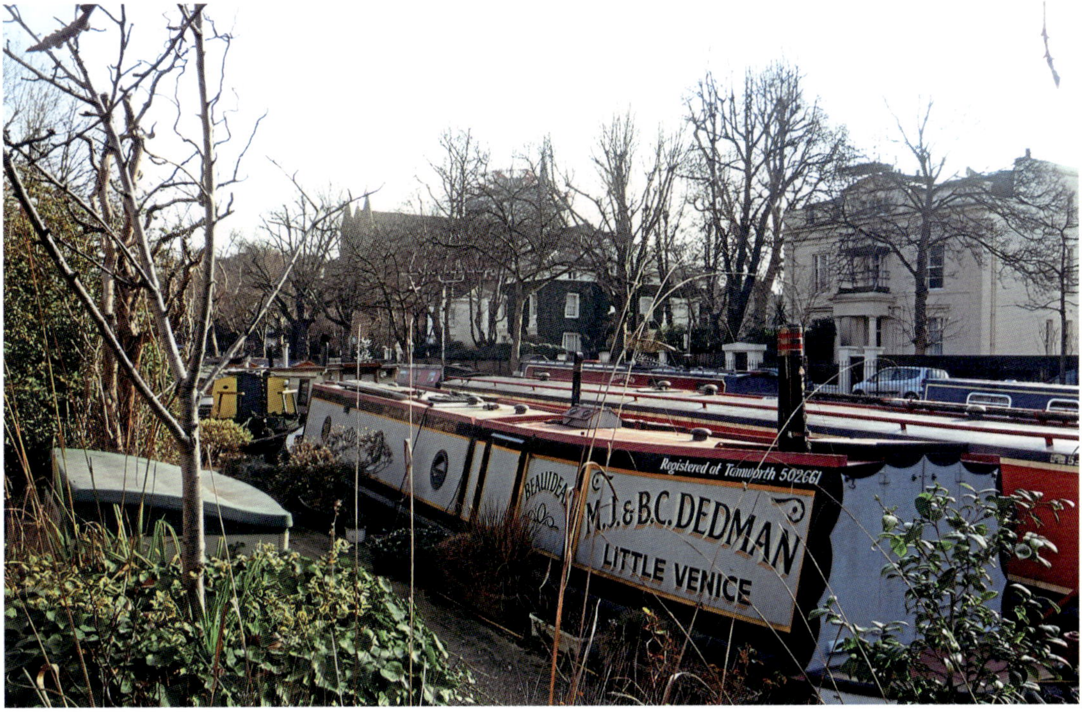

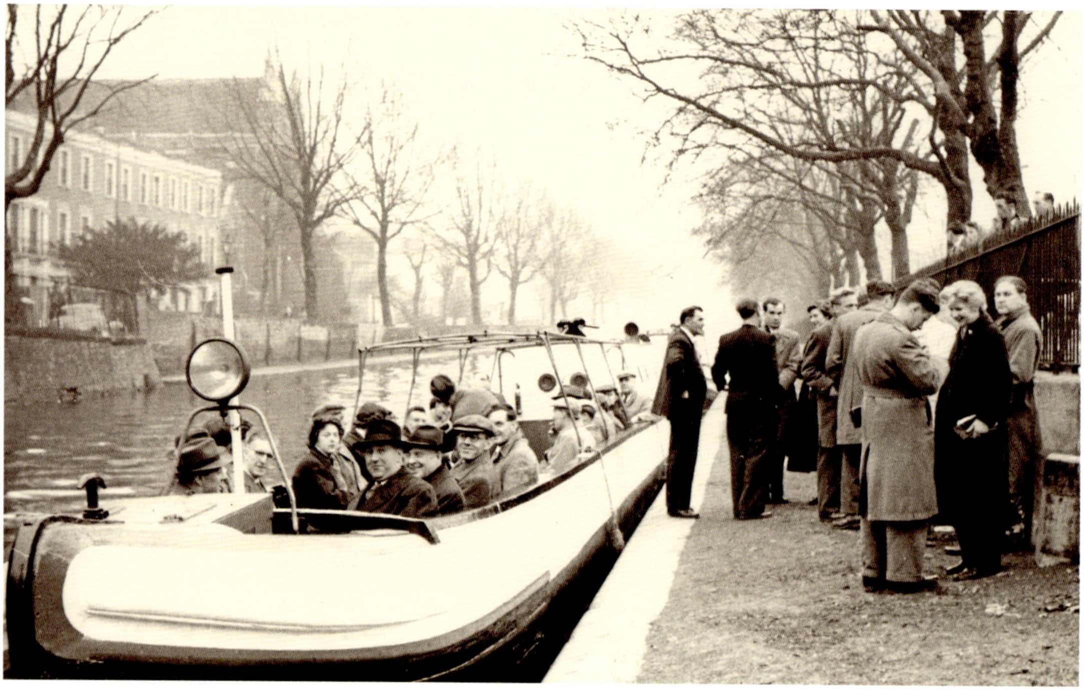

Regent's Canal at Blomfield Road ('Jason's Trip'), 1956

The post-war years saw a rise in leisure activities on the canals; 'Jason' made its first trip in 1951, giving its passengers a unique view of aquatic London. Here, above, a private party has booked a voyage. This is the point where the canal narrows prior to entering the Maida Hill Tunnel.

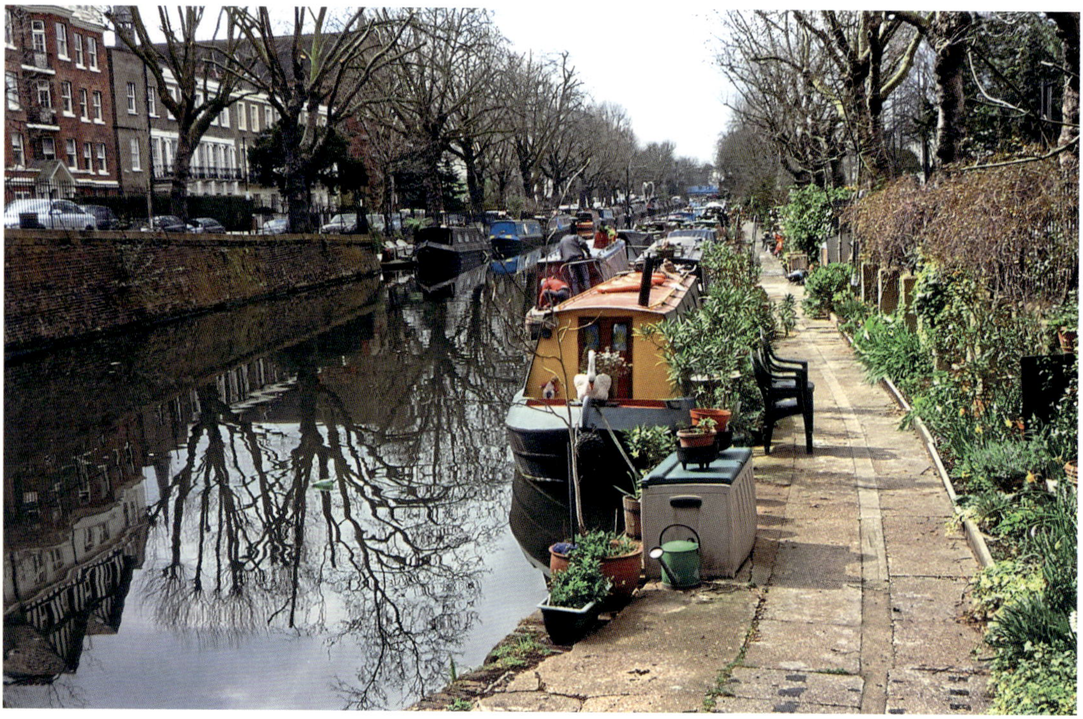

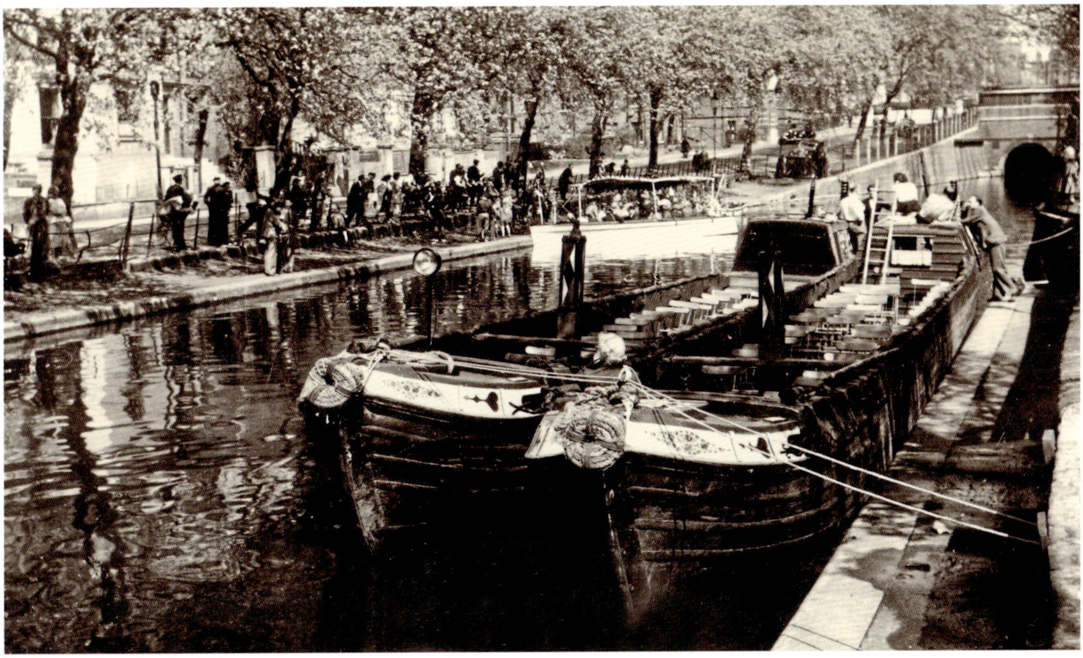

The Canal from Maida Avenue, 1949

In the image above a sunny spring day has stimulated activity on the canal, close to Maida Hill Tunnel where a restaurant sits above the waters. Modern attractions in Little Venice include a theatre barge and a floating restaurant in Browning's Pool while Rembrandt Garden is a peaceful waterside amenity, the former site of war-damaged houses.

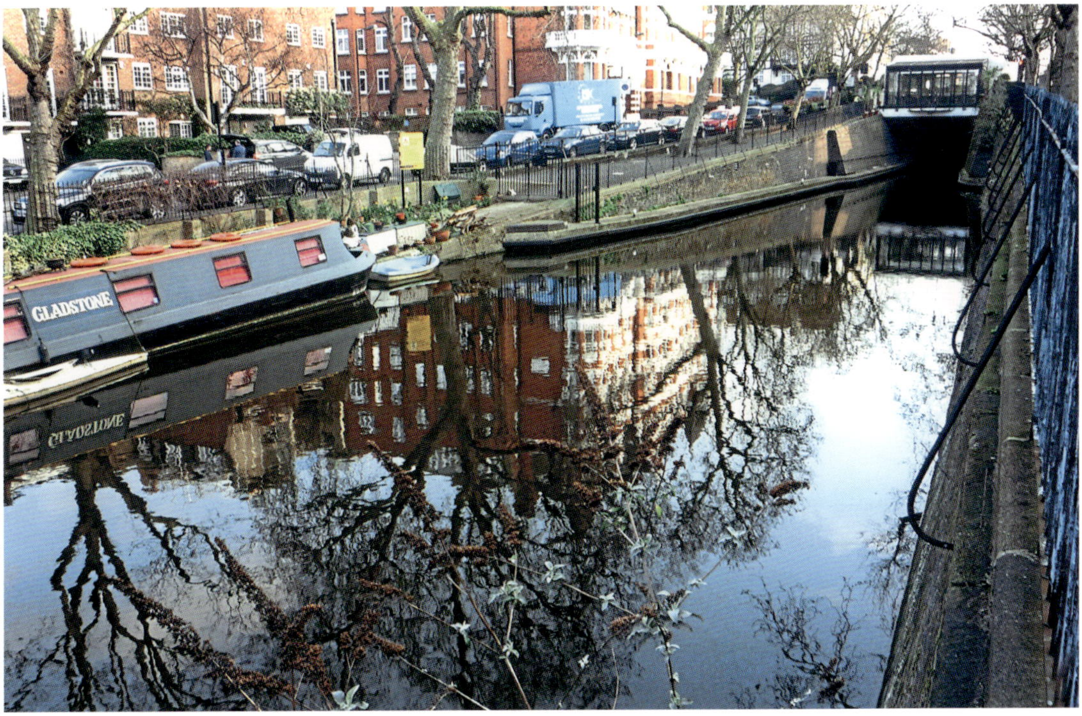

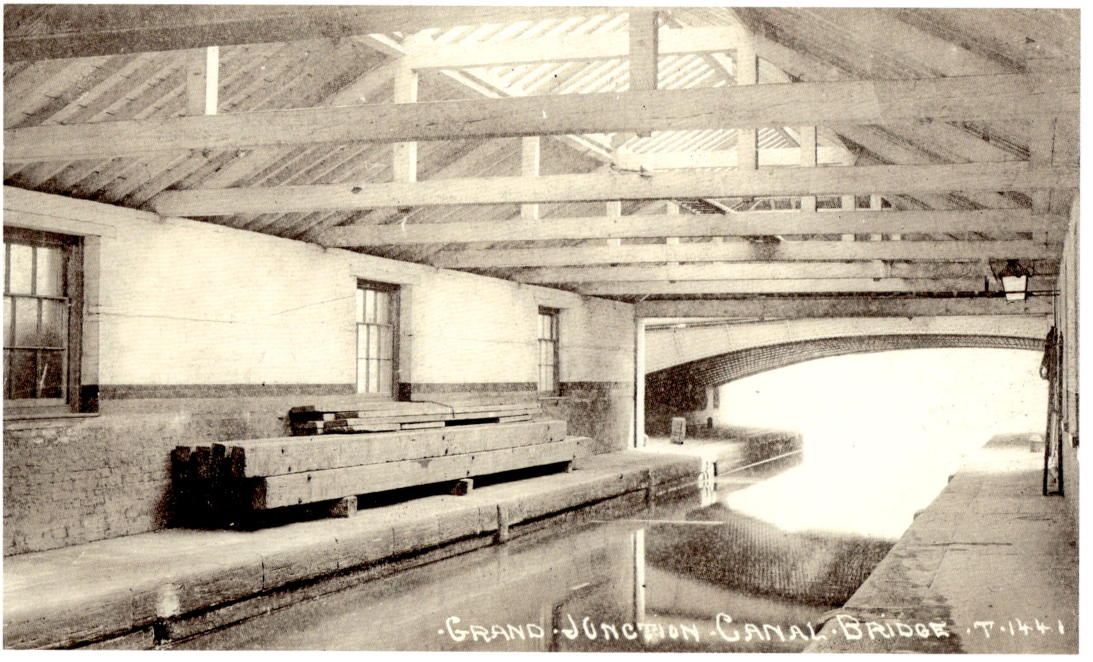

The Weigh Bridge and Toll House, Grand Junction Canal, *c.* 1906
It was here that working boats had their cargoes weighed in order to calculate the amount of the toll to be levied for further passage along the waterway. Having passed this point and under the road bridge (built in 1899) the boats entered the Broad Water or Browning's Pool, a spacious harbour often filled with working boats awaiting access to the freight terminals at Paddington Basin.

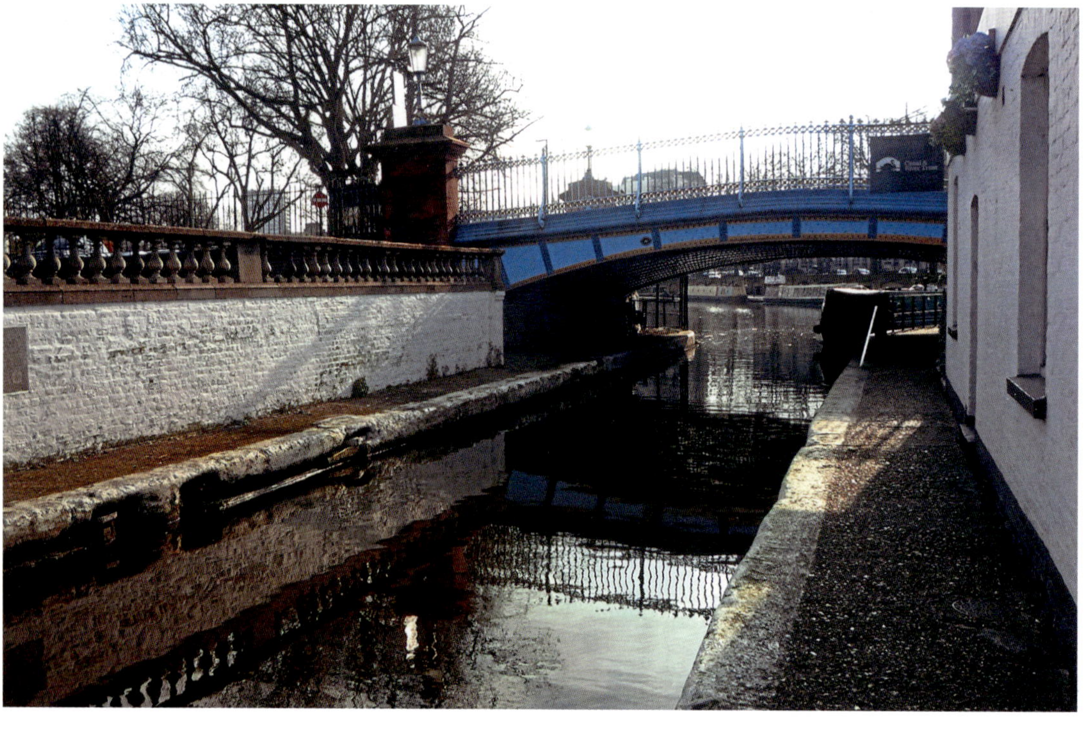

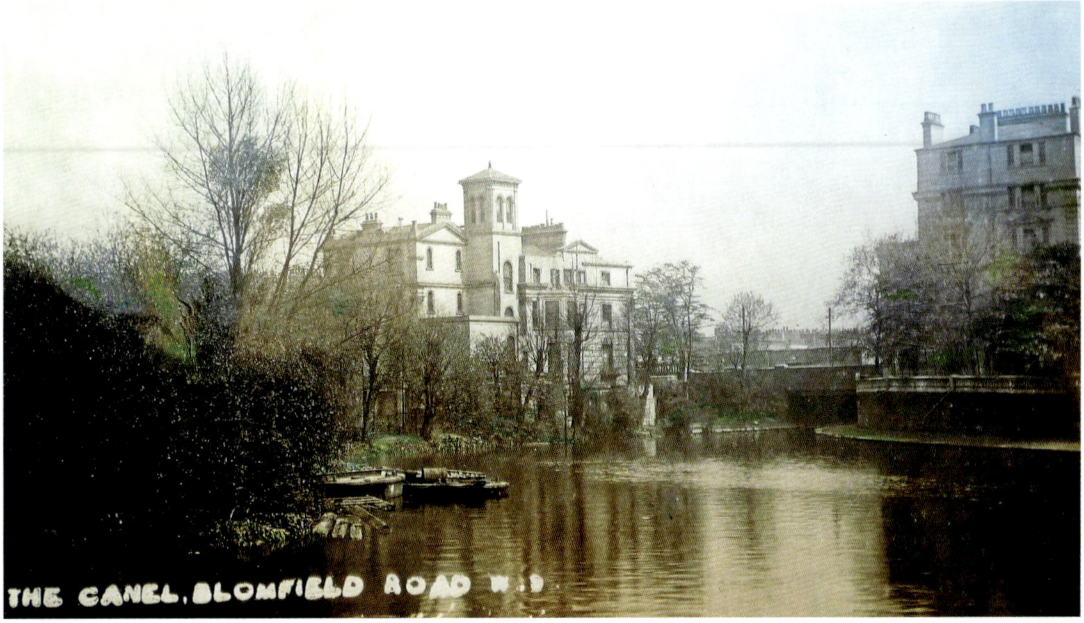

Browning's Pool from Blomfield Road, *c.* 1912

The one-time harbour at Paddington and the meeting point for three branches of the canals. Browning's Pool was named after the poet Robert Browning, whose house overlooked the waters. The term 'Venice in London' is attributed to Browning but 'Little Venice' came in 1934 in a novel by Margery Allingham. The Italianate architecture of the mansion overlooking the Pool at Harrow Road strengthens the illusion that something of Venice had been somehow transplanted into London.

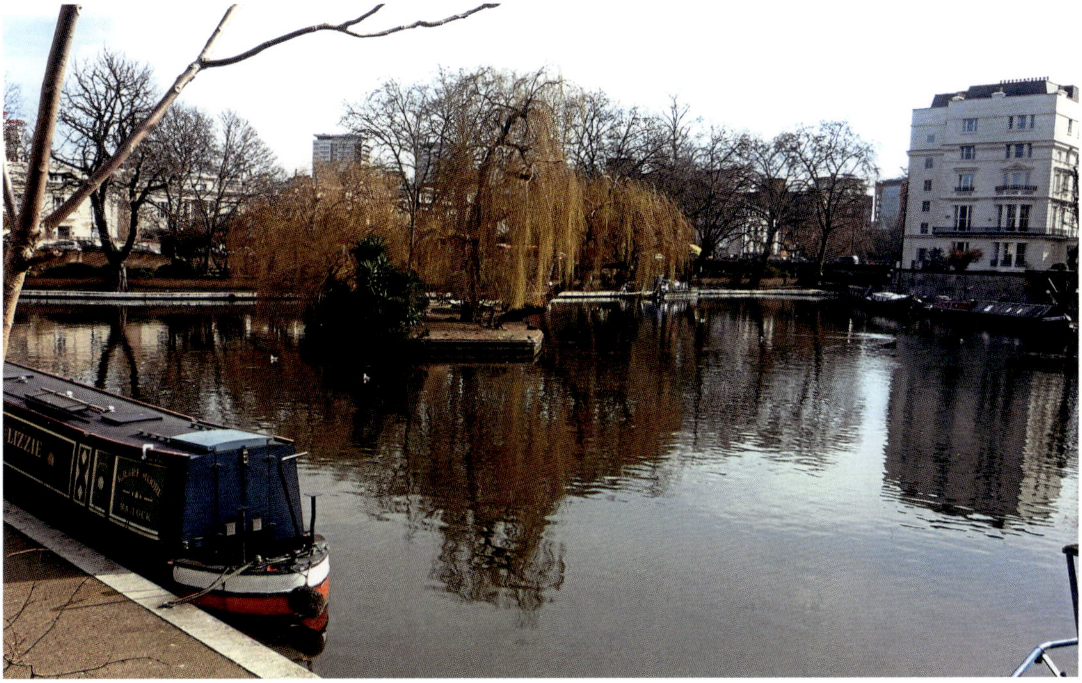

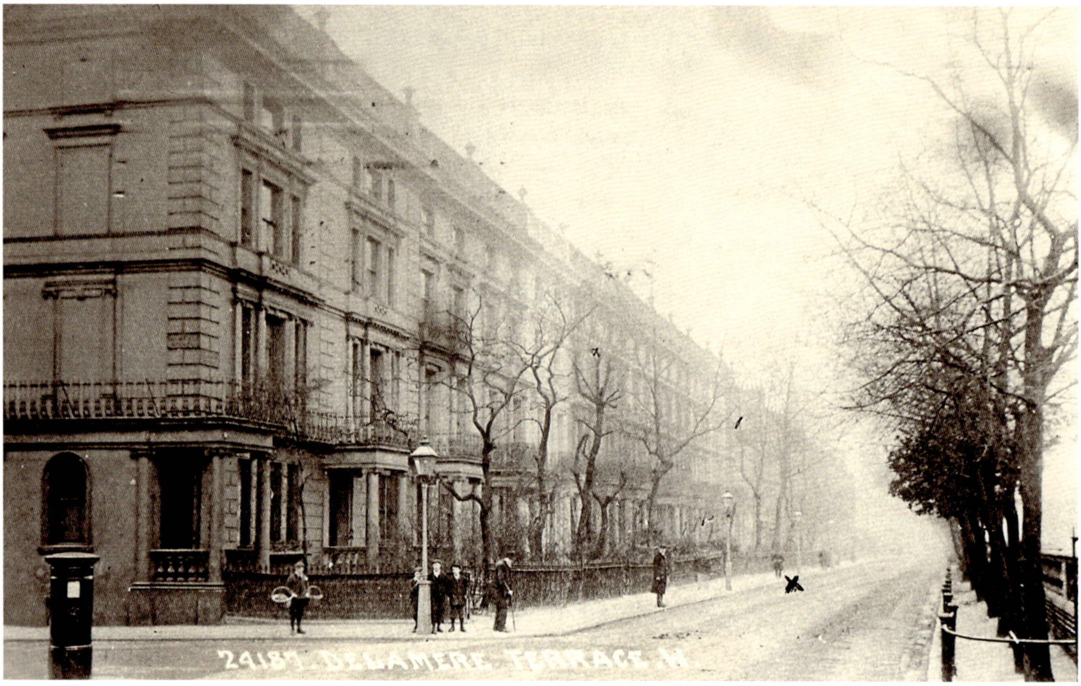

Delamere Terrace from Blomfield Street, *c.* 1906
Residents of the old houses in the above image would have enjoyed an enviable outlook over the waters of the Grand Junction canal, but as conditions declined the area was rebuilt as part of the Warwick Estate.

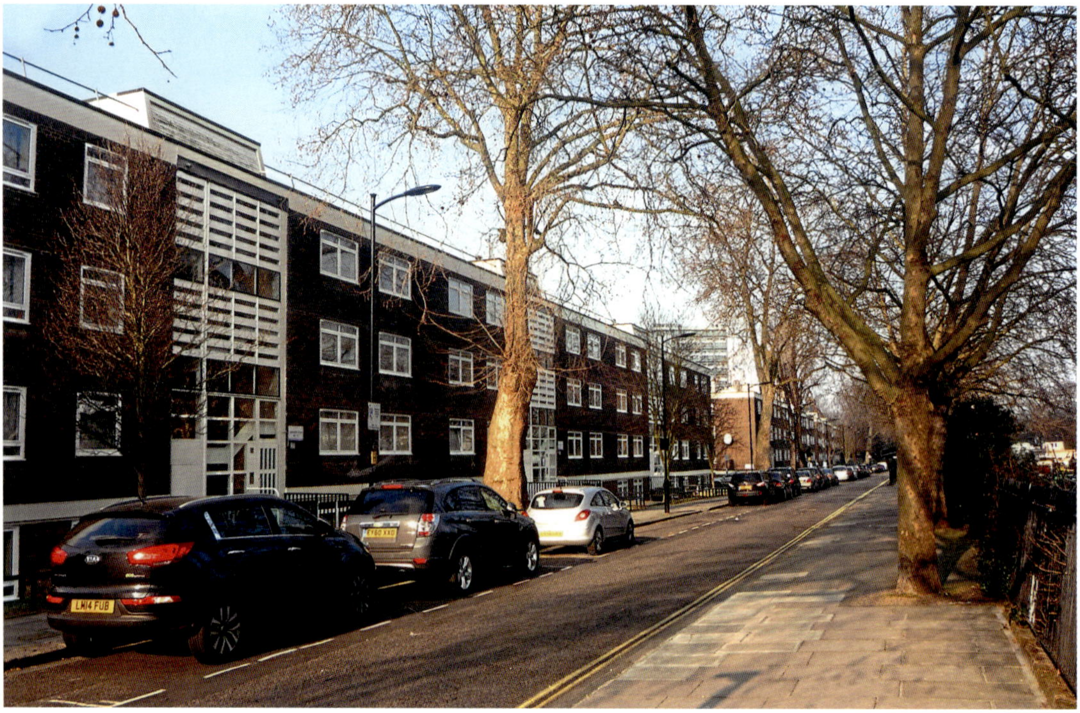

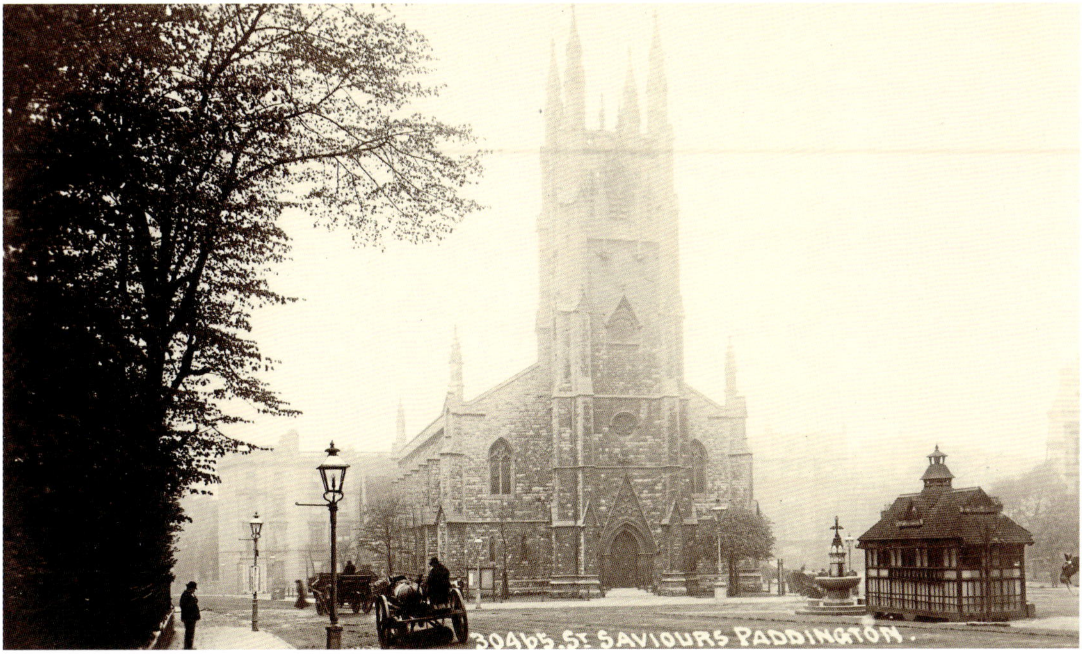

St Saviour's Church and the Site of Warwick Avenue Tube Station, *c.* 1906

This was once one of the widest residential streets in London, its majestic view from the canal closed by St Saviour's church. The image above pre-dates the opening of the Bakerloo Tube's extension from Paddington to Kilburn Park, which came in 1915. In this street of grand houses, the new station had no surface buildings other than a pair of staircases that went down to the booking hall and were guarded by decorative iron railings.

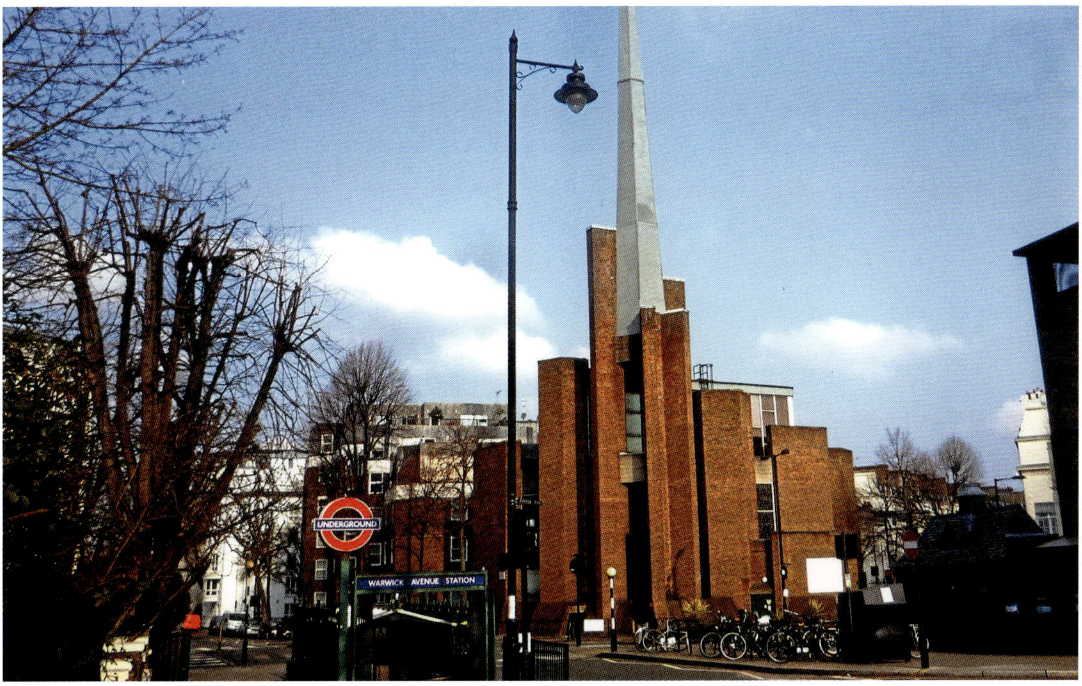

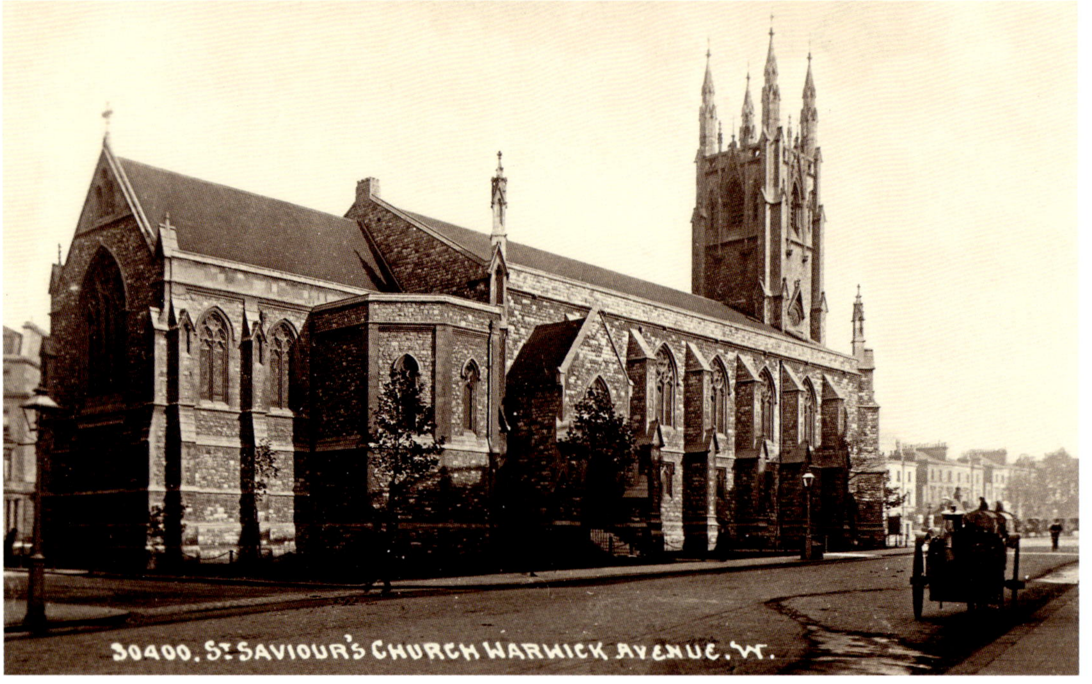

St Saviour's Church, Warwick Avenue, *c.* 1908

A grand church faced in Kentish Ragstone, dating from 1855. Replacement of the church became a necessity in 1972. A smaller St Saviour's took its place in 1976 and the rest of the site was then taken up with new flats. The original church was designed by Thomas Little.

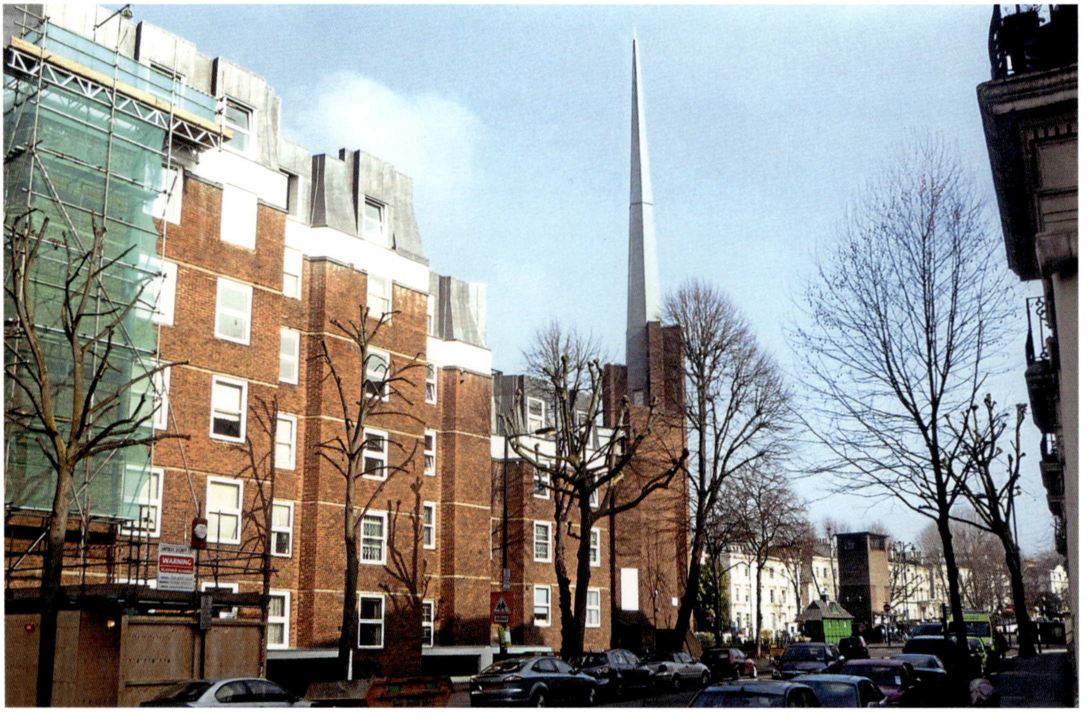

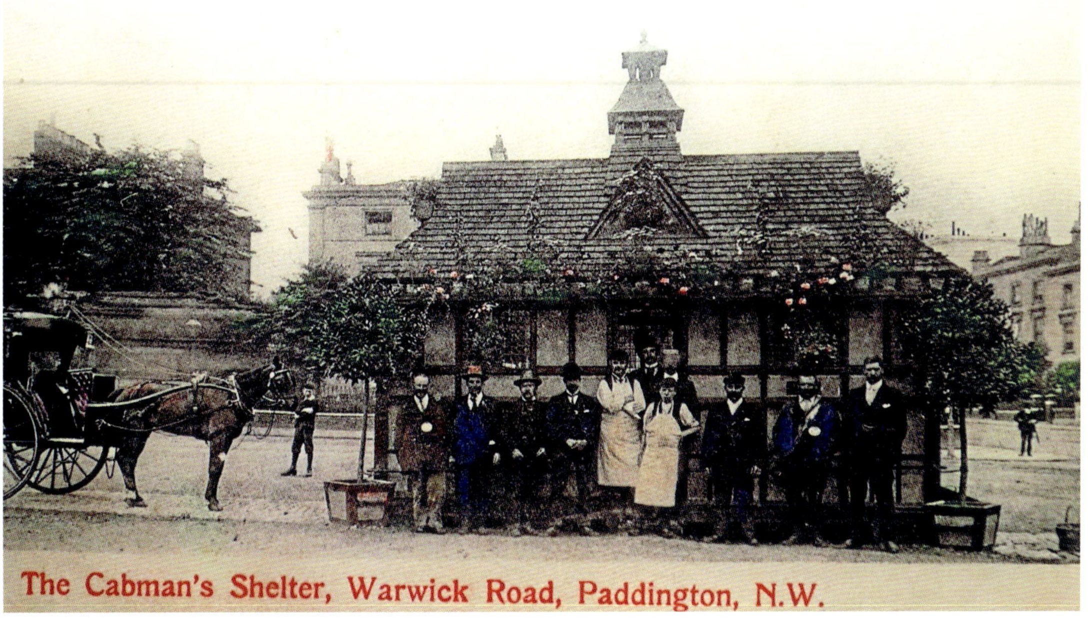

Cab Driver's Shelter, Warwick Avenue, *c.* 1905

These iconic and much-loved wooden shelters date from the days when hansom cabs and 'growlers' (four wheeled cabs) served the city. Lovingly maintained in the present day, examples are scattered about central London – this one was restored in 1994.

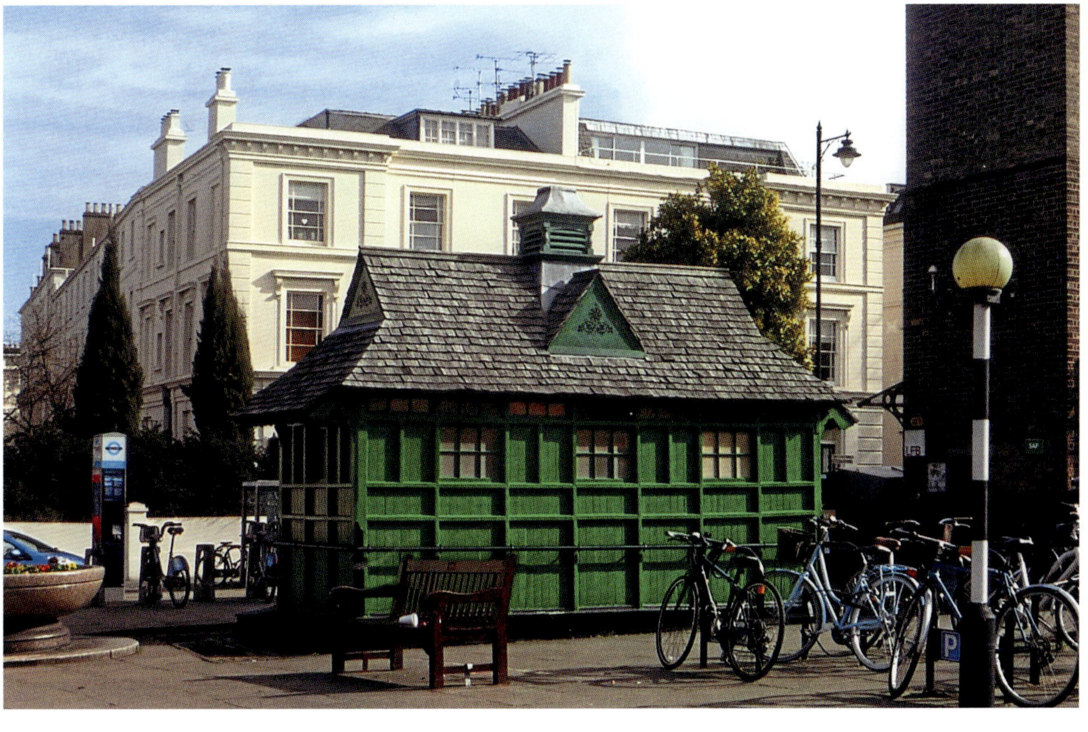

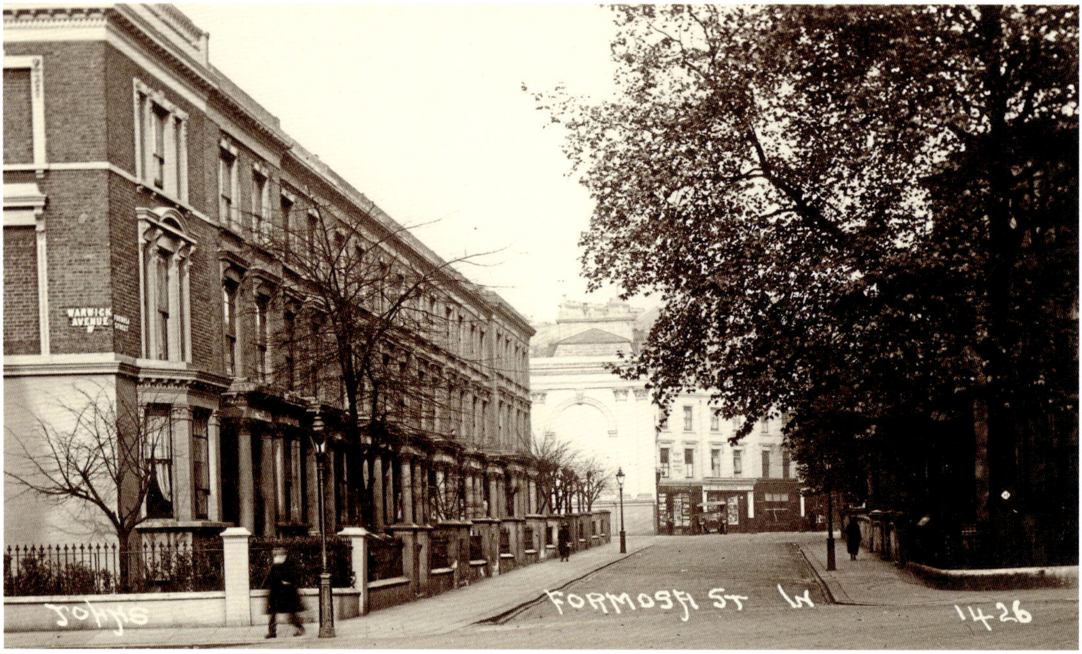

Formosa Street from Warwick Avenue, *c.* 1920
A residential terrace leads into Formosa Street's Regency-style shopping centre, which has served the canal-side community since the mid-1800s. The stucco-fronted shops here reflect the elegance of the local houses.

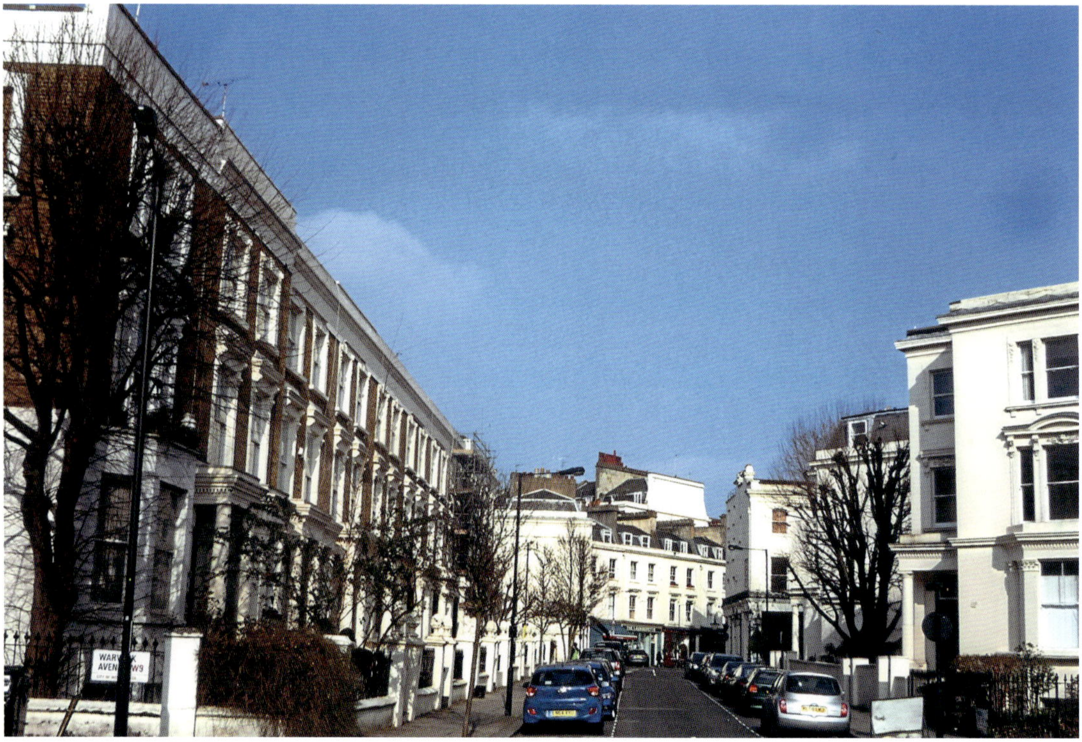

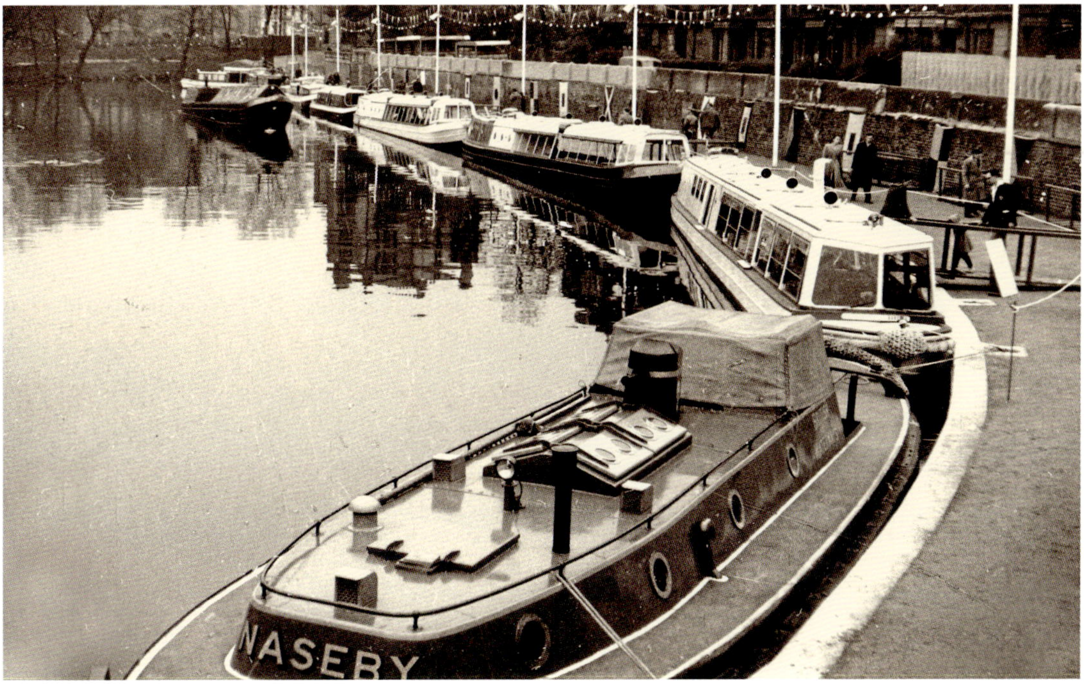

At Browning's Pool, Little Venice, 1959

Above, a line of pleasure boats moored in Browning's Pool as a working boat draws alongside. The background shows a few of the original houses in Warwick Crescent (where Robert Browning once lived), then in their final years. The rebuilding of the properties was completed in 1966. A restaurant boat is currently moored here and there is a waterbus service to Camden.

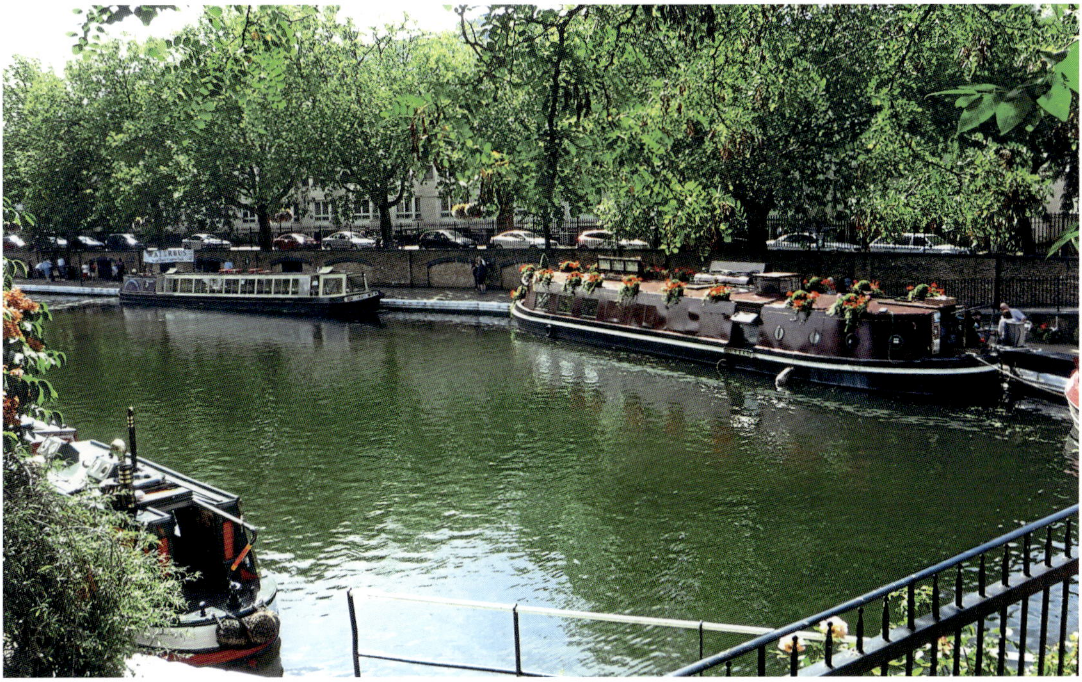

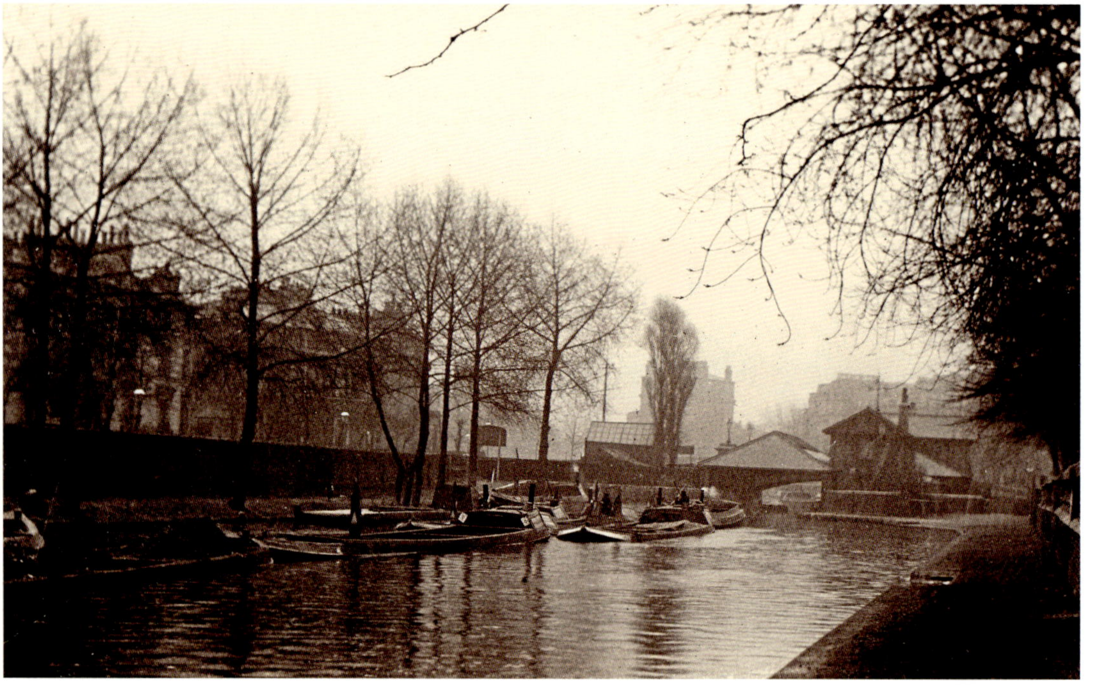

The Grand Junction Canal at Delamere Terrace and Blomfield Road, *c.* 1905

The above image shows working life on the canal; a bank of barges are seen awaiting passage through the weighing facilities at the Toll House on a drab winter's day. There would often be congestion here at busy times.

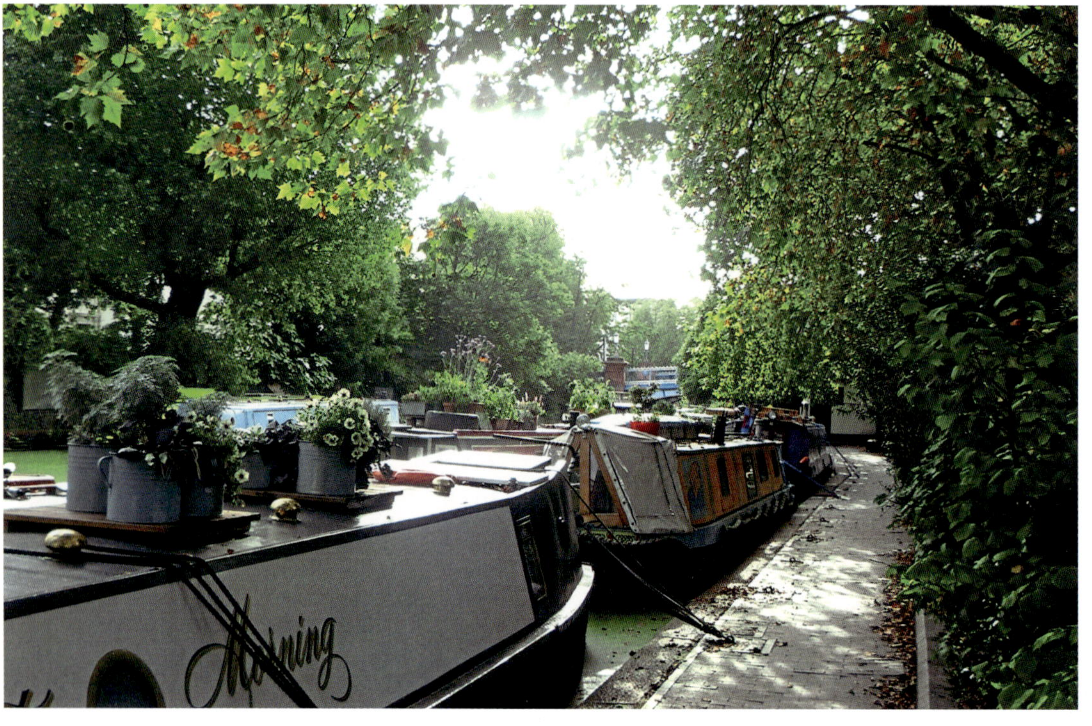